Starting and Running a Winery

by Thomas Pellechia

ALPHA

A member of Penguin Group (USA) Inc.

ALPHA BOOKS

Published by the Penguin Group

Penguin Group (USA) Inc., 375 Hudson Street, New York, New York 10014, USA

Penguin Group (Canada), 90 Eglinton Avenue East, Suite 700, Toronto, Ontario M4P 2Y3, Canada (a division of Pearson Penguin Canada Inc.)

Penguin Books Ltd., 80 Strand, London WC2R 0RL, England

Penguin Ireland, 25 St. Stephen's Green, Dublin 2, Ireland (a division of Penguin Books Ltd.)

Penguin Group (Australia), 250 Camberwell Road, Camberwell, Victoria 3124, Australia (a division of Pearson Australia Group Pty. Ltd.)

Penguin Books India Pvt. Ltd., 11 Community Centre, Panchsheel Park, New Delhi—110 017, India

Penguin Group (NZ), 67 Apollo Drive, Rosedale, North Shore, Auckland 1311, New Zealand (a division of Pearson New Zealand Ltd.)

Penguin Books (South Africa) (Pty.) Ltd., 24 Sturdee Avenue, Rosebank, Johannesburg 2196, South Africa

Penguin Books Ltd., Registered Offices: 80 Strand, London WC2R 0RL, England

Copyright © 2008 by Thomas Pellechia

International Standard Book Number: 978-1-59257-818-4
Library of Congress Catalog Card Number: 2008927332

13   8 7

Interpretation of the printing code: The rightmost number of the first series of numbers is the year of the book's printing; the rightmost number of the second series of numbers is the number of the book's printing. For example, a printing code of 08-1 shows that the first printing occurred in 2008.

Printed in the United States of America

Note: This publication contains the opinions and ideas of its author. It is intended to provide helpful and informative material on the subject matter covered. It is sold with the understanding that the author and publisher are not engaged in rendering professional services in the book. If the reader requires personal assistance or advice, a competent professional should be consulted.

The author and publisher specifically disclaim any responsibility for any liability, loss, or risk, personal or otherwise, which is incurred as a consequence, directly or indirectly, of the use and application of any of the contents of this book.

Most Alpha books are available at special quantity discounts for bulk purchases for sales promotions, premiums, fund-raising, or educational use. Special books, or book excerpts, can also be created to fit specific needs.

For details, write: Special Markets, Alpha Books, 375 Hudson Street, New York, NY 10014.

Publisher: *Marie Butler-Knight*
Editorial Director: *Mike Sanders*
Senior Managing Editor: *Billy Fields*
Acquisitions Editor: *Tom Stevens*
Senior Development Editor: *Christy Wagner*
Production Editor: *Megan Douglass*
Copy Editor: *Cate Schwenk*

Cartoonist: *Shannon Wheeler*
Cover Designer: *Bill Thomas*
Book Designer: *Trina Wurst*
Indexer: *Johnna Vanhoose Dinse*
Layout: *Chad Dressler*
Proofreader: *John Etchison*

Contents at a Glance

Contents

Introduction

The great songwriter Irving Berlin wrote one called "Everybody's Doin' It Now." He was talking about the turkey trot, a dance craze of the turn of the twentieth century, but today, Berlin's title could very well apply to starting a winery because everywhere you turn, in cities and in forests, everybody seems to be doing it.

It wasn't always this way, but in the past 30 years, the generation born after World War II has done a great deal to bring wine into the North American culture. So much so, that wine consumption, which has been on the rise over that time, took an even sharper upward turn in the past decade. Retail shops across North America have decreased the size of their spirits offerings to make room for wine. Down the street from the retail shops, the latest tasting bar has opened its doors. Not long ago a wine-by-the-glass restaurant program was the exception; today, it is the rule. And wine aficionados from every walk of life are changing careers to feed their great passion. Many of them are starting a winery to satisfy a combination of love, enchantment, freedom, and the potential for financial self-sufficiency.

Together, the rash of start-up wineries plus a new round of corporate interest in wineries is unequivocal proof that wine has made it into the North American culture. Wine consumption growth projections point to the undeniable fact that wine is here to stay.

After thinking about and drinking wine for so long, perhaps after making wine at home, is it time for you to take the next step? If the answer is yes, or even maybe, this book is for you.

How This Book Flows

To lead you from the beginning, literally, of wine to your own wine, this book is divided into six parts:

Part 1, "Before You Take the Plunge," explains why the wine industry is attractive. After some history, two case studies, and self-analysis, you'll be ready to decide if this is a business for you.

Part 2, "Laying Your Foundation," gets you going on the legwork so you can see your dream take shape.

Part 3, "Laboring in the Vineyard," is where the legwork morphs into the real work. You'll understand grape growing and winemaking better, and you'll learn the multi-levels of the wine business.

Part 4, "Getting It All in Place," explains the equipment, staffing, and training necessary for success.

Part 5, "The Fruit of Your Labor," takes your product to the people. You've produced that first bottle of wine, now you'll learn how to let the world know about it.

Part 6, "Making Wine into Success," brings you full circle. You've got it all working at peak, and the time has come to consider your legacy.

In the back of the book, you'll find more information to help you along the way to making your winery dream a reality, including a glossary; helpful forms, worksheets, and charts; and further resources you can drink in.

Extras

Throughout this book, you'll find additional info in sidebars that highlight and complement portions of the text. Here's what to look for:

Master of Wine

These boxes share some tips and helpful advice.

Sour Grapes

Heed the warnings in these sidebars.

The Winepress

These boxes contain fun trivia information I bet you didn't know.

def•i•ni•tion

As the name implies, these boxes contain definitions of terms used in winery-speak.

Acknowledgments

I've been in or connected to the wine industry since 1985. I've tried to stay on top of its growth and changes, but that is a job no one can do alone.

When I accepted the task of writing this book, I immediately called upon some wine industry friends and contacts for information, plus a few people I hadn't met yet but was glad when the opportunity came my way.

Special thanks goes to Gerald White, Ian Merwin, and Tim Martinson at Cornell University; Finger Lakes winery owners Scott Osborn, Gene Pierce, and John Zuccarino; Susan Spence of the New York Wine and Grape Foundation; and, in California, winery consultant Cary Gott, plus the Netbooks company's Doug Baum.

Special Thanks to the Technical Reviewer

The Complete Idiot's Guide to Starting and Running a Winery was reviewed by an expert who double-checked the accuracy of what you'll learn here, to help us ensure that this book gives you everything you need to know about starting and running your own winery. Special thanks are extended to Cary Gott.

Trademarks

All terms mentioned in this book that are known to be or are suspected of being trademarks or service marks have been appropriately capitalized. Alpha Books and Penguin Group (USA) Inc. cannot attest to the accuracy of this information. Use of a term in this book should not be regarded as affecting the validity of any trademark or service mark.

Part 1

Before You Take the Plunge

Wine is as old as civilization, it fills you with passion, and it makes you want to produce your own. That's not a bad idea, especially now that wine consumption and the wine industry in the United States are on a meteoric rise.

In Part 1, I tell you what's going on in the wine industry and help you discover whether becoming a wine industry entrepreneur is the right choice for you. You learn how it all began, analyze the way others got into the business, discover how you can tap into the wine industry, and get a glimpse into your future. By the time you get to Part 2, you'll know whether you're ready to sink your feet deep into the vat.

Why Wine?

In This Chapter

- ◆ Passion, commitment, and perseverance = results
- ◆ A matter of symbiosis
- ◆ Wine through the ages
- ◆ What America thinks of wine
- ◆ Profiting from the wine boom in America

There's an old adage about wine:

> You can make a small fortune in the wine business, provided you begin with a large one.

Most people start a winery as the result of their passion and love for wine. Others start a winery because they see a good business opportunity. By marrying the two reasons, the chance for success at starting and running a winery is greatly increased.

Just like forming any other business, starting and running a successful winery takes passion, commitment, and perseverance. The legal roadblocks alone are formidable. But don't let that scare you. This happens to be a good time to get into the wine business, provided you do it right.

Why Now?

Wine consumption is growing fast, and many have been cashing in; even people who didn't start with a small fortune. The rise in wine consumption makes it easy to imagine the hundreds of people you can satisfy by producing and selling wine, and how great it would be to be your own boss while doing it.

Imagining is the first step. This book shows you how to take the next step and the steps after that, but first let's get a handle on exactly what's going on in the wine world, what this product is all about, and how the United States wine industry fares in the marketplace.

The Old U.S. Wine Market

In the past, the wine industry served two major U.S. consumer markets: the well-to-do and the immigrant poor. The American working and middle classes stayed with beer and martinis. The people with money mainly bought European wine, leaving domestic wine producers to serve the rest of the market with cheap, bulk wine. That was the image of American wine. The situation kept American per-capita wine consumption dismally low in comparison to other major industrialized nations, ranking 39 out of 50.

Oh, how times have changed. Today's wine consumption and production in the United States is larger and better than ever before.

The New U.S. Wine Market

In the mid-twentieth century, the American wine industry was like a train leaving the station, slowly building momentum. By the turn of the century, the throttle was wide open and the wine train barreled at full speed ahead as the number of wine consumers in the United States grew and kept on growing to the tune of three times its size in the past 25 years.

As per-capita U.S. wine consumption rose, the domestic wine industry found itself competing for the larger share of three major consumer wine markets:

- The affluent
- The middle class
- The next generation

The growth in wine consumption is the result of a number of factors, not the least of which is a higher standard of living among many Americans and a lot more leisure time. The information age has noticed wine, too. Never before have so many magazines, newspapers, books, movies, and now the Internet focused so much on wine. Never before have so many wine classes and special wine tastings blanketed the country. It all began with a major event in 1976, which I'll get to later in the chapter.

Right now, this is the general breakdown of the market for wine in the United States:

◆ The affluent buy what are called ultra-premium wines at prices between $25 and three digits per bottle.

◆ The middle class drink the $15 to $25 wines in large quantities.

◆ The new generation drinks wines under $20 but gradually learns more and enters the middle class both in income and in wine preferences.

Never before has the opportunity for wine sales in multiple markets been greater than it is today, and never before have so many avenues opened for domestic wineries to surpass their European counterparts in wine sales in the United States.

Whatever the motive for growth, entrepreneurs have taken notice that wine industry analysts see good things in the future for domestic wine consumption. In the middle of the twentieth century, the number of wineries nationwide was in the high hundreds. Today, the number is in the thousands—5,000 and counting. For the first time in the country's history, commercial wine is produced in all 50 of the United States.

Before you get ready to add one more winery to the growing count, take a few minutes to understand what makes this product tick and why we love it so much.

The Winepress

In a 2007 wine industry report by the consulting firm Gomberg-Fredrikson, the reasons cited for a now 15-year drastic growth curve was noted to include publicity about the potential health benefits of red wine, an increase in younger consumers, increase in women with high incomes, and better wine marketing, especially the labels with pictures of animals on them.

What Is Wine, Anyway?

If you take clusters of freshly picked grapes, throw them into a large tub, and store them at room temperature, within minutes a mass of fruit flies will swirl around the rotting fruit and a puddle of juice will start to settle. Soon, maybe the following day, a heady aroma will rise, and the juice will be on its way toward becoming wine, without you having done anything to help it along.

Grape Juice with a Kick

According to U.S. federal regulations, *table wine* is a grape beverage containing between 7 and 14 percent alcohol by volume. When mature, grapes are the only fruit that can produce a beverage like that without human intervention. Wine is neither brewed, like beer, nor distilled, like spirits. Wine is simply naturally fermented grape juice.

But grapes can't make wine completely alone; they need the help of yeast.

All About the Yeast

Fermentation begins when the yeast starts to consume grape sugar. Wine begins when the meal produces alcohol, carbon dioxide and heat, plus the transformation of other byproducts—what chemists call phenolic compounds (including the ones that are supposedly good for your health). These compounds also produce the wonderful aromatics that send wine writers to the thesaurus for adjectives.

def•i•ni•tion

Fermentation is simply a food decomposition process. Products like wine and cheese produce decomposition favorable to our senses. Fermentation also unleashes a multitude of aromas and compounds.

Master of Wine

Dozens of studies over the past 50 years show that chemical compounds in wine with names like quercetin and resveratrol may contain antioxidants that are beneficial to your health.

The yeast involved in the winemaking process is in the same family as baker's yeast: *Saccharomyces cerevisiae*. It's a natural single-celled fungus that flourishes in the great outdoors—this particular yeast seems to mostly live within reach of oak trees.

Yeast microorganisms thrive on vegetation, so it's a cinch that they've been around far longer than humans; for that matter, so have grapevines, which date as far back as 60 million years. (Archaeologists have found grape seed remnants in Paleolithic caves. Scientists aren't sure whether those seeds represent a simple dessert of grapes or a cave dweller's equivalent of a good red wine to accompany a mammoth dinner.)

For thousands of years, grapes made use of the symbiotic relationship between the ambient yeasts of nature outside the grape skins and the sugar inside them. These days, however, most winemakers apply commercially hybridized yeasts to the process. But if they didn't, ripe grapes would still be able to ferment within the alcohol range necessary to produce legal table wine.

Some Legal Stuff

Did I mention that in the United States wine is a so-called "legal drink"? Oh yes, it takes not one, but a minimum of two permits to produce, distribute, and sell commercial wine. (You'll learn how to get them in Chapter 5.)

As you sit there scratching your head about our modern world of regulations, consider this: the ancients understood the power of wine immediately, and just like modern governments, they knew a revenue stream when they saw one. Ever since its discovery and cultivation, wine has been a simultaneous source of joy and revenue. It's been regulated throughout the ages in one way or another by church and state, which often was the same entity. It was no different with how wine got to America.

How Did We Get Here from There?

There must be as many legends about wine's origin as there are wines in the world. Dionysus, the Greek god of wine, brought grapevines to Earth in two separate legends. Ancient Semites, Egyptians, Etruscans, Russians, and Chinese all had their legends, too. One of the most common legends comes from Persia, and it makes some sense.

A Wonderful Poison

The Persian King Jamsheed loved grapes so much that he stored them in jars marked "Poison" so no one else would eat them.

One of Jamsheed's exiled—and, therefore, depressed—brides saw the jars marked poison. She drank the puddle of juice at the bottom of a jar, hoping to do herself in. Instead, the liquid picked up her spirits. She ran back to the king to report her findings.

Impressed, Jamsheed passed a law that from that day forward, grapes would purposely be made into this new liquid, which he called wine, and which he regulated.

Discovery in the Fertile Crescent

Legend notwithstanding, grapevine cultivation and controlled wine production developed about 8,000 years ago, while the earth was warming from its most recent ice age. The more hospitable climate allowed hunter-gatherers to stray. The group that discovered gardening and husbandry landed in Mesopotamia, which became more commonly known as the *Fertile Crescent*, the area that includes modern-day Iraq plus parts of Syria, Turkey, Armenia, and Iran.

The Winepress

Mesopotamian priests in control of commodity warehouses developed *cuneiform*, a pictograph to keep track of important inventory for trade, like wine. Cuneiform became the first written language to express complex thoughts, and the first words may have been about wine, which shows up in the earliest writings of the ancients.

The first major agricultural crop of Mesopotamia was barley, which was also used as currency. The first drink was beer, which was often produced from barley, but wine was not far behind. But unlike common beer, wine was quickly given high status. The general public didn't get to drink it much; it was reserved for a community's ruler and his priests.

As groups broke away to form new communities, extensive trade developed among them. Because it was important for religious practices, wine became a premium commodity for trade; regulations to govern its production, traffic, and price swiftly followed. They weren't kidding with their laws back then. In Babylon, anyone caught selling fake wine or overcharging for wine was thrown into the Euphrates River as punishment.

Within a few centuries of its discovery, commercial wine spread vine cultivation throughout the known world, first from the Middle and Near East, to northern Africa, and then east to Asia and west to the edges of Europe.

Much of the spread of the wine trade was due to the first itinerant seafarers, the Phoenicians, a group with roots in northern Syria. They were among the earliest to make big profits from wine, about 5,000 years ago. Their profits financed building new colonies from North Africa to Spain. The wine trade made ancient Phoenicians so wealthy that they founded their own country, Carthage, in North Africa, where Tunisia is today.

The Classics

Later, wine, grain, and olives became classical Greece's version of a "big three" economic powerhouse. The Greeks gained their love and knowledge of wine from trade with Phoenicians around 1300 B.C.E. Wine became so important to the economy of the Greek islands, where the best wine was made, that stringent controls were put into place to guarantee its quality.

Through the cult of Dionysus, the Greeks became the first to bring wine into everyday common use. Becoming a grape farmer was one in a long list of Greek cultural status symbols. Then, when classical Rome took over where Greece left off, wine remained a potent and dominant economic force, as did the regulations governing its production, distribution, and taxation. Roman governments accepted wine as payment for taxes, and even Roman senators and nobility grew grapes or ran wineries.

The fall of Rome and the subsequent rise of Islam did much to reduce the power and influence of commercial wine in the East. But its wide use for religious practices in the West, especially for the Christian religion, helped commercial wine survive the so-called Dark Ages, as Christian monks of Europe kept wine flowing into the Middle Ages.

Wine became one of the most prized European commodities. During the late Middle Ages, the wine industry often employed the population of whole regions on the European continent. The stuff ran like blood in the Old World—sometimes literally—as wars broke out over its commerce, taxation, and generally marvelous favorable revenue stream, not to mention land claims.

Still, wine made many medieval landowners wealthy, and it kept a few kingdoms solvent, too. As it became a more important source of tax revenue, regulations governing its production and distribution continued to tighten.

Kings exacted taxes at ports of call before wine was offloaded. Politicians who owned taverns or were connected to wine importing created legislation that restricted importing wines from rival nations. And wine adulteration became a major problem—stretch it with water or juice and you could double your profit. Better still, sell a concoction that tasted like wine but had no grape juice in it, and you could become rich!

The Winepress

Wine was implicated in the 100 Years' War between Britain and France (1337–1453). The fight began near the prized section of Bordeaux, which Britain owned through royal marriage and France wanted back for its wine revenue.

Failure, Success, and Shutdown in America

In the late fifteenth and early sixteenth centuries, Spain's conquistadors journeyed across the Atlantic Ocean with wine onboard their ships—and it's a good thing, too. When the Spaniards landed in the areas around Mexico, New Mexico, South Carolina, and Florida, they found no wine production.

At first, the new settlers were commanded by Spain's royalty to use wine from home, but delays and other problems forced the settlers to plant vines and produce their own wine. Most of the wine was for religious and personal use; the only commercial wine was sold to support religious missions.

Meanwhile, without a wine industry of its own, the British crown had grown tired of French and Spanish wine taxes, so when the British set sail for the New World, part of the colonizing charter was to establish a commercial wine industry abroad. The first attempt took place at Jamestown, Virginia. It was a dismal failure.

The Winepress

In 1839, a French immigrant named Jean Jacques formed what is today the oldest continuing winery in the United States, Brotherhood Winery, in New York State's Hudson Valley region.

In fact, until well after the American Revolution and into the mid-nineteenth century, commercial wine hadn't gained a foothold in North America, not because the colonists and revolutionaries hadn't tried. They didn't like the wines indigenous American grapes produced, but they had trouble getting their European transplanted vines to produce.

It took until 1830 before anyone in the Untied States came close to creating a successful wine business, and that limited success developed outside Philadelphia, at York, Pennsylvania. A few years later, success struck in Cincinnati, Ohio, followed by Hermann, Missouri; Blooming Grove, New York; and Anaheim, California. The American wine industry began to flourish at the time of the California gold rush, in 1849 and 1850.

Most early commercial wine went relatively unregulated. American citizens could buy wine in bulk if they wanted to or in small lots drawn from a barrel, and they could have the wine shipped from overseas directly to their homes. (Neither is possible today without a permit.)

The wine industry was growing, but the Civil War got in its way. After the war, beer and whisky edged out wine. Meanwhile, an anti-alcohol movement began, lasting about 75 years, and then the movement culminated in 1920 with the Volstead Act—Prohibition—which edged out *all* alcoholic beverages.

The legislation came with a provision that allowed producers to sell sacramental wine for religious purposes. Any wine that was produced before the law could be kept in inventory, presumably for the day when the law would be repealed. Plus, the head of every household was allowed to produce up to 200 gallons of wine for personal consumption each year.

Rebirth

Prohibition lasted 13 years, until the 21st amendment to the U.S. Constitution repealed it in 1933. But Congress was painfully aware that Prohibition had spawned a vast criminal alcohol network. To stem the tide, congressional legislation gave the states the right to regulate and control commercial alcohol within their borders. The states jumped on this right quickly, putting into place a startling variety of restrictions, controls, taxes, fees, and general hoops through which wine producers, wholesalers, and retailers must jump.

While the regulations may be frustrating—and also formidable—the growth of the wine industry in just the past 30 years proves that the hurdles are not insurmountable. With new commercial wineries opening their doors throughout the United States almost daily, the industry promises to stay around for a long while.

The Winepress _____

To start a winery today, your first task is to learn how to jump through the hoops and navigate the controls. The best way to start is to read the federal and local requirements. (See Appendix C for a listing of federal and state alcohol control authorities.)

It Keeps Growing ... and Growing ...

Today, the wine industry includes many large wine companies, even corporate conglomerates, yet the majority of American wineries start out small. Many begin as family operations and remain that way over successive generations. In fact, it was a few small wineries that sparked renewed interest in American wine in the 1970s, kicking off a revolution that helped create a growing wine writing and magazine industry as well as the establishment of wine bars across the national landscape. With each new venture came more exposure to wine, and more consumption.

In the past half-dozen years, bulletin boards and blogs dedicated to wine have popped up online like grapevine flowers in June. Plus, even with the hodgepodge of regulations from state to state, online wine retailing grows.

Remember that U.S. wine consumption ranking of 39 among the leading industrial nations 30 years ago? Since that time, the pace of wine consumption has steadily picked up steam. At the last count, Americans consumed approximately 720 million gallons of wine annually, representing about $24 billion. In 2005, wine sales in America outpaced beer sales for the first time since before the Civil War, and in 2006, wine sales beat beer again. Consumption is expected to continue to grow at least for the next decade, and the United States is projected to rank in first or second place by the year 2010. (It would easily be in first place were it not for China, another booming wine phenomenon with a seeming endless population count.)

The Winepress _____

In Paris in 1976, a few California wines took top honors over their French counterparts. The landmark event was made more important by the fact that the judges were all French. Thus began the American wine boom.

What Are You Waiting For?

A chunk of the growth in the wine industry is coming, and will continue to come, from individual vineyard and winery operations, plus a growing trend of wineries that work out of cooperative and custom crush facilities. In this book, you discover how you can start and run a winery under the traditional bricks-and-mortar method or in the fast-growing custom crush method.

If you're ready to become part of the bright future of wine, the following chapters tell you what you need to know to succeed. But before you begin this business, you need to take stock of your personal assets. Chapter 2 helps you find out how.

The Least You Need to Know

- ◆ Wine is as old as civilization.
- ◆ Since its discovery, wine has been both a spiritual and economic powerhouse, and it has been regulated and taxed.
- ◆ Between the fall of Rome and the nineteenth century, Europe was the major wine-producing continent.
- ◆ Starting in the nineteenth century, the United States became a major wine-producing country.
- ◆ The American wine industry is experiencing steady and rapid growth, and you don't have to be a large company to get in on it.

2

Ready for Some Hard Work?

In This Chapter

- ◆ Can you really do this?
- ◆ The ins and outs of the business
- ◆ The government and other intrusions
- ◆ Step 1: go to work

You have to be serious-minded and ambitious to start and run a winery. Don't get me wrong—it's good to have dreams. Dreams are the starting gate to success. But whether you dream of getting back to the land or of an invitation to serve your wine at the White House, the hard reality is that just to get a winery started can be a long, tedious, and frustrating task.

Look at the often-difficult experience of applying for and getting a permit to produce and sell wine as a training ground. Indeed, the challenges and demands of running a winery can make it seem like a day at the beach.

You'll certainly need that passion mentioned in Chapter 1, but you also need a refined work ethic and a capacity for overcoming hurdles—and that's just to get the winery started. After you've put in the hours of research, after you've overcome the bureaucratic hurdles, and after you've obtained your permits to open your winery doors, you then have to run what is a complicated yet rewarding business—or more accurately, three businesses. (I'll get to that later.)

Take Stock, Now

Before you proceed, you need to take stock in your personal abilities and, yes, in your faults, too. Review the following list of important questions. Your answers will guide you and firm up your baby steps toward starting the business. It's a kind of personality test, so be honest. Later in the chapter, I go into more detail concerning these issues.

Am I prepared to give myself over to starting and running a demanding business? Only the wealthy can start and run a winery by giving it a few hours a week in between "real" responsibilities. Starting a winery means changing your life; it means you have to give yourself over.

Can I calmly handle challenges when they include matters beyond my control, like the weather, equipment failures, etc.? Wine is an agricultural product. If the weather doesn't get you one year, it might the next. And you haven't dealt with temperamental equipment until you've met a tractor or an electronic wine press. Challenges like these can do damage to profit, but they can also do damage to your health, if you let them.

Am I a people person? Much of the wine business is dealing effectively with people, from your farm employees, migrant farm workers, office employees, wine cellar employees, and tasting room employees to distributors, retailers, restaurants, and the always-fickle general consumer public. Be honest with yourself. If you don't like working with people, or if you become too stressed by talking all day long to people with different attitudes from yours, you may need to find a partner who can handle it.

Can I make it through the frustrations of dealing with bureaucrats? Sometimes it might not seem so, but bureaucrats are people, too. You will deal with all the trappings of both federal and local bureaucracy, from the permit application process through the everyday operation and reporting requirements of a winery. If you have trouble dealing with rules and the people who enforce them, or if you're impatient, you could burn yourself out before even getting the business started.

Sour Grapes

The distance between the dream, submitting the applications, and opening your winery door can be vast. Depending on the state you start your business in, it can take as much as a year before you have all the permits in place. Don't give up!

Do I have the risk-taking gene that will let me borrow a lot of money if I need it? A winery is capital intensive. Unless you're independently wealthy and willing to put all your money in, you're likely to have to borrow large sums of money either to get your business going or to keep it growing. If a string of zeroes after a number makes you nervous, you should stop to consider.

How long can I wait for success? Most small businesses don't show a profit for three to five years. Prevailing wisdom is that wineries don't break even until a minimum of five years, and they aren't securely in the black until about year eight. You must have extreme patience.

Be really honest in your answers, because you can spend an awful lot of money only to find out that you've made serious mistakes or you're not cut out for a certain aspect of the process. If you need to take on a partner, find out right away. Maybe it will help you decide if you know a little about how the wine business functions.

How the Business Works

A winery is neither a 9-to-5 nor a Monday-to-Friday business. It needs every bit of attention, every drop of sweat, and every ounce of brainpower any other business needs, and maybe more.

When you operate a vineyard plus a winery, you're in more than one business; you're in three:

◆ Agriculture

◆ Food production

◆ Entertainment

Viticulture Is Agriculture

On the agriculture side, grapevines need year-round tending, and their schedule is set by the weather, not by a clock. The same goes for harvesting grapes. You can—no, you *will* suffer many setbacks with *viticulture*. The type of setback often depends on where you are, because many agricultural problems start with the weather. But the weather is still only one part of it.

Vineyards are subject to myriad ecological problems such as insects, fungus, and the guy next door's bad agricultural practices wafting into your domain.

Plus, government controls require ongoing classroom training, licensing, and inspections to be sure you know how to safely use and dispose of chemicals. You'll also need

def•i•ni•tion

Viticulture is agriculture specific to growing grapevines. Because grapevines can flourish in a variety of climates, the farming methods for viticulture are equally varied.

training in establishing and watching over safety programs for farm and wine cellar workers.

Unless you come from an extremely large extended family, or you live in a community with an abundant stream of energetic and available farm workers (unlikely these days), viticulture at peak times often means relying on migrants, which requires good management and organization skills, not to mention the possibility of learning a second language.

Finally, the grape harvest begins in late summer and early fall, depending on your location. It's best not to process picked grapes under a hot sun, so working later in the day at harvest time is a given. After the grapes are picked, you'll move into the winery business.

Wine Is Food Manufacturing

Tons of grapes coming off vines and into the winery will keep you awake at night as they threaten to overwhelm your winery staff and your winery equipment. (And some of the equipment is almost certain to use the occasion to break down.) Then, after the grapes are crushed and fermentation begins, winemaking becomes babysitting, carefully keeping watch over a baby that neither sleeps nor takes weekends off.

Whether or not you are the winemaker, you'll find yourself worrying over the wine because by the time you take in your first grape harvest, you will have studied enough about winemaking to know how so much can go wrong in a process that keeps scientific researchers endlessly employed.

The Winepress

While much is known about it, fermentation is not an exact science. Few professions are as bad as winemaking when it comes to unintended consequences.

While you worry over the new wine, last year's wine might be on the bottling line, giving you something else to think about. And because harvest and fermentation take place at the height of the tourist season, you'll have to direct your attention to the entertainment side of the business, too.

That's Entertainment

You can make prior arrangements with tour groups, but general tourists travel on their schedule, not yours. Your visitor center and tasting room needs to be staffed and ready.

Don't stay up too late the night before worrying about the wines, because you'll need to be fresh and ready to give that bus group a tour, speech, and something to eat while they taste wine. Or that night you might be needed at a local restaurant, where a dinner pairing your wine with the food was sold to the tourists for an evening with you as the entertainment.

Throughout the year, you may even host special events such as barbecues or particular wine themes, sometimes with other wineries, sometimes on your own, and sometimes with entertainment. At these peak times, you'll have to increase tasting room staff and your own supervisory hours to keep up with the traffic.

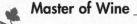

Master of Wine

As you establish a quality wine production line and product, it pays to develop a quality presentation, and that means contact with customers.

Perfect Peoplework

Every business requires human interaction, and the array of people a winery operator deals with is brisk. There's the migrant workers in the vineyard, cellar workers in the winery, the office staff, the retail/tasting room staff, and perhaps a staff of salespeople for on the road. You'll also deal with a variety of people in the distribution and sales pipeline (and of course, the ever-present bureaucrats). In addition, you'll deal with equipment and packaging representatives, print and Internet designers, printers, office suppliers, an attorney, accountant, insurance agent, and perhaps a bank manager or maybe some investors.

If your winery is small, you may find yourself dealing extensively with the public. There is none so demanding as a customer with cash or credit card in hand. Even with seemingly boundless capacity to take on whatever comes your way, an irate, sometimes irrational customer can tip the nicest person over the edge, and that could be you. As I mentioned earlier, if you're not a people person, consider the benefit of bringing on a partner who is.

Piles of Paperwork

Every businessperson contends with paperwork, of course. A great deal of the paperwork is now done on a computer, but someone in the office still has to make the entries. When you start a small business, you'll likely be the one to initially fill out employee forms, schedules, and much of the bits and pieces of paper required for an effective day-to-day operation. But a winery gives you an added burden: government regulations.

Battling Bureaucracy

As well as being a segment of the food production business, wine is a source of both federal and local revenue. Therefore, bureaucrats seem to be all over the place. They inspect for cleanliness, demand taxes and fees, and seek forms that must be filled out right on schedule and exactly to their detailed specifications—sometimes on a specific paper color. And just when you think you've mastered the requirements, the regulators come up with a new set of regulations.

> **Master of Wine**
>
> When you apply for a winery permit, federal and state governments provide many regulatory documents. Read them, follow them, and don't throw them away. Set up a library of regulatory material—you'll need it.

You need to deal with bureaucracy calmly and accurately or you can waste vast resources of your energy and a whole lot of time, not to mention the loss of money in fines. One day in the future, you may pass off this function to an operations manager, but in the eyes of the government, the owner is always the one responsible.

The Waiting Game

Depending on the type and size of your winery, it may take from $100,000 to millions to start the business. In either case, it will also take money to keep the business going. Putting money into a start-up business is called *capitalizing*.

To keep the doors open while the business grows, you need to capitalize the business to run it for a few years, and that includes paying your own salary over those years, or asking a moneylender or an investor to make a revolving line of credit available.

The amount of money usually involved in starting and running a winery is quite a risk for many. The fact that a winery generally takes longer than most start-up businesses to show a profit keeps the risk intense.

Just One More Thing ...

Okay, so you have what it takes to work nearly all day every day, year-round. And sure, you can stay calm in the face of bureaucracy. You can also manage all kinds of people or you have a partner who can. You don't fly off the handle when something unforeseen happens. And you have or can raise the capital necessary to keep a business going until it makes a profit. You are dead serious about starting and running a winery. Now we can talk business.

Well, not quite. There's just one more thing: do you like the outdoors?

Location, Location, Location

Just a few separate grapevine species account for about 10,000 different wine grape varieties. They don't all do well in the same location. Your decision where to start your winery might be based on the kind of grapes you want to grow. Wine is produced in each of the 50 states, so you have a fine array of climates, topography, and lifestyles available to you. On the other hand, where you choose to live might determine the kinds of grapes you can grow.

In Chapter 10, you learn the general qualities that allow you to grow certain grapes in certain climates. For now, what you need to know is whether or not you can stand certain climates.

Go Get Your Hands Dirty

If you plan to build your winery from the ground up, literally from your own vineyard, you certainly can read up on grape growing, but no book will make a city person understand what it's like to go rural, and no book can tell you what it's like to work outside on a farm in either the extreme cold or the extreme heat of a place you haven't visited or spent some time exploring.

There's really only one way to find out what it's like out on the farm: work on one. Vineyards require year-round maintenance, so vineyard work may be one of the easiest jobs to find—so go find one. You probably won't even have to get dressed up for the interview, but it would help if you have gardening or other outdoor work experience. Maybe a brief read-up on how grapes grow would give you just enough knowledge to show you aren't exactly a complete novice. At the least, bringing some knowledge to the interview shows that you have initiative.

It's not a bad idea to tell the interviewer about your dream of starting your own vineyard. Many farmers are sharing people, and many once had their dreams. Besides, it will make the vineyard owner feel more secure about your desire to learn and to work hard.

If you can take the time, choose more than one location, so you can work in different climates and experience what a migrant worker experiences.

> **Master of Wine**
>
> Ads in local wine region newspapers are a good source for finding jobs in a vineyard and winery. Wine industry trade magazines, both in print and online, are an even better source for job listings. (See Appendix C for a list.)

Whether or not you work in different locations, you should work a complete vineyard cycle, from pruning in winter (to set the crop size for the next vintage), to tying vine tendrils in spring (to keep them upright as the grapes add weight), to thinning and suckering vines (cutting off bottom shoots that can sap energy) in summer, to fall harvesting. That will give you a definite idea about a particular climate and teach you how to handle farm employees, too.

The Winepress

If you decide a vineyard is not for you, don't worry. You can't make wine without grapes, but there's no law preventing you from buying grapes from someone else for your winery (in Chapter 12, you learn why and how).

After the experience of working the vineyard cycle, you should know whether or not you can cut it as a farmer and if owning and running a vineyard is for you. At the very least, by working in the vineyard, you'll gain an understanding of how the source material for your wine is grown and produced. The experience will also help you make decisions about the grape varieties that interest you and that you might want to grow.

It's All About the Wine

Okay, you've worked a vineyard and you know whether or not it's right for you. Now we can talk business, right? Almost. There's just one more thing, really: what do you know about making or selling wine?

Winemaking 101

If you've never made wine at home, you should. You can learn winemaking from books (see Appendix C for a short list), but there's nothing like hands-on winemaking to fully understand the process.

The University of California, Davis Campus, is arguably the premier teaching school for winemakers in the United States. The university offers an online winemaking course (wineserver.ucdavis.edu). Cornell University in Ithaca, New York, offers winemaking courses (www.nysaes.cornell.edu/fst/vb), and other schools have started to offer courses as well.

Custom Crush

Today, there's a way to make wine that begins online and ends in a cooperative winemaking facility. *Custom crush* is a growing approach to starting your own wine business, which does not include running either your own vineyard or winery. Still, the approach may offer basic knowledge that could show you if you have what it takes. The fee you pay for this experience is far less than it would cost to start a winery, and in the end, what you learn could save you money.

In Chapter 17, you learn the details about this wine business method known as custom crush, but you can get a glimpse of it at www.crushpadwines.com.

Get Into the Cellar

You can augment book and online learning by working in a winery as a *cellar rat*, the assistant in the wine cellar. It's a job that covers every part of winemaking, from harvest to bottling. Many young winemakers come up the ranks by serving first as the "rats."

While you gain winemaking knowledge, the cellar also gives you experience with the large equipment of a winery—something no book can give you. Working in the cellar gives you the chance to develop ideas for how you'd like your winery laid out.

Become a Seller

It's been said that before you even think of sending in your application for a permit to produce wine, you should know exactly where and how you'll sell the wine you intend to produce. That's not a joke; it's good advice.

Try for a staff job at a winery behind the tasting bar or as someone who takes wines to retail shops and runs wine tastings for the consumer. Or get a job selling wine for the winery direct to retailers. If working at a winery is impractical, get a job as a sales representative for a local wine distributor selling to retail wine shops and restaurants. Or work in a retail wine shop to learn how to sell to consumers. If you have a background in sales, make it known during your interview.

Keep in mind that employers make an investment of time and money in their new hires. You'll have to determine whether or not a conversation should take place about your future dream to start and run your own winery. It could be a deal breaker, or it could show the interviewer that you are passionate about wine and might perform better than someone who just wants a job.

The benefits of working in the wine business before starting up a winery can mean at the very least that you'll avoid making the most basic mistakes and at best that you'll avoid the whoppers—the ones that can cost you a great deal of money and maybe

Master of Wine

Each state mandates how wine is distributed to the retailer and sold to the consumer. Working within the system is a good way to discover the ins and outs so you avoid writing anything in your start-up proposal to bureaucrats that will delay the permit process.

your whole dream. If you know exactly where you'll sell the wine that you haven't even produced yet, you are ahead of the game.

Okay, you have what it takes to be in a demanding business, and you're willing to spend time to learn by working outdoors, indoors, or in a cellar to discover what you need to know to help you start and run a winery. Are we ready to talk business? I think so.

Let's start with a case study. In Chapter 3, you learn what can happen when you do not do your homework, and what can happen when you do.

The Least You Need to Know

- ◆ Starting a winery is a tough job; running one may be even tougher.

- ◆ Honestly assessing and adjusting for your shortcomings is one way to avoid big mistakes.

- ◆ Before starting a winery, determine where you want to live.

- ◆ It's a good idea to learn how grapes grow, but you don't need to own a vineyard to operate a winery.

- ◆ It's a great idea to learn the basics of wine production and sales—knowledge you'll definitely need later.

3

Two Cases of Wine Start-Ups

In This Chapter

- ◆ Don't let the dream cloud reality
- ◆ The wrong frame of mind leaves you open to serious mistakes
- ◆ The right frame of mind helps you find solutions to setbacks
- ◆ Which business hat will you wear?

So far, I've talked a lot about your responsibility for making the dream come true. You've been able to handle it. In fact, you are certain you can handle it or you wouldn't be reading Chapter 3 already. Or maybe you didn't read the first two chapters. Maybe you figured you already knew all that stuff about wine history and how tough it is to start a business. Or maybe you simply want to get going right away. However you got to this point, this chapter presents you with one more taste of reality. At the end of the chapter, you'll be encouraged to make a choice.

Following are two real-life cases of two men who started their own wineries.

Case Study 1: Thomas the Dreamer

As a child, Thomas loved to sniff his next-door neighbor's recently emptied wine barrels. He tasted his first wine, cut with water, at 7. By age 19, he was the only kid on the block with a corkscrew.

As he became an adult, his passion for wine grew. By his mid-30s, he was in a successful career in the audiovisual presentation industry. He had amassed quite a lot of knowledge about wine, consuming and reading all he could.

Let's Start a Winery!

Thomas's wine passion got a boost in 1979 when he was assigned to work on a visitor center audiovisual piece for a California winery. After a few hours with the president of the wine company, Thomas developed a desire to get into the wine business—possibly even start his own winery. He began to make wine at home, and he signed up for a few winemaking and analytical classes.

> **Sour Grapes**
>
> Before the 1980s, it wasn't easy for an individual to start a winery. During this time, only a few states began to loosen controls for small family farm wineries to thrive, limiting where a person could start a small winery.

One evening over dinner, Thomas told his wife that he wanted to quit his job and start a winery. She surprised him by saying she thought it was a great idea. He had absolutely no idea how to go about getting a winery started, but he thought he was smart enough to find out. Plus, his passion, he figured, would get him there.

Most of the momentum in the wine world took place in California. But with savings that didn't measure up to the price of California land, Thomas had to look elsewhere. He knew that his home state, New York, had hosted a successful commercial wine industry for as long as California, so he took a drive to the Finger Lakes region in the western part of the state. He liked what he saw there and discovered that he could easily afford to buy land.

He bought a home on 11 acres with 6 of the acres planted to vineyards under contract with the Taylor Wine Company, New York's largest winery at the time and the most successful wine company outside California. The contract was for a specified grape tonnage that Taylor would buy from Thomas' vineyard. Thomas figured he could learn grape growing and have some income from it while he put together his winery business plan.

As he was buying property, a round of inflation had boosted interest rates to a shocking
18 percent. Thomas took out a mortgage
anyway. The wine company promised to
renew the grape contract. At the same time,
however, the increased wine consumption
across the United States was benefiting
California wine producers but was not ben-
efiting East Coast producers. In fact, it was hurting them. He didn't let that bother
him because he intended to produce premium wine, and he did have the promise of a
renewed contract.

The Winepress _____

In the early 1980s, wine consumption in the United States
was on the rise, especially
among the baby boomer population.

A Financial Setback

Within weeks after moving into his new home, Thomas received a letter from the
Taylor Wine Company. The winery was feeling pressure due to the economy and
competition with California. Because the contract for grapes was with vineyards under
the previous owner, and because the company needed to cut back grape purchases, the
company decided not to renew the contract with Thomas after all.

Thomas worked hard to learn to grow the
grapes that year and then scurried to find a
market for them. Inflation had also affected
the cost to grow grapes, which increased
at the same time wineries reduced the prices
they would pay for what had become a grape
oversupply in New York. He lost money on
his first crop.

Master of Wine _____

Sophisticated wine consumers consider wines pro-
duced from Old World grapes
more elegant than wines from
so-called Native American grape
varieties of the New World.
California produced the former;
New York was known for the
latter. (See Chapter 10 for more
detail about the grape varieties.)

In the meantime, Thomas created a business plan using information from the
Small Business Association and Cornell
University's local cooperative extension program. He aimed to seek financing for his
start-up winery, but although his business plan looked good on paper, the two separate
local bank managers he approached were unimpressed.

To the bank managers, his business plan did not prove he could draw a salary from the
business and make a profit. With no visible means of support, they didn't believe he
would be able to pay back the 18 percent interest on his mortgage, let alone another
loan for the winery. To make matters worse, in the bankers' minds, Thomas had no
small business track record.

Sour Grapes

To a bank, an individual borrower with no large capital to back him or her up is an unsecured risk and not someone they're eager to loan money to.

In addition, the bank managers pointed out that Thomas was asking for money to enter an already risky business that had just become riskier. And it didn't help his case at all that an influential consumer wine magazine, *Wine Spectator*, had just put out an issue with a picture of Finger Lakes vineyards being bulldozed on the cover.

A Change in Plans

Thomas scrapped his business plan. He set out to start a winery on a smaller scale, using his remaining savings. He also took a day job, as his new plan was projected to provide him with no salary for some time. The plan included letting the vineyard go, so for the next three years, he pulled up another section of vineyard until the vines were gone. He expected to replant as soon as possible in the future.

He couldn't build a new winery, but a small house with a two-car garage directly across from him was for sale at a bargain price. Thomas bought it. Interest rates began to fall at that time so he used the purchase of the small house as a way to instigate renegotiation for a more favorable deal on his home mortgage.

And Now, About That Winery ...

Without the help of an attorney, Thomas navigated the federal and state winery permit application processes. The frustrating task took nearly a year, but when it was over, he was ready to go. All he needed was a supply of grapes and some winemaking equipment.

Sour Grapes

According to many industry experts, a winery producing fewer than 5,000 gallons each year has a hard time showing a profit. It has to do with economy of scale—the costs to operate often outpace the price you can get for your wine.

After doing more number-crunching, Thomas figured he could afford to produce about 1,000 gallons of wine in his first year. He also decided to forgo the equipment to crush and press grapes. Instead, he contracted with a local business that grew grapes and sold juice to home winemakers. Unlike red wine, which is fermented before the grapes are pressed, most white wine is pressed and then fermented as juice. Thomas's decision to buy juice limited him to producing only white wine.

He invested in a few small stainless-steel tanks, some smaller glass storage vessels, a pump, and a bottling line that consisted of a small stainless-steel gravity-fed filler that filled four bottles at a time. He also bought himself a hand corker. He insulated the two-car garage and installed a sink and water line. He set up the house with a storage area off to the side and remodeled the kitchen into a tasting room.

Reality Strikes

By the time he was ready to produce his first wines, Thomas was out of money. But he kept his day job and managed to keep the winery going on a shoestring budget. He hired someone to work in the tasting room on weekdays. On weekends, when the traffic was at its greatest, he rounded up his wife and any family members he could get to help in the tasting room.

In spite of having produced a couple of award-winning wines over the years and a customer base that continued to slowly grow, Thomas kept having to chase his financial tail. He was unable to get ahead of the bills and severely overworking himself.

Thomas's Mistakes

What did Thomas do wrong? First, he didn't do his homework. It's good to have dreams, yes. But to invest your money and your life in a business takes more than just desire. Thomas failed to thoroughly research the New York wine industry. He was blindsided when his vineyard contract was not renewed.

He also didn't understand the financing. Agriculture is a beacon of risk—vineyard land isn't much in the way of collateral security to a banker. When the bank turned him down, Thomas could have considered seeking a partner or private investors, but it never entered his mind because it was his dream to start a winery. The thought of sharing his dream got in the way of considering financing alternatives.

Thomas also forgot the salary part. If the business you operate is not part-time but it can't pay you a salary, you're already in a hole. Keeping a young business afloat takes steady cash flow. You don't want your day-job salary to be the source of new funds for your business.

 **Sour Grapes**

A person without a track record in a small business is at an added disadvantage with bankers.

And then he got off on the wrong foot. Thomas had no grape-growing knowledge or training. He also had no idea how the grape-growing market worked. He broke his back that first year to grow grapes and to find a market, and all he got for his effort was financial heartache. He would have been better off to disregard the vineyard until his winery business was established. In addition, while the growth in wine consumption was in white wine, the interest in red wine was actually stronger among the big spenders. Being forced to produce white wine limited his sales and his customer base.

Finally, he had an insecure ongoing supply chain. In the eighth year of running his winery, the general region faced a bad vintage and a reduced crop. The grapes Thomas bought came from a fellow who ran a home winemaker's supply business. His home winemaker customers came first, so they got juice and Thomas got none.

In an almost textbook timeline, Thomas's winery lasted eight years without ever showing a profit. He was forced to close the business.

Case Study 2: John the Businessman

His grandfather made commercial wine, but the passion never rubbed off on John. Instead, John did well in the oil supply and real estate development businesses. But realizing he was away from his family too often, he sold his businesses in the late 1990s with the idea to start a business that would keep him close to home.

John made a decent profit on the sale of his businesses. He had a few months to figure out what to do with the money before giving to the government what he thought would certainly wind up to be too much in taxes.

Where to Put His Money?

Seeking to put money into another business at the lowest possible taxable liability, John settled on agriculture, which, thanks to some benefits in New York connected to agriculture, provided him an avenue to shelter some of his profits. He remembered his grandfather's wine, so he decided to start a vineyard and winery, which especially benefited from state government programs at the time.

The Winepress

During the inflationary period of the 1980s, farming was hit particularly hard. Farmers were heavily in debt to banks and farm bureaus to cover the cost of the expensive equipment necessary to supply the large wineries with the necessary grape tonnage. Because farms were on the verge of failing, states enacted beneficial tax and lending programs to help them.

John did his research. He discovered that the Northeastern wine industry was taking a good turn, plus he discovered a particular area that was booming in new winery growth. He found land in that area, packed up his family, and moved from the Mid-Atlantic region to New York.

His plan included buying land, planting a vineyard, and building a solid, modern winery in an area that had been averaging one new winery each year for the past decade. John also knew exactly what kind of wine he would produce. He had researched and discovered that the market was on a sharp increase for certain red wines, and because he would be competing with already-established wineries that produced mostly white wines, he would offer his target market something different.

A Financial Setback

Planting the size vineyard and putting up the building he wanted, with equipment, would take all the money John had available—$2 million. He knew he had to take care of an income for himself, so he went to a bank seeking a revolving line of credit he thought would tide him over during the ups and downs of the start-up business.

The money John could put into the business impressed the bankers, but they also noticed that it would likely be gone before he made his first sale. They were uninterested in the vineyard and winery equipment as collateral, and because he had no track record in agriculture, to John's shock, they said no to revolving credit.

> **Sour Grapes** _____
>
> Bankers prefer to give secured loans, but their idea of security doesn't always include real estate or specialized equipment for a particular industry. You'll often need to prove you have access to liquidity (cash) as collateral. If you can't, they might not lend to you.

A Change in Plans

John changed his plans. Instead of building and equipping a winery, he decided to build a modern wine warehouse facility plus a tasting room. He sought a source for wine he could bottle under his label. He decided to concentrate on selling wine before he produced it.

John found a source for bulk wine about 300 miles away. He wasn't thrilled about the distance, which he knew would add cost and aggravation to doing business. Nevertheless, he applied for the federal and state winery permits, signed a contract to buy wine in bulk, got his labels approved by regulators, had the wine bottled 300 miles away, and moved it to his tasting room to sell.

With wine to sell, John planted a vineyard knowing he had three or four years to build the business before his first grape crop was ready. He did everything the cooperative extension people suggested, plus he listened to a few neighboring farmers who told him about *grow tubes,* which would give him two years worth of vine growth in the first year.

Another Setback

By the end of spring, John's vines were in the ground and growing. With the help of his wife and children, John continued to build wine sales at the tasting room throughout the summer. In late summer, he lifted the grow tubes from the vines as had been instructed, and he scraped soil to create hills around the vines to protect the roots for winter.

The winter proved to be among the worst of the decade in the Northeast. In one day, an overnight temperature drop from above freezing to sub-zero killed more than half of the area's vines. Luckily, the hilling John had done around his new vines protected their roots. That spring, his vineyard was back on track. Unfortunately, the summer was rained out, and his infant vines literally drowned. John ultimately lost the vineyard, but he did not lose the business. His wine sales at the tasting room were growing as planned.

The Importance of Flexibility

John made an agreement with a group of investors to share in some vineyards that secured an annual crop of grapes for his wines, which John now produces under his supervision at the facility 300 miles from the tasting- and salesroom. He also decided not to distribute his wine to retailers and restaurants but to sell all of it from his tasting room, giving him full markup.

The distance between the source of grapes, the winemaking, and the warehouse/ tasting room is a small logistical annoyance, but it was a perfect solution for John. His winery has been operating for four years as of this writing and is showing a small profit.

John's Correct Moves

Even when forced to change plans, John made the right moves. First, he did his homework. Because John selected the wine industry not to feed a romantic notion, but strictly as a business decision, his research was rational. He saw a local region on the rise in winery growth and knew that was a good place to start his business.

John also understood the financing. He knew he would need a way to earn a salary while he was building his business. But he didn't consider that banks would be reluctant to provide him with a revolving credit line. Knowing the business would be the only way to pay his salary in the first couple years, he changed gears. He spent less money on the start-up than he had originally planned not by compromising but by coming up with an alternative. The money he saved by changing plans went toward paying him a salary while he built the new business.

John thought about sales before thinking about production. The second biggest mistake after undercapitalizing a product business is to place emphasis on production without figuring out how and where to sell the product. By first building a modern tasting- and salesroom and processing wine elsewhere, John built his wine sales before he bought one piece of expensive equipment.

Finally, John established a reliable supply chain. His business relies on a contractual partnership with investors in the vineyards and in a winemaking facility.

John's winery pays him a living wage, and he is seeing a profit each year, which he is plowing into the earth, to replant his vineyards.

Make Rational, Not Emotional Choices

The true stories in this chapter illustrate what can happen when you don't do your homework and when you do. The stories also illustrate how starting a vineyard makes an impact on plans for a start-up winery. In Thomas's case, bad timing coupled with a lack of understanding of the nature of the grape-growing end of the wine business proved lethal. He was unprepared for the financial loss that first year in the vineyard, and it had an effect on his ability to move forward financially. John's initial failure in the vineyard was weather related. He couldn't control it, but he should have known it was possible. He managed to bounce back, but the vineyard problem still made an impact on his plans for the start-up.

The Winepress

Running a vineyard is farming. Vineyards are the source of winemaking, but you don't have to be a farmer to run a winery.

Both Thomas and John had to change course, but because he was scrambling, Thomas made his decisions in a "seat of the pants," fashion. It's possible that if he had abandoned the vineyard when the contract was canceled he might have saved both money and energy he could have applied to thinking more clearly. He might have been better off from the start to operate a small winery without a vineyard. When the time came for him to change plans, he failed to consider taking on a partner or investors, holding on to his personal dream, which by then was slipping away.

John thought his setbacks through and looked for viable solutions, whatever they turned out to be. If John hadn't tried to get a vineyard started that first year, he might have had enough money to put into buying more wine and building more market for his wine, which could have given him quicker growth in the winery. But he had enough money at the start to see him through a small setback, and when he was faced with having to change plans, he was also quick to sign on with some investors—a business decision that was based on the realities he faced.

Before sinking your money into the start-up, carefully consider the three parts that make up the wine business (remember these from Chapter 2?): the vineyard, food production, and entertainment. It's possible to start in one of the three, in a combination of two of the three, or in all three. Whether you have the stamina or temperament for each is important. But more important is whether or not you have the ability to make business decisions and to secure the financing.

In Chapter 4, you get a glimpse into what your day would be like running a complete winery, from vineyard to tasting room. Then it's time to carefully weigh the decision to choose the business you want to be in, and the role you want to play in that business.

The Least You Need to Know

- You must do your homework. Always.

- If you can't raise enough money from a bank, don't rule out alternatives.

- Trying to start a winery while holding down a day job isn't impossible, it's just not recommended.

- Because you're producing a consumer product, start the business with sales in mind.

- You don't need to grow grapes to produce wine, but if you don't grow them, you need solid agreements to buy them.

Chapter 4

Choose Your Own Adventure

In This Chapter

- What operating a vineyard is like
- What operating a winery is like
- A glimpse at a day in the life
- Your role in the business
- The importance of a good staff

Now that you know what to look for when you start a winery, the time has come for a glimpse into what you'll face as you run one.

Grapes and wine definitely hold to a schedule: grapes flower in spring, grow in summer, and are harvested in the fall; wine is fermented in the fall and is produced through the winter. But except for the hours you open your wine tasting room and the timely submission of taxes and forms, just about everything else in the business is variable.

In other words, when you get out of bed in the morning, you often have no idea what will come your way that day at work—or how much of it! This chapter explains what some of your days at your vineyard will be like.

What's Your Choice: Winery or Vineyard?

I've said it before (I know, more than once), but I have to say it again: running a winery is running three businesses. It can be done well and profitably, but it has to be thought out, planned, and staffed for success.

Wine is a consumer product, so every choice you make must be reflected in the image your business presents. That means when you grow grapes, be certain the grapes are top quality. And when you produce wine, be certain the wines are premium value. High-quality grapes provide the raw material for great wine. How the wine turns out, and at what price it is available, is up to the producer and winemaker to determine.

> **Master of Wine**
>
> Wine people have a saying: great wine is made in the vineyard. Put your effort into producing or procuring high-quality grapes, and you have half the job done.

When you pour wine for visitors, make the finest presentation. Your winery visitor center and tasting bar is an interview room: the customer is interviewing your product. Everything the customer sees and hears augments what he or she tastes.

Break down the three parts of the business and then make a choice whether you will be in all the business or in a part of it.

Running a Vineyard

If you worked a couple cycles in the vineyard, as suggested in Chapter 2, you should know by now whether running a vineyard is right for you. If you do plan to grow your own grapes, you'll need to remember a few important things:

It takes time. It takes three or four years before a new vineyard produces mature grapes for wine, and it takes another two or three years before the wine is in the bottle and on shelves.

It takes money. In Chapter 7, you'll get the numbers. For now, be aware that planting a vineyard means no return on investment for a minimum of four years but probably more like six years. Time is money.

It takes specialized knowledge. Grape growing is horticulture; it is as much science as it is farming. If you aren't schooled, get a horticultural consultant to help you begin and hire an experienced farmer/horticulturist to manage your vineyard.

It takes long-range commitment. When you decide what to plant in a vineyard, you can't easily change vines if the market changes its affection for certain wines.

If you want to run your own vineyard so you can claim it on your labels, your decision to run a vineyard may have more to do with marketing than with the reality of agriculture. This is the right time to have a serious talk with yourself about your motivation.

Sour Grapes

On their labels, many wine producers boast that all their wines are the product of their vineyards. In the twenty-first century, the marketing benefit of this claim seems to have become negligible.

Running a Production Facility

It's been said, maybe in exaggeration, that in the 1950s, when Lucy and Ethel stomped grapes in Italy on the *I Love Lucy* show, they set back the vision of the Italian wine industry 100 years.

When you commit to producing wine in the twenty-first century, you'll either commit to a mini industrial revolution or go back in time. Sometimes the choice you make is personal; sometimes it's marketing. Winemaking is a scientific craft. You can't hurry wine, you can't legally doctor wine, and wine doesn't always turn out according to plan. Your job is to give the product every benefit it needs, and that means understanding the technology behind the science.

Modern winemaking technology is costly. Even if you don't scrimp or cut corners, machines can cause you to lose money. Learn to understand the technology or have someone close by who does. Wine has its timing; machines don't.

Going back in time may have its benefits. Doing things less high-tech may help you maintain high quality. For example, instead of pumping from tank to tank, moving wine by force of gravity prevents excessive oxidation. In the bargain, you'd have fewer machines to break down.

Producing wine is complicated. You may need to consult a few professionals. In Chapter 8 you learn why and how to find them.

Running a Full Winery

By "full winery," I mean the one described in the crystal ball later in this chapter, the one that is agriculture, manufacturing, and entertainment. Obviously, when you run all three businesses, you meet the characters of each head-on.

Building a Brand

Learning how grapes grow, how wine is made, and how to market wine is necessary, but you don't have to run either a vineyard or winery to use the knowledge. You can apply what you know to running a brand or brands.

In Chapter 17, you learn how to let someone else source grapes and make the wine for you. Then all you have to do is sell it. This happens to be a growing end of the wine business, especially on the West Coast. It's called custom crush.

Make It a Hybrid

If you don't want to stay within the lines of only one part of the wine business, you can pick the parts that best suit your finances and your temperament. You can …

- Be a grape grower only and still get your name on wine labels.

- Grow grapes and produce wine for others.

- Produce wine only for others.

- Grow grapes and build brands but not produce wine.

- Produce wine, operate a tasting room, and build brands that others produce for you.

I cover each of these in more detail in future chapters, especially in Chapter 17, but before you go there, let's take a look at what a day in your business might be like if you decide to run a full winery.

A Day in Your Future Winery

You are in the early years of the business. It's spring, and you're planting vines you bought from a nursery. You're also preparing the already established vineyard that came with the property for the coming growing season.

Recent rains have taken a chunk out of your schedule in the vineyard, but the forecast looks good for a while and you intend to make up for the lost time. Today is the first good day in a long time, and you want to make use of every minute.

Rising Before the Morning Sun

Your alarm clock blares before the sun rises. There's no time for breakfast, just some juice and coffee. For morning energy, you can have a piece of the cake that you left in the office refrigerator the night before when you knocked off at 9 o'clock.

Your planting schedule is running behind. You have a couple acres remaining to plant, and you hope that extra migrant labor force will be waiting for you when you arrive at work.

You pull into the long driveway toward the vineyard. As you pass the winery, you smile that you were smart enough to erect the building at the end of the road that leads to the vineyard. Moving grapes to the winery minutes after picking them certainly has lowered logistical costs. More importantly, the grapes don't deteriorate, and they're fresh and clean when they enter the press.

It's not quite daylight yet, but when you look up ahead, even in the subdued light of dawn, you can see that no laborers await you at the end of the road.

A car pulls in behind you. It's your vineyard manager. Luckily, he's always on time.

> **Master of Wine**
>
> For a better chance at maintaining product quality, a winery should be as close to the source of grapes—the vineyards—as possible.

Dealing With No-Show Workers

Your vineyard manager says the extra crew won't be able to work as expected. Just like you, they lost time during a recent three-day rain. The team leader miscalculated when they would be finished working the vineyard down the road.

Your manager got a small crew of old-timers together, and he thinks, with extended hours, the job can be done. Of course, it might cost a little more in overtime pay ....

The morning looks to be beautiful, and the forecast looks good. Your manager needs to get the vineyard ready for its pre-bloom antifungal spray. He can't stand around wasting any more time. You roll your eyes and head for the office.

Some Good News

The new crew shows up within minutes. You know most of the people. They'll get the job done, whatever it takes. You chart the work for the day, assign a work supervisor, and distribute vineyard tools.

It's daylight, about 45 minutes past your originally planned starting time, but at least work has started. You grab a few bites and notice that the cake from last night is semi-fresh. Things may be looking up!

Another Boot Hits the Dirt

Just as you settle down to a cup of coffee and to collect your thoughts, your vineyard manager walks in to explain that he had to call Ernie. Ernie repairs tractors. You don't like where this is heading.

The vineyard manager isn't sure why but the *PTO* (*power take-off*) isn't working properly. You know that if he doesn't spray the vines soon, and it rains, risk of fungus infection can ruin flowering, and that can reduce this year's crop. You can only hope Ernie fixes the problem.

def•i•ni•tion

A **power take-off** (PTO) is a spinning rod fitted on the back of the vineyard tractor. When a variety of vineyard equipment is attached to it (separately, of course), the PTO enables the attachments to perform a variety of tasks like spraying, mowing, and digging holes.

Master of Wine

The U.S. Treasury Department's Tax and Trade Bureau (TTB) regulates what goes on a wine label. An industry of lawyers has sprung up in Washington, D.C., to handle label approval by "walking" your submission to the TTB office. It costs, but using one of them helps speed up the process and, maybe, avoids mistakes.

The phone rings. Ernie was sidetracked by some-one else's tractor problem, but he's on his way. Another half hour is lost, and you feel the day slipping away … which reminds you to open yesterday's mail.

In the mail is a returned wine label application. You didn't catch that the printer used the wrong font size for the government-mandated warning information so the TTB (the U.S. Treasury Department Tax and Trade Bureau) denied the label approval. You'll have to resubmit the application. You'll get to it later.

Just as you get on the Internet to check the weather for tomorrow, the planting crew supervisor walks through the door. There's a discrepancy between the number of vines and the number of grow tubes. A grow tube must be stabilized around each plant, so it needs to be set in place around each new vine as it's planted. Planting had to stop.

Neither the vineyard manager nor the supervisor know what you ordered, so neither can just pick up the phone, call the nursery, and make arrangements. You place a phone call to the nursery; they have your order. You send the supervisor to the nursery. You make a note: delegate more work, like placing orders, to the vineyard manager.

More time has slipped away. The clock has inched to 10 A.M. Because the vineyard crew started so early this morning, they break for lunch. You take a look at their work and see that they are less than halfway through the day's planting schedule. You call your wife to say good morning, which you never had a chance to do, as she was fast asleep at the hour you got started.

Ernie has arrived and says that there's nothing wrong with the PTO. The problem is in the gear stick that engages it. He can rig it to work today, and he can come back tomorrow with the parts and fix it like new.

Sour Grapes

Some horticulturists warn against grow tubes. They claim that the benefit they give—speeding up the first year's growth—can backfire as the greenhouse effect inside the grow tube can develop tenderness or weakness in the vines, making them unable to survive winter.

Your vineyard manager knows he has to get the spraying done before the sun is too strong. He hops on the tractor, skipping lunch. He is one of the best people you've hired.

The Tasting Room Is Calling

You finish the last piece of that cake in the refrigerator and pour yourself another cup of coffee. The coffee is good, but you have to put it aside for now as a new employee just arrived for her first day behind the tasting room bar. Your tasting room manager is at a hospitality industry sales and marketing meeting, so it's your job to orient the new employee.

You didn't get a chance to go over her credentials, but your tasting room manager told you she is well versed in wine and only needs an orientation in how your tasting room operates. It sounds simple enough, but because you're so busy, and you're not very good at customer interaction, you've given over the tasting room to your manager—you

Master of Wine

The wine tasting bar is your winery's theatrical stage. People come to be entertained. Make the presentation at the bar the highest-quality one you can.

don't even know where she stores the corkscrews, which of course are right where they ought to be—on the counter next to the wine refrigeration.

In the middle of the orientation, the phone rings. It's your distributor placing an order for a pallet of wine to be picked up tomorrow. While you're talking with the distributor representative, you notice that a couple have walked into the tasting room and are standing at the bar waiting to be served. If only you could afford to hire a traffic manager!

You hustle the distributor rep off the phone and get over to the tasting bar.

The Winery Is Calling

While you deal with the visitors in the tasting room, the cellar rat taps you on the shoulder to ask a question. He was racking some wine, moving it from one tank into another, per your earlier instructions, when the pump broke down. He'll repair it later. Right now, he needs to know if he should use the pump you had connected to a separate hose leading from another tank. He didn't want to move anything without knowing why it was there in the first place.

Had you told the cellar rat your intentions for that other pump, he wouldn't have been afraid to touch it without your knowledge and you wouldn't have lost another half hour. You make a note: delegate more responsibility to the cellar rat.

On your way to your office, you see a bus pull into the driveway with a load of people. Just before you go into a panic, you see your tasting room manager's car trailing behind the bus. She remembered the bus tour and hurried to get back to the tasting room. She's as good as your vineyard manager, and aren't you happy about that?

As you look out the window and notice a threat of rain, the phone rings. It's the local Chamber of Commerce chief reminding you about the dinner tomorrow and wondering how much donated wine he can count on from your winery.

You try not to imagine what can happen for the rest of the day, and you wonder whether you could run this business without killing yourself.

> **Sour Grapes**
>
> Being in business also means being part of a community, so it's good to join local business organizations. However, a joke told in the wine industry is that on any given day, you could give away all your wine by responding to product donation requests. Carefully consider the promotional benefits of making product donations.

Where Do You Fit In?

Most people with the drive to run a business are achievers, and some are overachievers or Type A personalities. Type A people are driven to succeed. If they have a touch of the Type B personality in them—attention to detail—they can achieve wonders. But they can also perform *too* well for their own good.

The biggest mistake Type A people make is to not take time to be sure subordinates understand their instructions. When those instructions aren't followed exactly, the Type A personalities often get angry and stressed and may complete the task themselves. Soon enough, the Type A business owner finds he or she is working too hard. It's a path to stress that can lead right to the intensive care unit.

It's your business, but one way to put it into jeopardy is to try to do everything yourself. However you formally structure your business (in Chapter 5, you learn the business structure options), and whether or not you choose to operate a vineyard along with the winery, you must decide what your job is at the company. You can pick more than one job, if you can handle it, but you should try not to do a zillion jobs just because you can't let go.

The CEO

A full winery contains a number of profit centers. The chief executive officer (CEO) is responsible for pulling the profit centers together and ensuring that the business plan moves forward. This is done by keeping eyes, ears, and mind fixed on all important business matters and by making decisions that answer to partners, investors, or the board of directors.

The CEO must build and motivate a staff who can be trusted and then delegate responsibility to the people on the team with confidence, holding them accountable for their assigned duties.

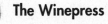 **The Winepress**

The CEO position is mainly for larger companies, to direct high-level strategy and overall growth. In small companies, the CEO will be hands-on, making most of the business decisions.

The CEO, Plus

In a winery, the CEO often is the winemaker. But I know at least three wineries where the CEO either is or started as the vineyard owner and manager. Under these conditions, the CEO runs one of the profit centers. That's fine, as long as the rest of the CEO responsibilities to the business and shareholders in the business are not compromised.

This chapter points out the challenges of running a winery on a daily basis. It also points out that you can run a demanding wine business without killing yourself, provided you know which business you want to be in, know your limitations, and build a competent staff, which you'll learn how to do in more detail in Chapter 16.

In the next chapter, you learn how to get the wheels turning to start your business. On second thought, wheels may be the wrong image. Get a good pair of walking shoes—you are in for some legwork.

The Least You Need to Know

- It's decision time: which of the three branches of the wine business do you want to be in?

- Be prepared to work long days and long nights.

- You will be called upon to make quick decisions minute by minute.

- It's decision time again: who do you want to be in the business?

- You can't do everything yourself and do it well, so find people you can trust for staff positions, and delegate.

Part 2

Laying Your Foundation

If you aren't sweating by now, you will be soon. You've got what it takes to do the hard work, now you have to put together the plan. In Part 2, I show you how to find the resources as well as the discipline you need to start your business. I lead you through the paces: the proposal, the applications, the decisions that will name and structure your business, plus your business goals. When you've finished Part 2, you'll know how to get your business plan in shape, what you need to do to name and register your business, and how to finance the whole operation.

5

Digging Into Business Decisions

In This Chapter

- ◆ Structuring your business
- ◆ Registering your business
- ◆ Finding a place for your business
- ◆ Following all the rules

The character and shape of a business depends on its principals and its legal entity. Whether the business has 1 owner, 2, 10, or 100, the nature of ownership determines how the business will be run and under which tax status.

By this time, I would be advising you to write a business plan, but that has to wait until Chapter 6, until after you decide some important things about your business. Where will it be? You can produce and sell wine in all 50 states, but not always in the same manner. Weather and regulations are unique to each location, and each location affects what it costs to start and run your business.

In this chapter, you learn how to structure your business and how to determine where you're going to run it. Are you ready to make some decisions?

Understanding Business Structures

Inc., *LLC*, and so on are not just business name appendages; they are legal identifications that represent how a business is structured. A business needs a legal structure to limit liability and pay appropriate taxes. And a business with more than one principal partner needs to work out the role of each.

It's possible to change a business structure somewhere in the future. How easy or difficult it will be to do that is partly based on the decisions you make when you create the structure.

Sole Proprietorships

In this simplest structural form, you are the sole owner and entrepreneur. You are in the driver's seat. You are the pilot of this ship. You have all the control. Feels great, doesn't it?

But the drawback of a sole proprietorship is your complete responsibility for all financial obligations of the business. If someone sues the business and wins the suit, either you or the business has to pay up. The same holds true if your business is bankrupted with debts outstanding.

> **Sour Grapes**
>
> As a sole proprietor, you automatically back up liability in the business with your personal assets. Depending on the state you operate in, that could mean your home.

To start a sole proprietorship, first you name it and then file for a business identification number. (I get to that later.) You can finance your business however you like, even from your own savings account or checkbook, and you can shut down the business whenever you please.

Tax filing is easy for a sole proprietorship. You use the IRS Tax Form 1040, Schedule C to file with your personal income taxes.

Partnerships

Two or more people make up a business partnership. It's like a sole proprietorship, only the profits and liabilities are shared among the partners. Partners are held liable just like sole proprietors, and they file their business taxes just like sole proprietors. How much each partner shares the gains and losses is spelled out by contract.

Partners not only share profits and losses based on their investment, but they may also share the workload. The contract covers everyone's responsibilities, too.

The two things a partnership contract can and must do clearly are …

- Provide a mechanism for revising it as situations change or arise.

- Spell out what happens to the shares of a partner who is severely incapacitated or dies.

Master of Wine

The partnership structure screams out for a good lawyer. Over time, one partner or the other may become unhappy with the arrangement for whatever reason.

An unexpected event to one partner can make the lives of the other partners quite difficult.

Corporations

Legally, a corporation is like a person. The corporation owns both its debts and its assets. It owns its products and fully paid-for fixtures and buildings. Shareholders in a corporation are generally not liable for its actions, and lawsuits against the corporation are settled with corporate assets. (Corporate officers can still be held accountable for personal actions, though.) The federal government recognizes two types of corporations: S corporations and C corporations.

An S corporation is designed for individuals seeking liability protection but who also want to handle the business as a partnership. The partners become shareholders and are officers of the corporation and/or employees. The S corporation pays no federal taxes. Shareholder employees receive regular employee W-2 tax statements, plus an IRS Schedule K-1 that reports annual taxable income from corporate profits (or deductions from losses), which they report on an IRS Schedule E with their federal personal income tax return. Individual states tax S corporations at their discretion.

A C corporation is a general corporation. Shareholders of the corporation who work there are also employees. Corporate profits are paid in taxable dividends to shareholders or not at all. Shareholders pay capital gains (or mount capital losses) on sales of stock. Because of the nature of profit distributions, a C corporation and its shareholders can be subject to double taxation on earnings.

Master of Wine

Corporations (and LLC structures, coming up next) are complex and paperwork-heavy. They are best administered with the help of a lawyer.

A corporation never dies. Shutting one down takes much paperwork.

Limited Liability Companies (LLCs)

The LLC structure offers shareholders the liability protection of a C corporation and the profit and loss tax status of an S corporation. The main drawback of an LLC is after you make your first couple of million in profits, it will be more difficult to take the company public than it is with a corporation.

Unlike a corporation, the LLC dies when its owners die.

Separating the Vineyard from the Winery

If you run a vineyard along with a winery, you should think of the vineyard as a separate business from the winery, even if you maintain the whole business under one roof, so to speak. As farms, vineyards are subject to a different set of business, employment, and taxation rules, especially at the state level.

The Winepress

Most agricultural communities have a state farm bureau as well as a university agricultural station that can assist you with the required government paperwork and maybe recommend the kind of professionals you need to help in specific financial and/or legal matters. Many wine regions have established promotion organizations that can also guide you in legal and financial matters.

No law prevents one of the winery owners from owning a vineyard that sells to the winery business. Of course, something like that would be part of the negotiation in, say, a partnership contract.

Location, Location, Location

Earlier I told you that starting a winery means deciding where you want to live. Of course, the weather is critical for running a vineyard. For running a winery, a state's regulatory climate is equally critical. Each of the 50 states has the right to control wine production and sales in its own way, so where you choose to start your business has a direct effect on the nature of your business plan.

The Fifty Unique States

The 21st amendment to the U.S. Constitution gives each state the right to regulate alcohol. States generally consider it a privilege to allow citizens to produce and sell wine, so they regulate commercial wine activity right down to how and when prices are listed and when business-to-business bills must be paid.

Here are a few ways state regulations can affect your plans:

Your sales forecasts may suffer. In some states, once you select a distributor for your wine, should you become unhappy with the service you receive, laws make it difficult for you to switch distributors. In alcohol regulation terms, this is called a *franchise state*.

Your marketing reach may suffer. Wineries may be restricted to signing with only one distributor.

The Winepress

The transportation or importation into any State, Territory, or possession of the United States for delivery or use there in of intoxicating liquors, in violation of the laws thereof, is hereby prohibited.

—21st amendment to the U.S. Constitution

Your profit margins may suffer. In some states, wineries can act as their own distributors to sell their wines direct to retailers and restaurants. Other states prohibit wineries from distributing their wines direct to retailers and restaurants.

Your distribution outlets may be limited by the state. States that restrict private retail ownership are called *control states.* They operate their own retail outlets, and the stores often don't buy wine from small wineries.

Your direct sales to consumers may suffer. In many states, wineries can operate more than one tasting room, in multiple locations, but this privilege may be severely limited in other states.

The ability to sell ancillary products may be limited. In many states, a winery can sell food through its tasting room and also operate a restaurant in its facility, but in some states, maybe not.

Your ability to sell to a national consumer market may suffer. At this writing, 35 states allow wineries to ship wine direct to consumers

def•i•ni•tion

A **control state** restricts private business from retailing wine to consumers. Generally, the state sets up a government entity to operate retail outlets with civil service employees who may or may not be trained in wine appreciation and sales. In control states, the state government, not private business, determines what appears on retail shelves.

across state borders, but with a variety of licensing and permits unique to each state that can make shipping wine a nightmare for small producers.

I've provided a list of the alcohol control offices in all 50 states in Appendix C. Get a jump on making your location decision by selecting three or four states you're interested in and send for their application for a permit. Ask also for a copy of the state's regulations. For an online list of the alcohol control boards, go to the U.S. Treasury Department Tax and Trade Bureau (TTB) website at www.ttb.gov/wine/control_board.shtml.

More Considerations for Choosing a State

A state's alcohol regulations certainly will affect your wine business, but so will other business climate considerations. As you narrow down your choices for a state of operation, seek answers to the following questions:

Where are the wineries in this state? Many states have more than one wine region.

What other tourist draws are there in each wine region? Knowing this information gives you an idea of the traffic flow you can expect in a particular wine region. For instance, if you draw a 150-mile radius around central New York State, you'll be within reach of approximately 54 million people.

What's transportation like in the area? Find out where the airports are, if there is a train station, where the major highways are, and what the secondary roads are like. This information is valuable in a state that allows wineries to have tasting rooms at multiple locations.

Which areas in the state are economically booming? It's well established that wine sales grow with the economy, and they grow even faster in communities and households with more disposable income. If you intend to distribute wine yourself, picking the location of your winery may mean being close to a certain segment of the market.

Which areas are economically careful? Sections of a region or state have an economic identity. A shopping mall is one measure of that identity. The type of stores in a mall, especially the wine and spirits shops, might indicate the wine pricing a community supports.

But don't stop with these questions. Add to the list whatever you think will have an effect on your wine sales.

Some of your questions can be answered when you talk with other business and winery owners. Other answers may require deeper demographic research from local and state government offices. Don't forget to check with local business organizations like the chamber of commerce.

The Price of Land

A winery is a business that takes up space. The space it takes up ought to be worth what it costs you to get it. Even within a particular wine region, land values can fluctuate greatly. They're generally based on access to recreation (a lake), the topography (a view), access to amenities (the nearest city), and the overall wealth or lack of wealth of a community.

In the case of wineries, land prices are related to the nature of the business. If other wineries grace the landscape and the tourist traffic is brisk, you can be sure the price of land will be equally brisk.

In the case of vineyards, the price of land is determined first by its viability for grape growing, second by its location, third by how good you are at negotiating, and fourth by what the business climate is for wineries at the time.

I mentioned earlier that for quality and control, its best to locate the winery close to the vineyard. But that doesn't mean they must be on the same parcel of land. The land directly adjacent to a heavily trafficked road may fit the winery's needs, but that land might not be best for the grapes.

> **Master of Wine**
>
> People like to see vineyards as they travel up the driveway to the winery. The vineyard that surrounds your winery need not be your only one or your most important one.

What's the Local Wine Industry Like?

What if you decide to locate your winery off the beaten path, all by yourself? Maybe in your research you uncovered something about potential growth in an area that others don't know yet, and because it happens to be close to an active wine region, you decide to risk it. But before you make the leap, consider that there may be something *you* don't know yet.

Check Local Zoning

What if the area you like isn't zoned for the alcohol business? Some states allow localities to regulate alcohol, and some localities don't tolerate its sale. The latter are called *dry* sections and may constitute counties, cities, or other localities.

The states with dry counties and/or cities are Alabama, Alaska, Arkansas, California, Colorado, Connecticut, Delaware, Florida, Georgia, Idaho, Kansas, Kentucky, Louisiana, Maine, Massachusetts, Michigan, Minnesota, Mississippi, New Hampshire, New Jersey, New Mexico, New York, Nevada (partial allowance), North Carolina, Ohio,

> **The Winepress**
>
> As of this writing, dry counties make up an estimated 10 percent of the United States; 18,000,000 Americans live in dry counties, and 35 states contain them.

Rhode Island, South Dakota, Pennsylvania, Tennessee, Texas, Vermont, Virginia, Washington, West Virginia, and Wisconsin. Kentucky alone has more than 50 dry, 30 wet, and 16 moist counties. (A *moist* county is a *dry* county with one or more *wet* cities within it.) In some states, such as North Carolina, a winery can do regular business inside a dry county.

Get to Know the Department of Environmental Conservation

Several years ago, it was perfectly acceptable for a winery to dump the remnants of pressed grapes (pomace) back into the vineyard, between the rows, or in a pile off to the side of the rows. It was believed to be good for the vineyard soil, and it may well be. But today, runoff into streams, rivers, and lakes is an ecological issue, and the pomace can't be dumped just anywhere.

Regulations fluctuate from state to state, and what's acceptable in New York may not be acceptable in California. Depending on the level of regulation, the costs involved in waste management can be substantial.

Regulating a state's ecology is generally the job of the state's Department of Environmental Conservation or agency of a similar name. That office should be on your list as one more source of information that's sure to make an impact on your business plan budget.

Your Local Health Department

Generally, because of the dishwashing of stemware, you'll need a health department permit for the sale of wine on premise and any water or food items you serve. Don't wait until you're ready to apply for your permit to contact the local health department. The time to do it is while you are investigating a locality for your business site, to find out what is required of your business.

What About Sales Tax?

Only five states don't have a state sales tax: Alaska, Delaware, Montana, New Hampshire, and Oregon. The other 45 states charge a sales tax anywhere from 4 percent to 10 percent as of this writing, and individual cities often add their own city tax on top of that. Of the 45 states that have sales tax, 39 states don't charge sales tax on groceries or food that's not cooked on-site.

No matter where you establish your business, you can't escape taxes, but maybe the difference between a sales tax or no sales tax, or a low rate from a high tax rate, will make a difference on the customer base you intend to target. Plus, collecting sales tax is one of the problems associated with shipping directly to out-of-state consumers. You can find updated sales tax information for each state at www. taxadmin.org.

The Winepress

Even in states where wine is sold in grocery stores, for sales tax purposes, wine is not considered a grocery item so it's taxed.

You've Found Your Spot ... Now What?

You've settled on the state and locality, and now you have to get a handle on what it will cost to buy, lease, or build. To do that, you need to have an idea of the size building you need for your winery. It's time to make a rough sketch.

First, Talk to an Architect

Having a preliminary architectural design in hand helps you better evaluate a property. It also helps you evaluate an existing winery for sale or a vacant building that interests you. (For a sample of a winery design, see Chapter 13.) You might get away with hiring a draftsperson for a building with a simple design, but an architect is better equipped to evaluate structural load and other technical considerations.

When talking with an architect, explain your vision for your winery as clearly and as comprehensively as you can, right down to the number of bottles and packed boxes of bottles you intend to produce as well as the number of people you intend to serve in your tasting room—and don't forget to consider the possibility for expansion.

Seek recommendations for an architect from wine industry contacts, the local business community, and national architectural membership organizations. For a listing of national architectural organizations, go to www.progressiveengineer.com.

Are You Ready to Buy?

If you discover a winery for sale that interests you, spend a few days there as an observer. If you're serious about considering buying the business, your request to look around will be taken seriously.

Bring your architectural sketch with you to evaluate how the winery meets your vision of *your* winery. Will you want to make an extensive overhaul in the existing winery?

Or will minor fixes bring it in line with what you want? This thought process also helps you establish the price you're willing to pay.

While there, take special care to get a glimpse into customer relations and sales activity in the visitor center and tasting room. You want an understanding of the winery's present market so you can evaluate its future potential.

Sour Grapes _____

No matter how inexpensive a winery is, buying a business that has a bad reputation with customers can hurt you in the end, even if you change its name.

The revenue stream is key for you to make an offer on an operating business. It's important to examine carefully the debts and expenses, but sales drive a product business. You may be able to make future changes that save costs and increase sales, but you're negotiating a price for the business based on its present costs and sales revenue.

Is Leasing an Option?

During your search, you might find a site with a vacant building and maybe a vineyard, too. If on examination you find it to your liking, you might consider leasing the property and the building from its owner. The business is yours, but the building and land is theirs.

Sour Grapes _____

Leasing an existing winery—just taking over running it—comes with a big drawback. If you run into trouble and need to renegotiate terms, the possibility for losing the business is greatly increased.

Leasing the building may lower your start-up costs, but it may also increase your operating costs, as most business leases come with annual escalating payment clauses. Consider the leasing option carefully, and get your financial adviser/accountant involved. (See Chapter 8 for how to choose an accountant.)

Let's Build It!

Okay, you've got the architectural sketch in hand and you've found a site on which to build your winery. You're ready to break ground and start buying lumber, right? No. You're ready for some more research!

Specifically, you need to find the answers to these questions:

- Does local ordinance and zoning allow you to build the business you want?

- Does the local planning board require environmental impact, traffic impact, and other impact studies?

- Does the community have any objections? (Try to discover objections before a public hearing takes place so you're prepared for them during the meeting.)

- Does the local building and fire department have any problems with your architectural sketch?

- Can you can get a building permit?

To get these questions answered, make an appointment with the appropriate local government. Usually, it's the local (city or town) planning board and other such named agencies.

Two Special Considerations

A winery has two special needs that must be carefully addressed:

- Insulation

- Waste management

Each of these issues is important to human health and the environment, and they're increasingly up for inspection by various health department and environmental agencies. For instance, is interior wall insulation made from potentially hazardous or benign material? Is there proper leach field and distance from a watershed for waste material? Addressing these issues to meet requirements can make a dent in what it costs you to get your plan off the ground.

Be sure to talk to many wine industry sources, including the local university's cooperative extension, to find out all you can about available materials, methods, and regulations governing insulation and waste.

More Business: Registrations and Permits

To you, the dream is fulfilled when you sell that first bottle of wine. But before you can do that, you have to fulfill the government's dreams. To do that, you must register with federal, state, and local governments and apply for permits.

Federal and State Registrations

The first thing your business needs is a tax identification number. If you are a sole proprietor, you can use your Social Security number as your tax identification for your business, or you can do what every other business must do: apply for an Employer Identification Number (EIN). Just like a Social Security number, the EIN is 9 digits long, but it is broken by a dash after the second digit, like so: 11-2222222.

> **Master of Wine**
>
> Get an EIN application at the IRS's business page, www.irs.gov/businesses/index.html and click on "Employer ID Numbers".

If you sell a product direct to consumers, you need to register for your state's Sales Tax Certificate. Check with your state's tax and finance department.

Some states also require that you get a certificate to buy or grow and sell grapes. Check localities; they may also require businesses to register with them.

Here are some other registrations you might need to check out:

- You may have to register for property tax assessments with the local assessor's office.

- If you serve food in your tasting room, you must have a permit from the health department.

- You must meet local code. For instance, you will need a parking area for tourists and buses; parking is a zoning issue.

- The local fire department issues an occupancy permit. It establishes the maximum number of people allowed, plus the number and location of exits.

Some code issues are "grandfathered," which essentially means that a building or location may have been up to an earlier code and has been exempted from having to meet the new code; the local inspectors will know about grandfathered codes, but you should be sure to ask the question and then read the code.

Alcohol Permits

To produce and distribute wine, you must first apply for a federal permit to the TTB on Form 5100.24. The plat, or layout, must accompany your application. (You'll see what a plat looks like in Chapter 13.) Applying for a federal permit to produce wine is relatively painless. You can start the process at www.ttb.gov.

After you acquire a federal permit, you are eligible to apply for a state permit to produce and sell wine. Many states issue permits based on your wine volume: the smaller the volume, the cheaper the permit.

Having a federal permit to produce wine does not guarantee a state permit. States are free to issue or deny based on their regulations. Because states consider it a privilege to gain this permit, the process can be difficult and lengthy; give yourself at least nine months. The list of state alcohol control boards in Appendix C provides the contact information you need.

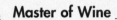

Master of Wine

Hiring an architect, researching the location, registering the business, and obtaining permits all cost money. Keep a running tally of your out-of-pocket costs. It's part of your financial accounting of what it costs to start the business covered in Chapter 6.

Now that you've selected the structure of your business, decided where you want to start your business, and applied for the necessary registration and permits, you're ready to create a business plan. That's the topic of the next chapter.

The Least You Need to Know

- ♦ Structure your business carefully—it's a matter of taxes and liabilities.

- ♦ States and regions within states have their own economic climates and their own view of alcohol regulations.

- ♦ State taxes and local zoning laws can affect your bottom line.

- ♦ Have an architect's sketch of your general ideas so that when you shop for a building site you can better envision whether or not your design will work.

- ♦ Environmental regulations may vary from state to state, but they are increasingly important everywhere.

- ♦ Register your business federally and locally, and secure every required permit before you open for business.

Chapter 6

What's Your (Business) Plan?

In This Chapter

- Why you must have a business plan
- Determining what you want
- Doing the research
- Where's the money coming from?
- You shouldn't go it alone
- Taking care of yourself

You know that old saying about "the best laid plans that can go awry ..."? You can be assured that going into business with no plan will give you a much worse outcome. Before you start a business, you should know why you are doing it and what you want to get out of it. One sure way to come up with the answers is to create a business plan.

A business plan sets you on your course and makes you focus on how to reach your goals. More important, your business plan makes other people—especially those you might be asking for a loan, an investment, a partnership, a building to lease, or equipment to buy on credit—understand what you're doing. This chapter shows you how to build your plan.

Mining for Information

I outline the sections of the business plan later in the chapter, but before you skip ahead and start writing your business plan, you have some work to do, so stay with me.

Someone once said that all writing is re-writing; he could have been talking about a business plan. Writing a business plan takes a lot of research and legwork, and the more you find out today, the more you'll find yourself readjusting what you found out yesterday.

As you learn the things you need to know about starting and running a winery from this book, plus the discoveries you make in your research, you'll be confronted with having to make adjustments to your business plan. Don't fight the adjustments, embrace them. You build a good business plan by mining for information and leaving no stone unturned.

What Do You Want?

Start your plan by thinking about what you want from your business. Think about and honestly answer these questions:

- Why do you want to own a winery? Is it for romance? Is it because you've heard how wonderful the business can be? What personal goals will running a winery meet for you?

- Now that you know what's involved with each of the three parts of the wine business, are you certain about your choice?

- Where do you see your business in the future: 1 year from now, 2 years, 3, 10?

- Are you interested in running a local, national, or international wine company?

- Do you know who your customers are?

- Do you want to distribute your wines widely, or would you rather sell all of them direct, through the tasting room, mailing list, and the Internet?

- Do you expect that everyone will automatically come running to your door, or have you thought about the ways you'll market your product?

- Have you identified a special niche or reason for customers to buy wine from you? Do you want to host educational programs, wine dinners, or some other extra service?

Don't dismiss this exercise as unnecessary for you and move on without honestly answering these questions. This is among the most important thinking you'll go through to start your winery. And be sure to keep your answers nearby so you can pull them out to remind yourself often along the way.

Check Out the Competition

You can produce the wines you like and then hope to sell them to people who make it to your door, or to people who find you on the Internet. A better idea is to know in advance not only who will buy your wine, but also where and how. In any consumer products business, you need to identify your market's geographic, economic, and age statistics. It's called *demographics*.

In a business like wine, competition is a fluid concept, so to speak. You may produce the same kind of wines that 5 or 50 other regional wineries produce, but the nature of winemaking means yours will always be separate and apart from theirs. Winery owners understand that although they're in competition with one another, they are in a communal business. The more wineries on "the street," the more traffic they create. You may be their competition, but grape growers and winemakers have reason to talk with you.

So go talk. Go meet the competition. Visit the wine region that interests you. Take in what you see during the winery tours and in the tasting rooms, and certainly taste the wines. Take special care to get a feel for how the wineries are laid out, and make notes while you're acting as your own sleuth, especially in the following areas:

- Road signage
- Vineyards
- Parking lot
- Product list
- Price list
- Number of employees
- Staff's collective wine knowledge
- Length of time in business
- Customer service practices
- General atmosphere
- Tasting room capacity

The Winepress

You can gain access to surveys and information regarding wine consumption demographics from Gomberg-Fredrikson, a private consulting firm (231 Ware Road, Suite 823, Woodside, CA 94062), www. freedemographics.com.

Keep detailed notes on each of the wineries you visit or create a spreadsheet (do this on your computer if you like) so you can compare data among the wineries.

Master of Wine _____

Most wineries are members of winery organizations that promote a "wine route" or "wine trail." Making the rounds on the trail is a great way to familiarize yourself with the competition.

Get the name of a principal in the business and call later to make an appointment to talk. When you meet, be on the lookout for answers to your sweeping questions; they'll give you an idea of the winery owners' general sense of satisfaction (for example: How do you like the wine business?). Answers to your precise questions will give you, well, precise information (for example: What do you think about another winery opening up nearby?).

Researching the competition is an exercise that lets you know how others handle their wine businesses so you can set more approachable, achievable goals as you build your business plan.

Capital Ideas

Let me stop beating around the grapevine and state the obvious: starting a business takes money. The business plan certainly is a tool to ensure that you cover all the bases to get your business started on the right track. It's also a powerful tool for you to raise capital (cash), especially if you aren't able to whip out that checkbook and write a check for a few hundred thousand dollars for a down payment on land, a building, or anything so costly.

Whether you are or aren't independently wealthy, you may need to raise capital for your business. You essentially have seven options or a combination of options from which to choose:

1. Savings

2. Retirement accounts

3. Equity

4. Family

5. Investors

6. Loans

7. Venture capitalists

The options you choose to raise money can affect your business expenses (you have to pay back loans), and they may affect the structure of your business. In Chapter 7, I go over financial matters in greater detail, but right now, you need to understand that the people and institutions with capital don't generally provide it for altruistic reasons. Your business plan is designed to comfort them, to set them at ease that you have thought of everything to keep their investment safe, and that you are serious.

To be sure you do think of everything, read on.

Pre-Start-Up Costs

While you have that spreadsheet out, get out a calculator as well. It's time to pin down what it's going to cost to get started, how much money you have, and how much more you might need.

A wine business has pre-start-up costs. That's the money you spend before you even get a permit to produce, let alone sell, wine. This is the money you spend just to find out if and where you can start the business. Pre-start-up costs must be included in the business plan. Examples of pre-start-up costs might look familiar to you:

- ◆ Research and travel expenses
- ◆ Architectural design fees
- ◆ Land purchase contracts and surveys
- ◆ Business registration/incorporation fees

These are the items you took care of in Chapter 5. Now, plug into the financial section of the business plan what your expenses were during the pre-start-up phase.

Start-Up Costs

Start-up cost is—you guessed it—money you spend to actually get started. These costs include the following:

- ◆ Applications for alcohol permits
- ◆ Down payment to an engineer and/or building contractor
- ◆ Consultant fees
- ◆ Mortgage down payment (or lease security)

Sour Grapes

Permits to produce and sell alcohol are part of start-up costs. Some of the permits and registration fees, especially at state level, become ongoing business operating expenses because they must be renewed at whatever regular interval set by individual states.

- Wine production equipment and office furniture

- Tasting room design, equipment, and furniture

- Utilities' set-up fees

- Vineyard plants, posts, and wires

- Motor vehicles, including a tractor and forklift

It's understood that the size of your winery determines the size of your start-up costs. But it's possible that you can overspend either by overbuilding or by making serious mistakes. It's best to spend a lot of time getting the start-up numbers as close to reality as you can before you take much, if any, action.

In some states, you may be able to save money based on the size of your start-up, and in other states, you may have to work within certain limitations because of the size of your business. You may also be able to reduce your start-up costs in the vineyard by utilizing state and local programs that help farmers. You can save a lot of money in start-up costs just by reading this book, but you'll save even more by meeting with your local cooperative extension agent and other officials connected to farming and the wine industry.

Operating Expenses

Operating expenses start the day you open for business, and they grow the day after. You will face two types of operating expenses: fixed and variable. Fixed expenses arrive like clockwork, such as monthly loan repayments; variable expenses may or may not arrive like clockwork, but they'll arrive all right, fleeting in and out of the daily workday.

Some of your most important operating expenses to plug into your business plan include the following:

- Payroll (Don't forget your own pay!)

- Rent, lease, loan, and mortgage payments

- Telephone and other utility payments

- Fungicide and herbicide spray material and consumables (string and ties to attach vines to trellis, staples to reattach loosened trellis to end posts, various nuts and bolts for minor repairs, protective clothing, etc.) for the vineyard

- Grapes, juice, or bulk wine purchases

- Winemaking and wine packaging supplies

- Cleaning and any food-handling supplies

- Promotion and advertising

- Website maintenance

- Delivery service

- Taxes on wine removed from the bonded warehouse

- Food and/or snacks for the tasting room

Understanding your operating expenses allows you to calculate the minimum amount you need to open the doors and keep things running month to month.

The Incoming Money

Your product is wine. Depending on the regulations in your state, you might also sell accessories, packaged foods, and gift items. If your plan includes, say, a restaurant in your winery, of course you need to focus on that, too. But for the purpose of this book, a restaurant is an add-on that can be considered after the winery is up and running. For the business plan, focus on the income generated by the wine.

> **Master of Wine**
>
> It's the business that needs start-up and operating expense money, and it's the business that needs to generate the revenue to pay the money back. You must plan your sales forecast.

When you put together your business plan, you have nothing to sell, so you need to create a sales forecast. To develop the forecast, you'll need the results of the demographic and legwork research you've been doing or will be doing soon enough.

The standard format for a sales forecast looks like this:

Sales forecast = M × G × TMS × AS × AV

I bet you're wondering what all those letters stand for, right? Here's the key:

M = market size, or the number of potential customers

G = growth rate, or the annual expansion of the wine industry

TMS = target of market share, or the percentage of market share you intend to capture

AS = average sale, or the value of each sale

AV = average visits, or a measure of repeat business

That's the general forecast format. Depending on state regulations, a winery can have three sales markets: wholesale (to distributors), retail (to stores and restaurants), direct (to consumers)—and that makes an impact on what your particular sales forecast will look like.

You'll need to scour for demographic information and wine sales information. That will mean making use of government and private resources. You might want to join a few industry associations that can provide valuable sets of statistics. You can find wine consumption information at The Wine Institute (www.wineinstitute.org), The New York Wine and Grape Foundation (www.newyorkwines.org), The Specialty Retailers Association (www.specialtywineretailers.org), and Appellation America (http://wine. appellationamerica.com).

In Chapter 18, you learn about how to sell to each market. For now, you need to reflect the sales value of each market you intend to service as a "best guess."

You're Not Alone

If you've never produced a business plan, it can seem daunting. It really isn't. Besides, you're not alone. Others have done it, and some have even produced information that will help you.

Remember those winery owners you met early on? Stay friends with them. Find out all you can about how they forecasted their sales. Also find out about the businesses you'll sell to and those you'll use as supply sources: local wine shops, restaurants, printers, small food suppliers, and office and farm equipment suppliers. If they're in or near the community where you'll establish your winery, many of them will be members of the Chamber of Commerce and other business groups.

Master of Wine

Subscribe to wine trade magazines. Get online, too. Join wine industry websites, and learn all you can from people who have been there and done it or are doing it now.

Join the Chamber of Commerce, and join other business groups. Do a lot of networking so you can evaluate the level of interest—and sales—your business can generate.

After you've joined the local business community and made some business friends, ask people if they'd like to become part of your personal advisory board.

Your Advisory Board

You may one day run a Fortune 500 company and, as the CEO, you'll answer to the board of directors. But you don't need to run a Fortune 500 to need an advisory board. Your advisory board is a group made up of people you know or people with whom you do business—a winery consultant is a good candidate for the board. All advisory board members should have business experience. That's the point of having them around. They're there to *advise* you.

You can have anyone you choose on your board. You can pay them for their services, treat them to dinners, or give them discounts on wine. However you compensate the advisory board, you should always treat it as strictly business.

Set the board up as a no-nonsense group, and be sure to make its members understand their responsibility to you. Have regular meetings, and run them like any other important board meeting, with an agenda, a flow, and a goal for results. You can do this by following General Henry M. Robert's *Rules of Order*.

The Business Plan

The time has come to sift through the all data you've compiled and put your business plan together. A winery business plan contains at least six parts:

1. *Title page.* This provides your general contact information such as the winery name and the name, address, and contact information of the owner(s).

2. *Executive summary.* This section is a one-page first impression intended for the banker or investor. The executive summary is up front, but it's written after the business plan is completed, because you won't know what to say until you have all the information.

3. *Business information.* This section describes your business, its products, its location, and general business conditions that will affect the wine industry nationally and in your locale.

4. *Marketing.* This is where your mission statement appears. In this section, you spell out your target market; your competition; your pricing, distribution, and sales strategies; plus your promotion and advertising plans.

5. *Management and operations.* Here you describe the legal form of the business, the skills of its managers and employees, and any other considerations for a successful winery operation. If you're working with a consulting winemaker and/or vineyard manager, this is the place to mention it.

6. *Financial information.* This is where you analyze and present how much financing you need and how you'll use the money. The owner's equity in the business is included in this part. You need also to present a minimum five-year financial projection plan.

See Appendix B for a sample business plan worksheet.

One Final Word

One of the biggest mistakes people make when starting a business is forgetting that they need to earn a living during and after they get their start-up off the ground. Remember to include in the financial portion of your business plan exactly what you'll need as a salary for at least five years into the future.

As I said early in the chapter, while putting together information for your business plan, the more you find out today, the more you'll find yourself readjusting what you found out yesterday. In fact, every chapter from now on includes advice and information you can use for your plan. Next up, Chapter 7 gives you the basics for establishing the financial part of your plan.

> **Sour Grapes** _____
>
> You need to earn a living while you build your business plan. Unless you can afford it, don't quit your day job until you're certain the income from your winery can support you. You never know what will influence your decision as you discover what it takes to start a winery.

The Least You Need to Know

- The purpose of a business plan is to keep you on the right track and help you raise the money you need.

- As part of building your business plan, keep up with the market and the other businesses like yours.

- Establish your target market, and determine what will make you better than the competition.

- Assemble an advisory board of successful businesspeople or entrepreneurs to help you overcome obstacles at minimum cost to you and to your business.

- You need to earn a living while you build your business plan, so don't quit your day job, and do build a five-year salary for yourself into the plan.

Chapter **7**

Money Makes the World Go Round

In This Chapter

- ◆ How to establish your financial needs
- ◆ Pinpointing your personal sources of financing
- ◆ External sources of financing
- ◆ The importance of forecasting
- ◆ Paying back what you borrow

Even if you have a small fortune you can use to finance your winery, you still need to do a financial analysis of your business, if only to remind yourself how much money it's going to take to get started and how much money you'll need to keep going until the first profits roll in.

When you want to raise money to start your business, the financial analysis is the most important section of the business plan you started in Chapter 6. I've seen bankers skip all the other pages and go right to it. The financial analysis serves one more purpose: depending on the state where you want to start the business, the alcohol control board might want to see exactly how you intend to fund the business, with a documented financial trail to prove it.

This chapter shows you where to go for financial backing and how to make plainly visible to others where you intend to get the money for your business.

How Much Money Do You Need?

If only there were simple answers to simple questions. To answer the "How much money do you need?" question, you need first to answer a few other questions:

Where will the business be located? The price of land as well as the cost of running a business varies from region to region, state to state, and within local areas.

Will you run a vineyard and a winery? You might want to raise all the money up front, or you might want to start the winery first and add the vineyard later.

Will you run only a winery or only a vineyard? Obviously, either way, the start-up costs will be lower than starting a full operation with both.

Will you establish a custom crush brand? This may be the lowest-cost alternative to getting into the wine business. (See Chapter 17 for detailed information about custom crushing.)

What size business do you want? If you plan to start big, you'll certainly need more money than if you plan to start small.

How quickly do you want the business to grow? You might want to accelerate the normal growth curve. To do that, your marketing and promotion costs will grow.

Do you have the amount of money you need? If you've got the money and you've chosen to use it, well then, there's nothing left to say here.

Can you get the amount of money you need without a lender? The money can come from a team of investors or partners.

Do you need to finance a portion of the business? If you can raise some money but not all of it, you'll need a plan for raising the rest of it.

The last three questions go directly to the issue of how much money you'll need, but you can't answer any of those questions without answers to the first six questions, and that takes a thorough analysis of establishing a wine business.

Of course, I don't know your answers to these questions, so to help you determine how much money you need, let's take a look at an example of a start-up winery that plans to produce wines with a retail value between $15 and $25 per bottle. Our initial goal should be a 10,000-case production at the end of five years. Production should begin in the first year at approximately 2,000 cases of 12 bottles each (around 5,000 gallons of wine), increase to 4,000 cases in the second year, and so on.

How Much for the Vineyard?

The cost of vineyard acreage varies so greatly across the United States that no standard dollar value can be pinned on it. Per-acre costs can be as low as a few thousand dollars or as high as hundreds of thousands of dollars. After you know where you'll buy land, you'll have to determine the size of your vineyard and then your total cost for it.

According to a 2005–2006 Cornell University study by Gerald B. White and Mark E. Pisoni titled "Cost of Establishment and Production of *Vinifera* Grapes in the Finger Lakes Region of New York (see Appendix B), a 50-acre vineyard of *Vitis vinifera* grapes (see Chapter 10 for a description of wine grapevines) yields about 11 rows and just over 800 grapevines per acre. To start this vineyard, you'll need a building and repair shop plus a variety of tools, a tractor, and other equipment. You might need to install drainage tiles, and you'll definitely need vineyard posts and a trellis system.

According to the Cornell study, the total cost to start the 50-acre vineyard is $1 million ($20,000 per acre). $600,000 covers the value of the land, building a shop and storage facility, and vineyard equipment. $400,000 ($8,000 per acre) is for site preparation and planting.

In the upstate New York Finger Lakes region, where the study was completed, the land value was set at an extremely low $2,500 per acre. In another location in the same state, the north fork of Long Island, vineyard land may start at $50,000 per acre. In Napa, California, you couldn't find land even at $100,000 an acre.

How Much for the Winery Building?

White and Pisoni, at Cornell University, also issued a winery business plan report. According to the business plan financial analysis, the cost of a building to start our example winery is approximately $485,000 (see Appendix B). The Cornell team expects to update the costs by the year 2009.

At the end of the first year, installation of a tasting- and salesroom, plus landscaping, adds $330,000 to the cost of the building.

How Much for the Winery Equipment?

To equip our example winery start-up with all it takes to produce the first 2,000 cases would require approximately a $205,000 investment. (Find a detailed equipment needs analysis in Chapter 14.)

At the end of the first year, the young 2,000-case winery would need a bottling line installed at a cost of approximately $123,000.

How Much for Marketing?

Among the first things to think about when you start your business plan is marketing your wine. Pinning down the cost of the vineyard, winery, and equipment is meaningless if you haven't thought about marketing. For that, the first year's budget is set at $10,000.

How Much for the Staff?

Staffing in the first year would be lean. It's possible for 2 people to operate a 50-acre vineyard efficiently, with hired part-time laborers as needed. Both full-time and part-time employees and consultants, with payroll taxes and fees included, will run about $80,000.

How Much for the Grapes?

Remember, when you plant a vineyard you must wait a minimum of three years for a viable crop. Until then, you'll either grow grapes from an existing vineyard on the property or buy grapes. In any case, the cost of *Vitis vinifera* grapes for the first 2,000 cases is estimated at $42,000, or $21 a case.

How Much for Operating Costs?

In their study, the Cornell professors estimate that the balance to cover operating expenses, including taxes and depreciation for the year, is $144,000.

What's the Damage?

To start our example business with 50 acres of vineyard plus a winery that produces 2,000 cases in the first year and is expected to grow to 10,000 cases in five years, the following minimum dollar amounts are needed from start-up to the end of the first year:

Vineyard: $1,000,000

Winery: $1,143,000

Expenses: $276,000

To operate the business while it grows over the next four years, and if you sell all your wine at your tasting room for full mark up (direct to consumers without a middle-man), less case purchase discounts, you'll break even in year 5 and be ready for expansion.

Year 2: $413,000 expenses

            $145,000 projected revenue

            $268,000 net expenses

Year 3: $527,000 expenses

            $373,000 projected revenue

            $154,000 net expenses

Year 4: $653,000 expenses

            $651,465 projected revenue

            $1,535 net expenses

Year 5:   Break even

How Much Money Do You Have?

When you know how much money you need to get the business going, you need to figure out whether you have all you need without breaking your personal bank, or whether you need to seek outside money.

Generally, your money will be in one or all of three places:

♦ Personal savings account

♦ Retirement account

♦ Equity

The fearless among us might be willing to take the plunge and use every dollar they have and convert every asset they have into dollars to start a winery. But that would be potential suicide. Carefully weigh how much money you really can afford to invest in the business, and if you come up short, start thinking of ways to raise the rest of it.

Your Personal Savings

We hear over and over in the news that Americans don't save enough money. Maybe you aren't one of those Americans. If you have personal savings, you may have built your account into something big enough to tap. But if your personal savings won't cover your needs for at least six months, the minimum "rainy day" savings, do not empty your account.

Your Retirement Account

Often, people view their retirement account as personal savings. It's better to think of the account as reserved for your retirement, for the time when you'll no longer be actively or gainfully employed. Emptying this account is a truly bad idea. But if it's large enough, you can borrow from it. To do that, you must know the rules.

> **Master of Wine**
>
> Talk to your financial planner or find out more about borrowing from a retirement account at Forbes Media Company's website: www.investopedia.com/articles/retirement/03/070203.asp.

You'll have to pay back money you borrow from your retirement account, with interest. But the interest you pay goes back into your retirement account. The downside is that you lose the tax-deferred growth on the money you borrow, plus you have to pay income taxes on the money you use to pay back the loan and the interest. Another downside is that some retirement plans go into suspension for a period of time after you borrow from them.

Unless you're borrowing for a primary residence, you'll have five years to pay back the money you borrow from a retirement account.

Before you go fill out the paperwork, know that not all retirement accounts even allow loans. You'll have to find out if yours does. Generally, you can borrow 50 percent of your vested retirement account balance or $50,000, whichever is less. An exception is made for accounts vested at or under $10,000.

Your Equity

After you invest in your business, you'll establish owner's equity, or the value of your interest in the business after liabilities are reduced. But you may already have equity in another business, in real estate property, or in other financial instruments you can use to help finance the start-up winery.

Equity has cash value, so you can convert your holdings into cash. If you do convert them into cash, the equity assets are gone. As an alternative, you can use your equity as collateral to borrow cash. Of course, you'll have to pay interest on what you borrow, but with each payment, you recapture some of your equity. A second mortgage on real estate is a common form of raising money through equity.

Financing Sources to Consider

Assuming you don't have the money you need to start the business and you've decided to seek financing, the best place to start is where the money is—and I don't mean that small tin box you've been throwing coins into at the end of each day for the past few years.

In the following sections, I cover some areas of financing you might want to consider.

The People You Live With

A relative is probably the most difficult person in the world to talk with about money. Still, if what you're proposing makes sense to someone in your family or your extended family of in-laws, you may be able to raise their interest.

You should treat the money you raise from relatives like any other source of financing. You can borrow and pay back with interest, you can sell shares in the business to them, or you can make them working partners.

The thing is, you won't know if you can raise money from a relative unless you ask, and that's the hardest part.

The People You Know

Look around you. You might be staring at a friend with money and nowhere to put it! You can put more than one friend together and make them silent partners or shareholders in the corporation. In each case, it's a good idea to offer them a dividend, maybe a certain number of cases of wine each year until profits are made and can be distributed.

Sour Grapes _____

A friend may not be as difficult to talk with about money as a relative, but be careful. Many friendships have failed over money. If you tap a friend or two for financial assistance, always treat it as strictly business, and do it in writing.

You can also make friends into investors, or people who give you money with the expectation that you will return it, with a profit for them.

Banks

The obvious choice for raising money is, of course, a bank. That's what they do … or is it?

Remember from Chapter 3 that bankers turned down Thomas and John, the two fellows starting wineries. Sure, there might be money in the bank vault, but it takes quite a lot of scratching and scraping to pry open the doors, especially when the banker sees a risky business. A banker's interest isn't to fully realize your dream but to make money on the money he lends you. If your business plan doesn't persuade the banker, you won't capture his interest.

Your business plan's financial analysis is there to not only show bankers the numbers but also to show them that you've done your homework and have figured out a way to pay back the money you borrow. Your case to the bank is helped along if you have a stable team of partners and you're able to invest a large portion of the money you need to get started.

The Winepress

The U.S. Small Business Administration (www.sba.gov) can help you with your financial plan and possibly help you find a bank for a small business loan.

Even if you have everything in place to persuade bankers, you'll still need impeccable timing. Bankers get scared when the economy is shaky, and they get cautiously happy when the economy is vibrant. Somewhere within that minuscule swing of emotional possibilities you might be able to persuade one of them.

Venture Capitalists

Or you can raise money from people who are in the business of betting on other people's dreams. Believe it or not, there *are* people out there who *want* to give you money. In fact, they spend their time looking for people like you.

Venture capitalists usually put together a pool of money from wealthy people or companies, or even pension funds, into a venture capital fund for the specific purpose of lending money to businesses. Generally, each fund is set up to lend to a specific industry.

Some venture capitalist funds offer more than just money. A fund can offer experienced people and good industry contacts. In return, the fund receives shares in the business and some control over it.

Sour Grapes

Venture capitalists can be a fantastic source of money, but the money comes with one large string attached to it. The fund holders are speculators interested in reaping a high return on the money they give. You will be under pressure to perform, and if you don't perform (in a relatively short period of time), you may find yourself having to pay the fund back in full or handing over the business to the fund.

The idea behind venture capitalism is for the fund to invest in a business that within seven years either sells shares to the public and is listed on the stock market or is sold off at a profit. In the end, the fund seeks as much as 20 percent interest on its investment per year. For that reason, venture capitalist money may be available only for a start-up winery with major national or international ambitions.

You can sign up online for a directory of venture capitalists waiting to hear from you. Start at www.venturedeal.com or www.gobignetwork.com.

It's All in the Forecast

If you don't have experience in the wine business, you'll need to be quite a fortune-teller to come up with reasonably good forecasts for your business. Luckily, you have studies available to use as a guide, like the one at Cornell University (see Appendix B).

The forecasting is to show lenders that you have a well-thought-out and viable plan. You do that by pinpointing when money needs to be pumped into the business and for what reasons. The forecast clearly lays out your expense and revenue stream and, through tracking your growth curve, shows when everything converges so investors can take money out of the business's profits.

When you build your financial plan for potential investors or lenders, it doesn't help to be creative. Not many jokes are thrown around during business meetings about money. Money managers are single-minded; they want to see the path to success clearly laid out before them.

Lenders also want to know that you've thought about potential unanticipated expenses. Being able to anticipate cash requirements is a necessity in the financial plan. For that reason, the forecast shows month-to-month activity in production, expenses, marketing, and sales.

When You Need Money In

You may need money for pre-start-up and start-up, or you may have enough of your own. Your financial plan should clearly indicate how much money you're seeking and when you'll need it.

In many cases, it's better to string out the cash infusions so you receive the money exactly when you need it and not before because interest calculations begin when the money is turned over to you.

When Money Goes Out

You'll also have to clearly document when you expect money to go out. (You may need this to support your claim that you need more money pumped in.)

Also, lenders want to be sure you aren't frivolously throwing money around before you have to spend it. They also know when interest calculations start, and they want you to be able to pay back that interest.

Paying Back Loans

Don't forget that the cost of borrowed money is a business expense that needs to be included in your financial plan. It would be a shame to think that you've made a profit only to discover that the profit is the result of you forgetting to include the loan expense in your forecast.

Besides, lenders really appreciate that you haven't forgotten them in your forecasting.

Paying Back Investors

Except for venture capitalists, you should treat investors just as you would treat a bank that loans you money. The difference between the two is that the bank generally only wants its money back with interest; investors may take something else.

When you sign up investors in the business, you will have formed a written agreement between them and the business. In that agreement, you might have come up with one or two creative ways to pay them back—in wine, or in shares of growth, etc. Every agreement you make to pay them back is a cost to the business and must be forecasted in the financial plan just like any other cost.

In Chapter 8, you learn how to get the professional help you need to start the business. In most cases, it's easier to find the professional help you need if you've already framed your business plan. You'll have a better handle on what you need, and the professionals will have a better handle on how they might help you.

The Least You Need to Know

♦ The state in which you locate your business has a decided impact on start-up costs.

♦ Your financial plan should take your business at least five years into the future.

♦ Your financial plan must take into consideration that new vineyards don't produce for a minimum of three years.

♦ Carefully weigh the options available to raise money for your start-up.

♦ When you forecast your start-up business, don't forget to include the cost of borrowing money in your expenses.

Chapter 8

Getting Help from the Pros

In This Chapter

- ◆ You can't start a complicated business alone
- ◆ Why you need an attorney, an accountant, an insurance agent, and more
- ◆ The government's role in your business
- ◆ What to look for in professional help

I've shown you how many hats you might have to wear to run your business. But I haven't told you how many hats it really takes.

You don't necessarily need an attorney, accountant, or insurance agent on staff, but you might need to hire them to get your business started. If you or one of your partners is neither a winemaker nor vineyard manager, you might need those consultants, too, at least until you get started. You might have to consider consultants for design, marketing, and technology matters, too.

In this chapter, you learn why you need professional help for legal, financial, and other important matters and how to get it.

You Need Professional Help

Specialized professionals are there to help you run smoothly and profitably in a variety of business segments. You need some of this professional help during start-up and some during normal business operations; often, it overlaps.

Because wine production is a regulated business, the first professional you should consult is an attorney, followed by an accountant and then an insurance agent.

An Attorney

Federal and local government will be your ongoing business partners. If you don't play by your partners' rules, you may get into trouble.

When you apply for permits to produce alcohol, you must guarantee that you have no criminal record, and if you did do something wrong in your lifetime, even as far back as your teens, you may need a lawyer to help you get the documents that will satisfy the regulators.

You might be smart enough to get by, registering your business with the federal government and the secretary of your state, but because a business is a legal entity with responsibilities and potential liabilities, a lawyer may turn out to be the indispensable resource for setting up the business and your written agreements with others.

A lawyer is there to keep you out of trouble by interpreting regulations, contracts, and leases. If you do get into trouble for any reason, a lawyer is there to get you out of it.

Master of Wine _____

Most attorneys accept a retainer payment method based on an hourly rate. You agree on a set dollar amount and use the attorney until you eat up the money and time. Be sure you receive detailed reports showing the hours spent.

An Accountant

A business must follow prescribed financial and accounting systems. Depending on your business structure, you'll have to choose an accounting method. The best person to help with that is, of course, an accountant.

An accountant is not a bookkeeper. The bookkeeper keeps the records, makes the entries, and may handle writing but not signing checks. The accountant handles the complicated issues like filing taxes, determining profit or loss, handling expenses and equipment depreciation calculations, long-range financial forecasting, and even scheduling when the business should seek increased funding.

An Insurance Agent

You can lose everything by accident, and every business comes with the risk of something going wrong. It could be as small as an employee's breaking a finger on the job or as large as a mass product liability claim.

Being underinsured can be a severe problem, and being overinsured can be wasteful. You need to be properly insured, and that takes a smart agent who knows your needs and understands your budgetary limitations.

> **Sour Grapes**
>
> You or another company official should make bank deposits or cash checks. But if you choose to allow an employee to perform that task, take out an insurance bond on that person, which is essentially a liability insurance policy should the employee vanish with your money or should the employee be caught embezzling.

How Important Are They, Really?

Later in the chapter, I go over some other professionals to consider for your start-up business. For now, I want to be sure you understand the importance of an attorney, accountant, and insurance agent because of the intricacies of dealing with federal and state governments.

Dealing With Federal Agencies

You might be able to wade through government documents and maybe miss only a little, but hiring an attorney who really knows the laws and regulations, and how to fill out the applications, gives you a better chance at missing nothing.

Federal alcohol application regulations are rather straightforward. Essentially, you submit your application as required to the Federal Bureau of Alcohol, Tobacco, and Firearms, Trade and Tax Bureau (TTB) and then you wait for an answer.

As part of the application, you need to show a plat, a drawing of your facility (see Chapter 13). Much of the rest of what you'll need to include can be taken right out of your business plan. But after you get the permit, you'll be subject to all kinds of operational compliance regulations that can easily trip you up. Consider contracting with a specialized compliance consultant; start your search at www.compliance-connect.com or www.csa-compliance.com.

The Winepress

As of this writing, you don't need to worry about the U.S. Department of Agriculture (USDA). Until recently, the USDA could only dream of regulating the wine industry. Because of its status as a source of excise tax revenue, wine remained subject to the Treasury Department. But a recent interest in wine labeling as food has stirred the pot, so to speak. Soon, wine will come with both nutritional information and ingredient labeling, just like other foods. Then the USDA is expected to make a pitch for jurisdiction. In the end, it's likely that wine will be subject to both TTB and USDA regulations, and that means more legal requirements.

Safety is a major consideration in the vineyard and in the winery. Each function relies on heavy equipment, not to mention materials in use for manufacturing like glass and chemicals. A winery must comply with federal regulations that govern the workplace; these are overseen by the Occupation Safety and Health Administration (OSHA).

In addition, because of the nature of migrant workforces, vineyard owners are subject to Immigration and Naturalization regulations. All businesses that produce food are subject to regulation by the Office of Homeland Security.

These agencies require things of you that can make dealing with an audit by the Internal Revenue Service (IRS) a day in the park, which shouldn't happen, but if it does, that's what the accountant is for. Your accountant is there to be sure you comply with all tax rules, and that especially means payroll (Department of Labor), and don't forget payment to migrant workers.

A winery is so heavily loaded with assets that a good accountant is essential to the tax planning of the business. Accountants don't have to be certified, but a Certified Public Accountant (CPA) brings a guarantee of credibility to the table. Unless a retainer is agreed upon in advance, a CPA generally bills on a per-job basis, from a set fee schedule.

Dealing With State Agencies

In most states, alcohol controls are about as simple as physics might be to a standard poodle, and they often make as much sense as the idea of a poodle doing physics. But you can't get around them. Some attorneys even specialize in the alcohol controls in their state.

Other state regulatory departments that can easily trip you up include the state's Department of Agriculture and Markets; the Department of Environmental Control; the Health Department; and the Department of Labor, Taxation, and Finance. Each of the state department offices is well versed in the methods of the Department of Silly Talk. Often, only an attorney can translate.

Dealing With Insurance and Bonding

In addition to regular business and liability insurance, federal and state governments require that a wine producer be bonded. Bonding is simply paying an annual fee as security on the value of your inventory, should the business default on tax payments.

There's also dram insurance, which is specifically for businesses that serve alcohol by the glass or sell it by the bottle. In some states, a winery is not required to have dram insurance, but it's advisable that the business be covered.

There's also mandatory workers' compensation insurance that insures employees against loss connected to on-the-job accidents. Workers' compensation is administered by each state in its own way and at a cost to the employer that varies from state to state.

Health insurance is the only insurance a regular agent may be ill equipped to handle. If you intend to provide your employees with health insurance, consider looking into your membership in the local chamber of commerce. Quite often, such organizations provide reasonably good group health insurance policies.

For your other insurance needs, a good insurance agent is able to put you together with the right overall insurance package that keeps your coverage up and your costs down. Most insurance agents are paid a commission (based on your premiums) directly from the insurance company.

> **Master of Wine** _____
>
> For a reputable attorney, look to the American Bar Association (www.abanet.org). For an accountant, check with the American Institute of Certified Public Accountants (www.aicpa.org). For an insurance agent, look to the Independent Insurance Agents and Brokers of America (www.iiaba.net/na/default?ContentPreference= NA&ActiveTab=NA&ActiveState=0).

Sometimes, the lawyer and accountant or the lawyer and insurance agent together will need to help you resolve an issue. Generally, these three professionals will take care of your specific legal, tax, and insurance needs so you can take care of the things directly related to your business—producing and selling wine. For that, you may need a few other professionals ….

More Essential Professionals

Instead of having a payroll before you have the business up and running, you can hire consultants to get you started in many of the important functions. Until your business grows, you may also want to hire consultants rather than employees in many of the business's operating functions.

The following professionals represent who you might call "the essentials."

A Vineyard Consultant

Before you plant a single grape, you'll need to know how and when to do it. If you're not a farmer, you should be sure the information you get from the local farm bureau and cooperative extension agents is given to a person who best understands it. A good vineyard consultant will save you a great deal of time and money. Fixing farming mistakes after the vineyard has been planted can be a monumental, and costly, task.

A Consulting Winemaker

Before you press a single grape, you will need to have an idea about the makeup of your product mix. You'll also need to know how to go about producing each individual product. If you aren't a trained winemaker, you need to get one.

In the modern wine world, winemakers with full-time day jobs often act as independent consultants for start-ups and smaller wineries needing an overseer. But if you aren't comfortable with sharing your business with someone who works for another business, a small industry of consulting winemakers flourishes, and you can hold them to a contract that prevents them from divulging your proprietary business information.

A Marketing Consultant

The market for wine is varied and vast. Even if you or one of your partners has a marketing background, you still might want to get the benefit of a marketing consultant specific to the wine business, if only for the value of the updated information he or she will have.

A Technology Consultant

Today, the Internet is used in the wine business to share information, find customers, and sell wine. Tomorrow, the Internet is expected to do it better than it does today, and it is expected to be the driving tool for the wine industry's success.

If you're not comfortable handling the Internet-related aspects of your business, get a technology consultant. He or she can implement your plans efficiently and cost effectively.

A Few More Professionals

These are ones you might need before you get the business running:

A banker. Your business will need a bank, especially when your business plan includes seeking a loan. To form a relationship with a banker, find out—from other industry people or from a wine industry organization—which banks in your area may be in the market to lend money to your business. Make an appointment, and bring your business plan. Even if you're turned down, you can learn from the banker.

An overall wine business consultant. In California, where the wine industry is at its largest and most intense, you can find a few companies as well as private individuals engaged in wine business consulting. These professionals walk you through the process, help you build your business plan, find you potential sources of financing, develop your marketing plan with you, and maybe even consult with you in the vineyard and winemaking functions, or at least help you find the right people.

Master of Wine

The University of California, Davis Graduate School, at Berkley, offers a wine consulting service program that puts its enology and business students on your case. Find it at www.gsm. ucdavis.edu/ExploreOurSchool/ index.aspx?id=1728.

An artist or designer. Small business owners are endlessly seeking ways to cut expenses. The one place where it's dangerous to scrimp is with the company's image. Trust me when I say that a professional designer will be worth your money.

A publicist or PR rep. Getting started is difficult enough, but letting others know you've started is even more difficult. You may be the face of the business, and you may be quite good at schmoozing, but do you know how to write a good press release, put together a great promotion event, or pick up the phone and make contact with the most important journalists or even politicians in your area? Those are the things a good publicist can do.

A packaging expert. Don't make the mistake of thinking that your designer can also develop your packaging. A designer might have great packaging concepts, but he or she might not be so great at math—and packaging is calculating. Plus, what looks good on a box might look strange on a cylinder, or worse, you might not be able to fit a round item in a square slot. Packaging experts can also save you money by making sure your product—the bottles—aren't broken during shipment.

Inventory and warehouse help. Have you ever heard of "first in, first out"? If not, you need someone to help you; if so, you need someone to make it happen. Inventory control and warehousing is logistics. Believe it or not, warehousing wine isn't just stacking pallets on racks; well, it is, but there's a right way and a wrong way to do it. Plus, there's always a way to do it that will save space and money.

Point of sale (POS) help. I'm not talking about the cash register system here—that comes in a later chapter—I'm talking about how to make people buy wine and accessories. Impulse buying is only one of the methods a good point of sale program needs to embrace. In fact, a good POS system should interface with your inventory control as well as with government reporting functions.

An event planner. You haven't forgotten the entertainment part of the wine business, have you? You'd be surprised how difficult it can be to plan a party for 100 people. You'd also be happy if you had a party for 100 people and most of them left the party carrying boxes of wine to their cars. A good event planner can increase sales as well as exposure, and maybe give you ideas on how to add more events into your marketing scheme.

Food service help. Food service often goes hand-in-hand with event planning, but if you plan to serve food at the tasting room, run a restaurant on the winery premises, or host sit-down dinners, you may need the advice of someone who knows how to do it, or you may need a relationship with a caterer. And you should talk to a food service consultant before you install your kitchen.

No matter who the professional, it's vital to get your responsibilities and the professional's in writing. You should also consider establishing a performance schedule, with payment parameters. In some cases, it will be necessary to have the professional sign a nondisclosure agreement.

How to Find the Help You Need

To select professionals, ask around and get some names, make a few appointments, and ask many questions. These people might be consultants, but you're interviewing them for an important job, so don't be afraid to ask as many questions as you need answered. If you receive vague responses, move on.

Following are the types of questions to ask when you interview professional consultants. What other questions can you add to this list? Don't be timid. This is important.

What's your experience? You need to know to what extent your professional help understands his or her field. You need also to know if the professional has experience with your kind of business. (A criminal lawyer may help you at a criminal trial but may be useless in front of the alcohol control board.)

What are your affiliations or connections? Sometimes the best advice is "I don't know, but I'll find out." You want to know if the professional you hire can indeed find out what he or she may not know offhand. Plus, each professional should be a member in good standing of at least one of the important national professional organizations in the field, especially the top three critical professionals (attorney, accountant, and insurance agent).

Will you keep me in the loop? Don't settle for a professional who's unwilling to explain the process to you. Remember, you're the one responsible for the business. You need to understand as much as you can about its legal and financial functioning, and you and other select staff members need to know what goes on in all operational matters connected to your business.

Recommendations may be the best way to find professional consultants. But the best recommendations may not come from your family doctor or your brother-in-law. Not that they can't know good people, but if they aren't in the wine business, they might not know the people with the kind of experience you need. Wine industry people are the best sources of recommendations for professional help. The next best sources may include other professionals.

Master of Wine

The respected industry trade periodical *Wines and Vines* magazine publishes an annual comprehensive wine industry guide, which includes listings of professional consultants. Check it out at www.winesandvines.com/template.cfm?section=directory. Also see Appendix C for a sampling of professional resources.

The professionals you can trust are, of course, the ones who are reputable and have particular knowledge of the wine business. Be sure any professional you hire is accessible. It doesn't do much good to hire a lawyer you can reach only by taking a three-hour flight.

I've been talking about your business as if it had no name. Oh, it doesn't? Well, in Chapter 9, you find out how to fix that.

The Least You Need to Know

◆ When your business plan is finished, start searching for professional help.

◆ Professionals help with legal, financial, insurance, and a variety of business needs.

◆ You need a written agreement that clearly spells out the responsibilities of each of the professionals you work with.

◆ Find professionals through recommendations and by checking with professional membership organizations.

Chapter 9

What's in a Name?

In This Chapter

- ◆ The importance of a good business name
- ◆ Establishing your image
- ◆ Brand naming and the federal government
- ◆ Protecting your business name and image

Your business has been gestating for eight chapters now. Now let's think of a name for it.

Naming your business is more than simply coming up with a catchy phrase or a twist on a theme or a pun—no, please, no puns. What you call your business is what will call attention to it. That name will become intricately tied to the image your business projects.

In this chapter, you learn how to think about your business so what you name it makes sense not just to you but also to your prospective target market.

Who Are You, Anyway?

Some people have a natural talent for naming a business. They can some-how see right into the essence and pull out its identity. Others aren't so lucky—we have to work at it. Too often, we don't work hard enough. We settle on a name that means something to us, something personal or cute. But a name we love may not strike a chord with prospective customers. To do that, a business name must reflect what the business is and how it can benefit the customers.

Think of these two business names: The Athlete's Foot and Staples. They quickly bring up images that say something about the nature of their business, and they also evoke an emotional response. You need that athletic footwear because you are an athlete, or shop here because we have everything you need to supply your office.

> **Sour Grapes**
>
> When a successful business named after the owner is sold, the owner usually loses the right to use his or her name. The name *Robert Mondavi* now belongs to a global conglomerate, not Mr. Mondavi. Keep this in mind when naming your winery.

Imagine a winery trying to entice tourists with a business name like The Private Collector Wine Club. Or how many serious customers do you think a name like Alcohol Heaven will attract to a winery?

You know you're unique, and you know your business will be a reflection of that uniqueness. You also know you'll be selling wine. Your next task is to get all of what you know about the business into a name and image so when others hear or see your business name, they'll know, too.

Get Their Attention

Of course, a business must reach out to customers, but in a winery, you'll also have customers reaching out to you, by visiting your tasting room. Before they open your door, your business name will have had to open the door to what customers can expect from you. The name will have to make them *want* to open that door.

> **Master of Wine**
>
> Your business name needs to be inviting and memorable, because before your visitors see your tasting room, or even your driveway, they may have seen your name in a brochure or a newspaper ad, or maybe on the Internet.

To get customers' attention, your business name should immediately tell others who you are and what you do. Simply sticking the word *Winery* at the end of another word or two may not be the answer.

It's a good thing you met some of those professionals back in Chapter 8, because now you may have reason to talk to a few of them. But before you do that, try some exercises to come up with a name for your business.

What Do You Do?

Yes, a winery produces wine. Still, not all winery owners share the same attitude about wine; neither do they produce the same kind of wines.

When thinking about a name for your business, your first questions for consideration are: *What do I think about wine?* and *What kind of wine will I produce?*

That takes care of you. The next step is to ask yourself questions that will take care of your customers. You can start by thinking about the target market you identified for your business plan. For instance, if your target market is the next generation, the name you choose for your business may have to include a reasonably identifiable reference to pop culture your target market will quickly understand.

Your business must have a position, not a moral or political one, but a position that places the company among similar companies, and hopefully above them. Will you produce a kind of wine no one else in your area produces? Are you offering wines in one price level or in many? Is your winery bigger, smaller, or different in any way from the rest in your area?

The Winepress

Toys "R" Us is one example of a business name that illustrates target market naming. The inverted *R* in the name is a perfect device for evoking an image of the company's market.

What Do They Want from Me?

No, we haven't come to the section where we start the lamentations, and there is no letter *h* in the word *wine*. This is where you consider your customers.

To help name your business, think about what your target market expects from you and then apply a variety of business names that meet those expectations. To get you started, answer the following questions:

- What do I offer to my customers that they need from a winery? Do they need low-alcohol wines? Organic wines?

- Do my customers want more red wine or more white? Sweet wines? Oaky wines?

- Are my customers willing to pay more for wine than they already pay, or do they want to pay less?

- Do customers want wine to pair with food or to sip and to contemplate?

- What kind of marketing messages do my customers respond to?

◆ When they come to my tasting room, along with good wine, what else are customers looking for?

◆ How do my customers see me as different from the wineries in my neighborhood as well as from wineries across the country?

◆ Do customers want my winery to be like an exclusive club?

With each question, think about your target market and then answer the question and write down a few business names that correspond to each answer. Ask your friends and family what they think of the names. Enlist members of your advisory board for their opinions. Talk to people in your target market group for their responses to the names. Carefully watch everybody's reactions to each name—if they get it, circle that name; if they don't get it, or if they ask too many questions before they get it, cross that name off the list.

Use Your Imagination

After you remove the names that don't work, go through the remaining names and start imagining things. Imagine each name on a large sign in front of your winery driveway; imagine it on smaller, directional signs along the road; imagine a newspaper headline with your business name in it; and imagine how it fits on a business card, as letterhead, on an envelope, on a T-shirt, on a hat, and most of all, on a wine label.

Imagine how the business name sounds when you answer the phone, when someone introduces you and your business to an audience, or when the presenter calls out your winery name at that White House ceremony.

> **Master of Wine**
>
> Your business name should be as concise, as descriptive, as easy to read, and as easy to say as possible—and did I say memorable?

When you've settled on two or three names, it might be time to talk to a marketing consultant for some final input. To be safe for the future, immediately register for a website domain for each name. A number of domain name organizations exits. The simplest way to find them is to go to Google.com, type in "register domain names," and read the information on a few of the sites. Google itself has gotten into the domain registration business.

You've Chosen a Name ... Almost

When you start and name a business, you can elect to go by an alias or fictitious name; it's called your *dba*, which stands for "doing business as." You simply register your main business name and list one or more names under which you will do business (you can also add a dba later). The dba allows you not to have to use your name as a sole proprietor, and it allows a corporation or LLC to operate under multiple names.

In the case of a winery, your business name may become your brand name, which makes it doubly important to select it carefully and then check to see if it's even available and not already taken by a winery on the other side of the state.

Registering Your Name

In some states, you must file the name of your start-up with the Secretary of State office. They will do a name trace to ensure that no other company in a similar business is registered in that state under that name. In other states, you will file the business name locally and so you will have to do a name trace on your own. You can start that process online at www.legalzoom.com or www.experian.com.

You cannot open a bank account without a registered business name and dba.

Brand Naming Restrictions

When you decide on your business name, you may also decide to establish separate brand names for your products. This can be tricky in the wine business.

Sour Grapes

Chapter 4 of TTB regulations and TTB Industry Circular Number: 2006-1 limits brand name selections for wine labels (see Appendix B). With alcohol regulations, words have specific meanings. For instance, TTB protects the name of a wine region, so using the region as a brand name is a no-no. It's best to read the regulations thoroughly before coming up with brand names.

Wine labeling is subject to international agreements. Under the agreements, certain words are either regulated or prohibited. Plus, labels are restricted from using certain American geographic names as brand names. This is where your lawyer might have to get involved in the process.

Designing Your Logo

It's not enough for people to speak your business name. For them to remember your business, they need to see it. What you see when you think of certain companies is their *logo*. It might be the image of a swipe, or the image of a puma, or it might be the images of the two big cola soft drinks. Each is an indelible image to remember—it is a logo.

def•i•ni•tion

A **logo** is your name in picture and/or graphic form. It can be a word in special font, a word as a graphic, or a word plus a picture or graphic.

A logo can be your name subjected to a special design treatment, or it can be your name with a design treatment added to it. Sometimes, the added design element becomes dominant over the name in the logo, and that's what people remember. Your business name and logo will be used for your every communication with customers, business associates, the press, advertising, promotion, and placement of your product in the market. There's nothing more important for your company's image than your name with logo.

Do you remember Thomas in Chapter 3, the one whose winery didn't make it? He certainly made mistakes, but one of his interesting moves was the name and logo for his business. Thomas's corporate name was The Cana Creation, Inc., and his dba brand name was Cana Vineyards. The name is a reference to a story in the New Testament of a marriage feast in a town called Cana, where water was changed into wine. Had Thomas succeeded with his winery dream, the name Cana Vineyards was nicely situated to appeal to quite a large potential market. The name was helped along by a logo image that incorporated grape clusters flanking the word Cana in a stained-glass motif. From its road signs and labels, people quickly got a message that this company was making a claim that its wines are among the best. The fact that so many in Thomas's target audience were familiar with stained glass may have made the logo extra memorable.

Thomas used a combination of talking with friends plus a professional designer to come up with his business name and logo. When you're ready to find a logo designer, here are the steps to take:

1. *Get recommendations.* An artist or illustrator isn't automatically a good logo designer. Logo design may include fine art, but it is commercial art.

2. *Clearly spell out your business concept and your target market.* Your designer needs to play around with many design elements. Knowing exactly what you want and who your market is will help images and ideas flow.

3. *Ask for at least three design concepts from which to choose.* Sometimes a designer gets all three right, and sometimes a designer needs to try out a few before getting one right. Quite often a designer has good ideas that show up in separate designs that can be unified into one.

Your logo needs to be readable as well as reproducible. It must remain legible in photocopies of letterhead; it must be clear and legible as a label on a shelf from a few feet away and as a road sign; and it must be easy to read from a moving vehicle.

Be especially alert to colors. Some colors look wonderful on original letterhead but don't copy well. Other colors may be fine on letterhead, but on a road sign, they might be washed out by the surroundings. A color that works well on paper may get lost on a store shelf. Here are some other color considerations:

♦ Black is the color of authority.

♦ White is a good background color to give words impact.

♦ Red, the color of wine, is a fine color to grab attention and works well in a road sign—be careful with it for moving video images.

♦ Purple, another color for wine, speaks to passion.

The Winepress

Logos that call upon the customer's experiences are particularly effective. As reported in a 2000 survey, at least 77 percent of the U.S. population might have been familiar with the marriage feast at Cana.

♦ Blue is the cool, restful, calming color. (I've been told blue is not recommended for wine labels.)

♦ Yellow is bright and stands out, which is why official road signs use it.

♦ Green, another road sign color, is the color of nature.

When you talk to your logo designer, mention that you know colors have their own personalities and attributes and you want the colors for your logo to express the character of your business and its products. Consider hiring your logo designer also as your label and packaging designer, provided he or she has the experience.

Trademarking: Protecting Your Stuff

Any word, image, or combination of words and images—a logo—can be trademarked. You can even trademark your own color (think *UPS*). A trademark is a unique identity that distinguishes your business from any other. The subject of trademarking is covered in both state and federal law, so you probably should talk to your lawyer.

It takes a lot of back and forth with the U.S. Patent and Trademark Office (USPTO) to register a trademark, but it doesn't cost much. If you can follow directions well and are patient, you don't need to hire a trademark attorney or consultant, but many people hire one just to be safe. USPTO provides information about trademark attorneys at www.uspto.gov/main/profiles/tmatty.htm.

In the end, filing for a trademark could mean the difference between agony and ecstasy; the agony of finding out that another business is using the same name as yours and the ecstasy of preventing another business from using your identity.

Master of Wine

When you apply to USPTO, a trademark search is initiated for you. To apply or for information, call 1-800-786-9199. You can apply online through The Trademark Electronic Application System (TEAS) at www.uspto.gov/teas/index.html. To do your own trademark search, take advantage of the Trademark Electronic Search System (TESS). Find it at www.uspto.gov/main/trademarks.htm.

Have you ever wondered what the difference is between ® and ™ in a logo? The ® means the trademark was registered with and approved by the USPTO. The ™ means the trademark was not necessarily registered, but it likely was researched and could be pending. Should you ever need to stop someone from an infringement, the ® is the one that counts the most. It covers logo image and all the goods and services listed in the application and approved for trademark, and it also establishes the exact date when the trademark was applied for and issued, in case the offending infringement tries to claim having gotten there first.

This chapter ends the multitude of preliminary thinking and activity it takes to get your winery business started. In Part 3, you get your hands dirty. You start to do the work that will make your business a reality.

The Least You Need to Know

- Naming your business takes a lot of thought and a lot of imagination.
- Remember who your customers are when you name your business.
- Your business name should be memorable and so should your logo.
- Don't hire just any artist to design your logo.
- Use the right colors for your logo so it stands out under a variety of conditions.
- Protect your business identity by registering a trademark.

Part 3

Laboring in the Vineyard

Your plan is in place, your applications have been filed, and your permits and trademarks are pending. That wasn't so hard—okay, so it was just a little. The next round will really be hard work, but it will be worth it because you'll start to see the business—*your* business—take shape.

Part 3 explains how to plant the vineyard and lay out the winery. We explore the climate, the grape varieties, and the people who grow grapes. We walk through a winery and get the flow of it from grapes into pouring in your tasting room. Soon you'll be ready to start shopping to fill your winery with the production equipment that will get you started.

Chapter 10

From Grapes Comes Wine

In This Chapter

♦ Finding and laying out a vineyard

♦ The importance of climate and setting

♦ Discovering the many grape varieties

♦ Deciding what to plant

This might sound obvious, but you can't produce wine without grapes. Of course, you don't have to own a vineyard to produce wine, but you'd be hard pressed to produce your own bottle of premium wine without at least knowing something about grape growing.

If you plan to run a vineyard as part of your winery, in Chapter 2, I recommended that you get a job in a vineyard for experience. Now I recommend that you take grape-growing classes at the cooperative extension service in the wine region you've chosen to start your business.

If you still aren't sure whether you want to buy grapes or grow them, this chapter, plus the two chapters that follow, give you what you need to finally make the decision.

Laying Out a Vineyard

If you decide to grow grapes for your winery and you have a farming background, or you've gained grape-growing experience in the field, you already know what it's like out there. You probably also know that it takes three or four years after planting a vineyard to harvest your first crop. But did you know that after the first crop, your grapes will continue to mature and thereby change in quality?

That little bit of information is critical in making a decision whether to grow grapes or buy grapes when you start your winery.

To Grow or to Buy?

You can decide to grow grapes and still benefit from having mature grapes. It depends on which of the following courses you choose to take:

◆ *Buy an existing vineyard.* The benefit here is that if the grapes growing are the ones you want for your wine, you won't have to wait the three or four years it takes for a new vineyard to produce a viable grape crop. The downside is that the previous owner may not have handled the vineyard properly. Mature grapes still need to be tended carefully to maintain quality.

◆ *Find a plot of land partially planted to vineyards.* Select a vineyard growing grape varieties that interest you and that have proven themselves. It will give you a running start, a chance to have a crop while you plant new vineyards on the fallow parcel and wait for them to produce.

If you choose to buy fallow land and plant your own vineyard, first get the local cooperative extension agent or a vineyard consultant to help you determine the land's grape-growing potential. If you have no other vineyard, you can buy grapes while you wait (see Chapter 12). To determine which grape varieties will do well in your new vineyard and how best they should be plotted, you'll need an evaluation of your vineyard's soil types, topography, and climate.

Soil and Exposure

Grape growing is gardening on a large scale, and rule number one for a good garden is to have the right soil. Whether you're considering an existing vineyard or a fallow plot of land, get soil samples over to the nearest cooperative extension office. Tell the extension agent which grape varieties you have in mind for your land. The soil makeup will guide you by pointing out how much soil preparation may be required to start the vineyard and before each vintage begins or by showing you that you need to reconsider the grape variety you've chosen.

Gardening rule number two is to have southern exposure. Fruit ripens from exposure to the sun, which develops sugars. For the sun's rays to ripen a crop fully, southern exposure is best. But southern exposure may not always be available. A vineyard can thrive without southern exposure, but you have to prepare for it.

Cool, Clear Water

Grapes do especially well close to a body of water because rivers, lakes, and ponds affect air temperature, especially during early spring and autumn, when sudden frost can do damage. The larger and deeper the body of water, the better chance it has to make an effect on surrounding air temperature.

When we buy or rent a cabin on a lake-shore, we may not always get the best spot. Vineyards growing along lakeshores don't all get prime land, either. For example, bodies of water are important to the New York State wine industry. The Finger Lakes region is among the best wine-growing areas in the state. The lakes of the region are long, in a north/south direction. That means the majority of vineyards are exposed either to the east or to the west. They don't get full southern exposure. Still, the vineyards can do well. In a minute, you'll understand why.

> **Master of Wine**
>
> Grapes don't survive well in the arctic or in the tropics. Otherwise, grapes give back in wine what the climate puts them through. An extremely cold region will give you marginal wine. An extremely hot region will give you flabby wine. As you move from cold to warm regions, the crop goes from marginal to aromatic, and from hot to cool regions, flabby makes its way to leanness.

Mountains, Valleys, and Air Drainage

After you've settled on that parcel of land and you've decided how much of it will go toward vineyards, your next step is to plot the vineyard. You need to lay out exactly where the vines will go and which ones go in which location. The answers to the following questions will be your guide.

If you are near water, how far from shore is your vineyard? To reap the full benefit of a body of water's moderating effect, grapevines need to be reasonably close to the shore, and the air drainage needs to be reasonably unobstructed.

Does the vineyard slope, and if so, how steeply? Generally, a steep slope is better than a gentle slope toward a lake. But if it's too steep, the lower portion of the vineyard may reap benefits that the upper portion does not, or the other way around—the lower portion might benefit less if it's smack up against a wall of trees. A gentle slope might fare better in a valley.

How much vine spacing will your vineyard need? Two considerations govern vine spacing: air drainage and crop size. A good, steep slope automatically provides the condition for air to flow and drain rather than sit still and exaggerate temperatures as well as humidity, but if a forest surrounds the vineyard, extra care will be required in figuring out vine spacing.

Are you facing south, east, or west? If your vineyard faces south, it will get full daytime sun exposure. If it faces east, it gets rising-sun exposure. And a west-facing vineyard gets setting-sun exposure. The east-facing grapevines will ripen in a different time frame than the west-facing ones, and maybe in a different pattern, too. It's not advisable to plant on a slope facing north.

Your success with the types of grapes you grow and the style of wine you produce may hinge on a combination of these topographical considerations.

Understanding Micro- and Macroclimates

A *macroclimate* is the relationship between your plot of land and the general surroundings. Usually, regions are identified by their macroclimates. In grape growing, there are warm-climate regions, as in the bottom half of California, and cool-climate regions, as in the whole northeast of the United States. Many wine regions in the United States are given official federal appellation status for their unique climate and topography.

A *microclimate* refers to the specific spots within your plot of land that almost produce their own special weather. A small plot of land, as small as a few square feet, can be noticeably warmer or cooler than the overall region, or it can experience specific weather anomalies within your own vineyard. Microclimates can be a particular challenge or a wonderful benefit to grape growing.

How's the Weather?

Your grapes are outdoors all the time, day in and day out, in sun and rain, in cold and warm. The sun is one thing, but air temperature, flow, and humidity really make all the difference, and not always at the time of year you might imagine they should.

Grapes may be dormant in winter, but they aren't dead. Certain winter happenings, however, can kill them, or at least kill their bud nodes, those little bulges in the cane that are the source of spring bud break.

Remember that forest earlier, the one that might block the lake's effect from your front row of grapes? In winter, that forest could be your vineyard's best friend, especially if it's situated in such a way to buffer the vineyard against sudden serious drops in temperature. In most locations, you can keep on top of the weather online with a 10-day forecast. Check with the local weather station.

Sour Grapes

If you've done your homework, you already know that grapes have a shot at growing where you're planning to plant them, but you have no idea what the weather will be like from day to day, let alone year to year. Global climate change is now recognized as a challenge for grape-growing regions, threatening to alter the long-established character of grapes that have grown in particular regions for centuries.

Simply put, even with careful planning and research, the best-laid vineyard plans will always be subject to the weather, which is why knowing a little about specific grapevines will take you a long way toward establishing your wine product mix.

European Grape Varieties

Like all plants, grape varieties are members of a species. Wine grapes belong in the *Vitis* genus. In the subgenera *Euvitis Planch*, the first wines were produced from *Vitis vinifera sylvestris*. This wild species is believed to have originated in the Near East and western Asia.

Wild grapevines aren't good at producing grapes consistently from year to year because some produce male flowers and others produce female flowers. Relying on the wind or insects for pollination, and at the right time, isn't a good model for successful farming.

Luckily, nature isn't perfect. In its imperfection, nature must have provided ancient farmers with a few grapevines that managed

Master of Wine

A species is like a family. Grapevines within a species are identified as varieties within the family. Each family member produces a unique grape variety. An individual wine named after a grape variety is called a *varietal wine*.

The Winepress _____

It's estimated that 10,000 wine grape varieties spread their tendrils throughout the world. Europe is home to the majority of grape varieties, but North America is home to a majority of separate grapevine species.

to produce both male and female flowers and that would have been self-pollinating. Smart farmers among the group probably saw that those vines were consistent so they selected cuttings from them. In this way, thousands of years ago, ancient Mesopotamian farmers created a new species, *Vitis vinifera sativum*, a cultivated grapevine species that is still in use for wine today. And because Europe is where recent history made wine famous, today, *Vitis vinifera* vines are referred to as the European grapevine species.

How Do They Grow?

Generally, grapevines in all species grow in a similar manner: it's a four-part cycle that includes spring budding and flowering, summer fruit set, autumn fruit maturity, and winter dormancy. Cultivated grapevines have been bred to survive varying climates. *Vitis vinifera* began to favor warm climates generally, but over the centuries, it has been bred to survive cool climates as well. But not just any cool climate.

Even in the coldest reaches of the European Alps, southern mountain slope exposure can be quite warm in winter. And the temperature swings there may not be as violent as they are in, say, the Great Lakes region in the United States, which isn't mountainous. For that reason, *Vitis vinifera* vines have not been important in U.S. regions where the climate is erratic.

Being the oldest known wine grapevine species has given *Vitis vinifera* grapes a level of importance and they're in the highest demand. When you're selecting the state and location for your vineyard, you're likely to hear from the cooperative extension agent all about the local weather's effect on the grapevines you want to grow. If you happen to be in a frigid part of the United States, you might not hear much about European grapes.

European Grape Wines

To cover all the wine grapes that grow and all the wine styles the grapes ultimately become would take a volume of books. The following is a list of some wine varietals produced from the European grape varieties that enjoy high demand.

First up, the red wines, with their corresponding wine characteristics:

Cabernet Sauvignon	mainly powerful style
Merlot	softer, subtle wines
Cabernet Franc	lean and racy style
Pinot Noir	medium- to full-bodied (also used in sparkling wine)
Syrah	deep, peppery flavors
Grenache	light but spicy sensation
Gamay	light- to medium-bodied
Sangiovese	lean, leathery, and acidic
Nebbiolo	powerful, age-worthy wines
Primitivo	lush and fruity (cousin to American Zinfandel)
Tempranillo	earthy and dusty character

And here are a few of the white wine varietals:

Chardonnay	from lean to soft, depending on location (also used in sparkling wines)
Sauvignon Blanc	grassy and crisp character
Chenin Blanc	fruity, often a touch sweet
Riesling	versatile, fruity, and crisp (also dessert wines)
Gewürztraminer	extremely spicy and bold
Pinot Grigio	medium-bodied

European Grape Prices

Overall, the price any individual grape crop commands is based on local growing conditions and wine production decisions. When you forecast your income from the vineyard and wine in your business plan, you'll need to have good examples of the present grape prices in the location you plan to start your business.

> **Master of Wine** _____
>
> Demand for *Vitis vinifera* grape varieties is worldwide. In the United States, grapes from this species grow well in maritime climates and some desert regions. They are grown throughout the West, Northwest, and parts of the Southwest. They also grow in continental climates of the Northeast, Midwest, and other regions, where they are more fragile.

You certainly can't make wine without grapes, but you will never get the price you think you deserve for the wine without establishing the proper image. The quality image of *Vitis vinifera* grapes is what allows them to command the highest prices.

French-American Hybrids

Between 5000 B.C.E. and the nineteenth century, the offspring of the original *Vitis vinifera* vines ruled the wine world. In Chapter 1, you discovered that America didn't get into that world until the mid-nineteenth century. The reason for that was because each time European grapevines were planted in America, they failed to survive.

When the American wine industry finally developed, it was with grapevines native to North America. About that same time, American vines went to Europe for experiments. The journeys proved fatal. The first blow came in the early nineteenth century, and the second arrived mid-century. Each time, it was a grapevine disease that was previously unknown in Europe that got into vineyards through the American rootstocks.

> **The Winepress** _____
>
> A new grapevine created by joining two or more vines within a single species is called a *cross*. A new grapevine created by joining two or more vines from multiple species is called a *hybrid*.

Named *phylloxera*, the second disease nearly wiped out the whole of Europe's wine industry. Scientists spent many years seeking a cure. In the process, they developed a new grapevine species by crossing French *Vitis vinifera* with one or more vines from American species. The result was a French-American hybrid species.

How Do They Grow?

French-American hybrids were first bred as an answer to the disease problem. Scientists figured out that they might also be able to create hybrids to withstand specific climatic conditions, so a new grapevine-breeding industry developed, with a mission to create vines that could survive where *Vitis vinifera* couldn't. The aim was for the hybrids to produce wine comparable to European wines.

The hybrid breeding result was mixed, with some hybrid vines that do well in frigid and erratic regions and some that do not. Some hybrid wines come close to the style of their European counterparts, but many simply do not measure up.

French-American Hybrid Grape Wines

Rarely do wine professionals rhapsodize over wines produced from French-American hybrid grapes. Still, a few are known for producing decent products, often in a specialty classification like dessert wine.

Some of the well-known hybrid red grapes include the following:

Baco Noir	earthy flavors
Marechal Foch	fruity style
Chambourcin	probably the most Europeanlike of them all
Chancellor	medium-bodied

Here are some of the well-known French-American hybrid white grapes:

Seyval	versatile and often Europeanlike
Vidal	fruity and Europeanlike (also dessert wines)
Aurora	mainly for blending

Hybridizing still takes place in America, especially at Cornell University's horticultural school. Some of the well-known vines that have come from this effort include the following:

Cayuga White	quite fruity
Traminette	spicy, Europeanlike
Chardonel	light

French-American Hybrid Grape Prices

The prices wines produced from hybrids command are generally lower than prices for wines produced from European vines. As a result, the prices wineries pay for hybrid grapes is not as high as the prices for *Vitis vinifera* grapes.

> **Master of Wine** _____
>
> Wine professionals today generally agree that hybrid vines neither provide foolproof weather-hardiness nor do they produce wines that compete with their European counterparts. Their main homes in the United States are the Northeast, Midwest, and Mountain regions.

Many grape growers believe that the hybrids are as difficult to grow, but because some can survive certain icy, erratic winters better than European vines, the grape farmers haven't much choice but to grow them.

American Grapes

Just as the nineteenth-century root louse (phylloxera) blight in Europe came from America, so did the cure.

North America is home to a number of species in the *Vitis* genus, including *Vitis labrusca, Vitis rotundifolia*, and *Vitis riparia*. These native vines are generally resistant to the phylloxera that attacked European vines. The cure in the 1880s was to graft European vines onto native North American rootstock, to make them disease resistant. That propagation practice continues in nurseries today.

> **The Winepress** _____
>
> The American wine industry began in the 1830s relying heavily on American grapes until well into the early twentieth century. Catawba was the most successful American grape; it was the main ingredient in Midwestern and Northeastern sparkling wines.

North American wine grapes produce a forward, grapey kind of wine most wine consumers find overbearing. Still, the many failures at trying to produce European-type wines in America finally helped create an American wine industry built on these grapes.

Over the centuries, American vines cross-pollinated with one another and with some of the European vines planted here, resulting in yet another separate species, *Vitis labruscana*, which is considered a Native American grapevine species.

How Do They Grow?

The benefit these grapes brought to the wine industry was simple: they survived in climates where other species struggled to survive. In fact, the Native American species survives a variety of climates and has been planted in Europe, especially in Italy.

Today, Native American grapevines are used for wine in the South, Northeast, Midwest, and in marginal regions.

American Grape Wines

Measured nationally, demand for wines produced from American vines is low. Measured regionally, demand rises as you enter the regions where the grapes grow. Measured locally, demand rises relevant to local pride. This is crucial information for establishing a vineyard and wine business for certain communities as opposed to national ambitions.

Some of the names of American grapes may be familiar to you, and maybe their wines, too:

Concord	jammy wines
Catawba	grapey character
Norton	almost Europeanlike
Isabella	medium-grapey
Niagara	oddly petroleumlike
Delaware	fresh fruit character
Diamond	dry, clean
Scuppernong	cloying

American Grape Prices

Prices for wines from American grapes are generally low, even in regions where the grapes are popular. The demand for these wines remains mainly local.

The grape varieties you choose to grow for your business will of course be the result of what you've learned about the local climate and soil, but it will also be the result of that part in your business plan that sets your mission and your image. Which wines you produce is a direct reflection of which grape species you plan to plant.

In Chapter 11, you discover the various ways in which to run your vineyard.

The Least You Need to Know

◆ Whether or not you grow grapes for your business, you must know how, where, and why certain grapes grow.

◆ A vineyard is large-scale gardening that's subject to all the rules of gardening.

◆ Bodies of water are beneficial to producing consistent grape crops.

◆ Regional weather is important, but so is the weather in your specific vineyard site.

◆ Wines produced from the European grapevine species command the highest regard and prices.

Chapter 11

Growing Your Own Grapes

In This Chapter

- ◆ Starting and running a vineyard
- ◆ Determining who does the vineyard work
- ◆ The value of different grape-growing techniques
- ◆ What harvesting grapes can do to your wine
- ◆ The vineyard as a profit center

Great wine starts in the vineyard. No science has yet been developed that can help us produce a great wine from abused or ill-conceived vineyards.

As a wine producer, you'll strive to produce great wines. As a grape grower or grape buyer, your responsibility is to learn how to grow grapes in your vineyard that will produce the best wine possible.

In this chapter, you learn why vineyards are planted the way they are, why they are worked the way they are, and how to harvest them so they're in the best condition possible. You'll also discover how to integrate a vineyard into the rest of your business's balance sheets.

In Your Vineyard

The juiciest, most beautiful grapes you can imagine will grow in your vineyard. They will be sugary and lush, and they will drip like honey. ... Wait a second. ... If that's what your grapes look like, you're in trouble.

The next time you visit a winery vineyard, take a look at and taste a fresh grape. Wine grapes are generally smaller than table grapes, not near as juicy, and quite acidic. That's the way they should be. Table grapes are cropped for bigness; wine grapes are cropped for intensity.

The Winepress _____

The sweetness of a mature wine grape is referred to as its *Brix,* a term named after the man who developed a device that measures the approximate grape sugar percentage by way of measuring its specific gravity weight (see Appendix D).

Everything you do in your vineyard is to promote optimum grape maturity, and that does not necessarily mean overripeness. Winemaking depends on a prescribed sugar-to-juice, acid-to-pH ratio. You selected your vineyard site so your crop would meet winemaking parameters at harvest time. But winemaking also depends on a predetermined characteristic unique to each grape variety. In addition, the grapes need to be free from infections. All these measures combined reflect how the grapes were grown.

Into the Ground

You've already seen the cooperative extension agent to determine if and where you should plant the vineyard, and you have a general idea what the new vineyard will cost to get started (see Chapter 7 for guidance). Now you're ready to buy the grafted plants from the nursery that propagates commercial grapevines. (*Wines and Vines* magazine, in Appendix C, includes a listing of nurseries. Also ask your cooperative extension agent, plus other vineyard managers, for reputable nurseries.)

The Winepress _____

Cultivated wine grapevines are not a natural species. They may have many parents. They cannot be propagated from seed for fear of the offspring reverting to one of the parents rather than developing as the vine you want. For that reason, the vines are propagated either as bench or field grafts of individual vine material onto selected rootstock.

In Chapter 10, you learned about exposure to sun and to bodies of water, plus air drainage. Assuming you have had your soil tested and fertilized to suit your needs, determined your water and air drainage, your vineyard layout, your trellis system, and any other considerations the cooperative extension agent or consultant suggested, you're ready to plant your vineyard. (Planting the vineyard is a subject for a professional vineyard manager to tackle along with the local university cooperative extension agent.)

To get started, clear the site of weeds and map out the rows. You can do this by establishing the placement and length of the rows and then stringing a few rows for straightness. For detailed information on planting a vineyard see www.pawpaw.kysu. edu/Viticulture/Information/design_your_vineyard.htm.

Installing string guides.

After you determine your row length, vine spacing, and number of vines per row, you can mark the spots where your posts will go. Then it's time to go get the tractor. With the post-hole driller attached to your tractor's PTO (power take-off), dig post holes from 5 to 8 yards apart, based on the length of your rows and the number of vines you're planting in each row. After the holes are set, switch the equipment attached to the PTO to pound in the posts.

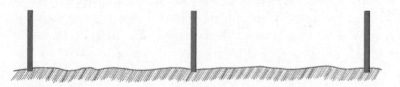

Installing posts.

After you select a trellis method suitable to your site, run the wires and staple them to the posts, tightening them on each end post.

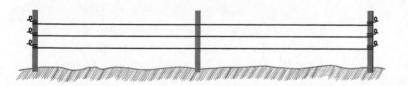

Installing wire.

Your next move is to plant the vines, which you'll buy from the nursery. There are a number of ways to plant vines, and you need a variety of equipment to do the work. Generally, you map out the planting in advance, using markers where each vine is to be inserted. You'll move along, inserting,

Master of Wine

Vineyard rows longer than 600 feet increase tension on the end posts and can cause the trellis to sag.

and piling soil, and you may have to string vine cuttings to the trellis to keep them growing upward. (If left to their own devices, vines will reach, crawl, and spread every which way.)

Planting vines.

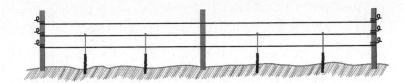

Which Vine Is for You?

Remember from Chapter 10 the root louse that devastated European vineyards in the nineteenth century? The fix was to graft European vines onto American rootstock. But the rootstock must be clean and American only, with no cross-breeding that might have even the slightest hint of vinifera in its bloodline. For this reason, the nursery you select to purchase your vines from must be reputable.

In conjunction with grapevine clonal selection, rootstocks are determined for climatic conditions as well as disease resistance. Talk to the cooperative extension agent about the rootstocks that are proven for your region. Read carefully the material the nursery and the extension agent provide. A mistake at planting can be extremely costly a few years down the road.

> **Sour Grapes**
>
> In the 1990s, vast stretches of California vineyards had to be replanted at great cost because the rootstock used was not resistant to the *phylloxera* root louse. The disease broke out in vineyards around the state.

The cooperative extension agent may have suggested that you plant your vines in grow tubes. In an earlier chapter I mentioned that grow tubes speed up the process toward establishing your first crop, perhaps by a year, but that they also present their own potential problems by creating a greenhouse effect that can leave the young vines in a weakened state during their first winter. One way to prevent that from happening is to be sure to remove the grow tubes by mid-August.

If you've done it correctly, you'll get to watch all summer as your new vines grow. What will you do in the vineyard after the vines are established?

The Four Seasons

The following is a quick rundown of the activity that will take place in your vineyard over each year.

Early spring   The ground is worked to prevent weeds, plus you'll have to pound back into the ground the vineyard posts that heaved from winter thawing.

Mid-spring   The spray schedule needs to be established to prevent fungus from infecting budding flowers.

Late spring   Flowers are bulging, which means minimal spraying until after they've fully bloomed.

Early summer   It's time to sucker the vines—cut away new growth at the bottom of the vines that can steal energy from the setting fruit. It's also time to position tendrils on the trellis for best exposure.

Throughout summer   A spray schedule is developed to fight fungus and insects, leaf thinning may be necessary for better sun exposure, some new shoots may have to be tied to the trellis, and weeds must be kept under control.

Late summer   A decision may have to be made concerning thinning the crop—dropping grape clusters to increase fruit intensity.

A few weeks before harvest   Spraying must cease and regular walks in the vineyard will begin to take samples to establish grape maturity.

Mid- to late fall   Each variety reaches maturity based on the style of wine you want to produce and harvest begins.

Late fall   The rows are prepared for winter (hilling in cold climates, clearing of debris, etc.).

Winter   After the vines have hardened off, pruning begins to establish next year's crop size, and the previous year's ties that held vine shoots to trellis are removed.

Late winter and into early spring   Remaining branches are tied to the trellis to position the new shoots and to prevent tendrils from crawling, as vine tendrils will.

As you can see, there's never nothing to do in a vineyard.

Who's Doing All This Work?

In our modern world, fewer and fewer families earn their living as farmers. Some of the older wine regions in the United States still have a tradition of family grape farms, but they are fast fading. As rural life fades from the landscape, in many grape-growing regions, it's difficult to find people who know how to work the vineyards.

At this point in your business, you'll need a vineyard manager on staff, and that may be someone with a university degree in horticulture. It's the regular day laborers who will be hard to come by. If you hadn't looked into the available farm labor force when you decided on a location, your future may be filled with long workdays and endless nights. (On the bright side, you'll build good biceps.)

Talk to local grape growers to find out how they handle seasonal vineyard labor. You may be sharing their farm hands, or you may be doing what's become an increasing practice in vineyards across the nation: hire migrant laborers.

The Winepress

According to the U.S. Department of Labor (www.dol.gov/asp/programs/agworker/report9/summary.htm), 23 percent of all hired crop farm workers were born in the United States, 75 percent were born in Mexico, and the rest were born in other countries.

In some wine regions, you can find vineyard management companies. They can provide the labor you need.

Migrant laborers generally do the shoot pruning, tying, pulling, and grape harvesting on a piecework basis. Your responsibility is to hire the labor contractor, lay out the workload, and pay the contractor a lump sum. You have to find either a broker or a recommendation for the labor contractor, which you can also do through the cooperative extension agent or other vineyard operators.

How Will Your Garden Grow?

Ask 10 gardeners a question about growing tomatoes, and you'll get 10 great ideas about how to grow tomatoes. The same holds for the intricate details of grape growing. Still, the overall choices for operating a vineyard generally fall into three categories of viticulture:

◆ *Conventional*   The way it's been done

◆ *Organic*   The reaction to the way it's been done

◆ *Biodynamic*   Back to the future

The organic and biodynamic methods are part of the modern "green" movement that today sweeps the wine industry. To decide on the grape-growing method that's right for you, gather information from the local cooperative extension, get some book learning on grape growing, and talk with grape growers in your area.

When making your decision, take the following factors into consideration:

♦ How you feel about the use of chemicals in food production

♦ How you feel about the potential danger to humans who handle petrochemicals

♦ How you feel about the earth

♦ Which grape-growing method enjoys greater consumer acceptance

♦ Which growing method provides the best-quality crop

♦ Which grow method is cost-effective and profitable

Conventional

Out of a total of 8,000 years of grape cultivation, what we call the "conventional" way to grow grapes has been in place for about 150 years. Before World War I, the majority of European grape growers probably didn't even own a tractor. Today, it's conventional to use a tractor, attaching equipment to the PTO to dig vineyard post holes, hill up soil around vine roots, pound posts each spring to put them back where they belong after winter heaving, and a host of other chores, including spraying the vines during the growing season.

Conventional grape growing is a combination of the effects of the late-nineteenth-century industrial revolution and the twentieth-century introduction of petro-chemicals to farming, with some truly conventional methods that have made their way back into the mix, like mulching between vineyard rows instead of using weed-killing chemicals.

Lately, many farmers wonder over the impact conventional farming has on the environment. What's more, consumers worry. Responding to consumers, "going green" has become a growing trend in viticulture.

> **Sour Grapes**
>
> When you choose the so-called conventional method of operating a vineyard, odds are that you'll handle a variety of petrochemicals. Most states' agricultural and health departments require special care for the use and disposal of the chemicals, from licensing those who apply them to licensing those who dispose of them as waste.

Organic

Even though some chemicals are allowed under a so-called organic scheme of grape growing, they're not of the petrochemical kind; they're considered to have come from organic material—elements found in nature that don't have to be refined or processed.

The Winepress

If you pass muster as an organic regime, you have the right to be certified. The word *organic* on a wine label has picked up a following, and so the prices you receive for your organic grape crop will reflect the growing interest in the subject. But you'll see in Chapter 15 how the word *organic* can be misleading.

To be an organic farmer, you must play by a set of rules that govern not only how you operate your vineyard but also how the vineyard next door operates and makes an impact on yours. If the guy next door uses petrochemicals, you may not be able to earn organic status because his spray material wafts over to your vineyard rows.

Under organic certification, it's perfectly fine to use copper spray and other materials that some people believe are bad for themselves and the environment. Many of these people have turned to another form of going green in their vineyards.

Biodynamic

This latest wave going through viticulture is from an early twentieth-century concept. We call it *biodynamic*. Under a biodynamic regime, no petrochemicals are used, making it organic. But what separates it from the organic method is that much of what constitutes biodynamic farming is akin to what can be called primitive thinking, and that isn't necessarily meant in a bad way.

def•i•ni•tion

Put forward by Rudolf Steiner, a European philosopher turned mystic, the **biodynamic** claim is to recognize the basic principles in nature that, when applied to agriculture, create balance and healing. Some people claim that biodynamic is organic farming with a touch of the occult. Incidentally, Steiner consumed no alcohol.

To be truly biodynamic, the grape grower must follow the cycles of the moon, the mystical nature of symbols, and the power of believing. Biodynamic farming calls upon the heavens at the same time it calls upon the beasts that walk the earth, whose hooves and horns are part of the ingredients in homeopathic concoctions that are buried in the ground, made into spray material, and burned almost as incense. Anyone who knows anything about ancient history might view biodynamic farming as the true conventional method, especially when the subject of the gods comes up.

It's a cinch that without the benefit of a tractor to farm them, the price of grapes surely would skyrocket. But operating a tractor doesn't seem to be a problem for those who go green—that mechanical beast is used in both organic and biodynamic farming.

Harvesting

No matter which of the three viticultural methods you employ, you'll make harvesting decisions based on weather, quality, and wine style. The harvesting methods available to you make up a short list of two:

- Mechanical
- Handpicking

The wines with the greatest reputation, and that command the highest prices, are generally produced from handpicked grapes. But that's not to say that all high-priced wine is produced from handpicking. The benefit handpicking has over mechanical harvesting is that it allows for a pair of eyes and a brain to make decisions about the quality of individual grape clusters. The benefit used to extend to how the rest of the vine was treated during harvest, but the latest harvesting machines can be quite gentle on them.

When to Harvest

The decision to harvest grapes always depends on the weather—both when the grapes were growing and at harvest time. Harvest for each grape variety falls within a general window of opportunity each year, but variations in the growing-season weather determine exactly when harvest begins, and the weather at harvest time determines when you can get into the vineyard to pick grapes.

It's at this time when a top-notch vineyard manager and winemaker work together to establish the optimum maturity for each individual grape variety. Determining when grapes are mature for harvest is a marriage of science and experience. The science is in the chemistry-reading instruments; the experience is in the feel and taste.

It's also at this time when handpicking grapes faces its challenges, especially when harvest-time weather is uncooperative. When nature chooses to go by its own schedule, desire must give way to reality. A major benefit of harvesting machines is speed.

When compared to handpicking, the harvester speed is phenomenal. It can make the difference between losing a crop from a sudden downpour and saving the crop by beating the deluge.

Mechanical harvesters are quite expensive and because they're used within a short time frame each year, investing in one may be beneficial only if you have hundreds of acres to pick or you hire your harvesting services to other grape growers. Mostly, you can hire independent harvesters to pick your crop.

Give Your Grapes the Time of Day

It's always best to pick grapes when they're at their coolest temperature for the day, and to get them into the winery for processing without the sun beating down on them. This prevents the grapes from breaking down and becoming infected with rots and molds.

Mechanical harvesters come with headlights, giving them an obvious advantage over handpicking.

The Vineyard as a Profit Center?

In Chapter 5, you learned that the vineyard should be treated as a separate profit center from the wine production and sales end of the business. Gerald White, Professor Emeritus who studies the economics of viticulture at Cornell University, starts his speeches with a question: "Do you want to make wine or make money?" He knows that the money is not in the vineyard; it's in the wine. He recommends that to make money in the wine industry, you should avoid running a vineyard.

Master of Wine

Many wineries make a profit while their vineyards lose money. A vineyard that loses money or stands still drags down the book value of your winery business. If you're running a vineyard as part of the winery, treat it as a separate profit center, making book entries every time the winery "buys" grapes from the vineyard.

It's possible to make a profit from growing grapes, but it's not something that most people set out to do. The vineyard is servant to the winery. Because it's agriculture, running a vineyard is a rollercoaster ride of good years and bad years. Even a grape grower producing a specific grape variety that's in short supply and high demand can lose the profit he makes in any one year if the following year is disastrous.

When you run a vineyard as part of the winery, the cost of growing your own grapes is no better than the cost of someone else growing those grapes. Your wine must compete in price with wines of comparable quality, so the way to look at running your own vineyard is that its benefit is in quality control and not in profit potential.

When You Need More Grapes

When you build a winery, you can take future growth into consideration either by overbuilding or by making sure you have enough land for expanding the business. To expand a vineyard, you'll either have to have bought much more land than you originally needed or you'll have to start looking for land. Even if you have the land you need, you'll still have to wait from three or four years for that first crop.

When you succeed at selling your wine and you need to increase production, you'll probably find yourself having to source grapes. Your job will be to find grapes of equal or better quality to yours, because you'll have to blend them into the wines you produce from your own grapes.

There's a right way and a wrong way to go about buying grapes from others. In Chapter 12, you discover how to become an informed grape buyer for your winery.

The Least You Need to Know

- ◆ Whether or not you run a vineyard, you should know how to do it so your wine benefits.

- ◆ Grapevines require year-round tending.

- ◆ Decide which of the three grape-growing methods—conventional, organic, or biodynamic—is right for you.

- ◆ Harvesting grapes is all about maintaining a high-quality crop.

- ◆ The vineyard and the wine have a symbiotic relationship.

- ◆ Don't expect big profits from growing grapes.

Chapter 12

Using Someone Else's Grapes

In This Chapter

- When you need to buy grapes
- Why you need to buy grapes
- How to buy grapes
- The cost of grapes in your wine price

Even with your own vineyard producing top-quality grapes at peak capacity, at times you'll find yourself needing to buy grapes. When you do shop for grapes, you don't get to stand around and squeeze the clusters, and no one asks the question, "Paper or plastic?"

The formula may seem simple: you need grapes, someone has the grapes you need, you order grapes from that someone, and you pay for the grapes you receive. It is that simple, provided you do everything the government, the seller, and your need for quality requires.

In this chapter, you become an educated grape buyer so the wine you eventually produce and sell is worth the money you ask for it.

Why Buy Grapes?

Anyone who wasn't born into farming but tries it quickly learns the many synonyms for the word *tenacity*, not to mention the word *hope*.

In Chapter 11, you learned that vineyard profits don't come easy. Yet as difficult as it is to make a profit, some achieve it. Mostly, they do so in one of two ways: either they grow on such a large scale that they're in a business that's more industrial than it is farming, or they grow the premium grapes that are in the greatest demand (the European grapes listed in Chapter 10).

The Winepress

The United States produces approximately 8 million tons of grapes each year. California accounts for about 90 percent of the total. Wine grapes make up nearly 50 percent of California's grapes.

Others grow grapes to sell to wineries for other reasons, too, like economy of scale. An extra acre or two might bring down the per-acre cost to grow, so some grape growers who own wineries plant more than they need. They might plant grapes they don't plan to use in their wines, but they know they can sell.

Some grow grapes for juice, for the table, and for raisins. This can be big business, but prices paid for these commodities can also fluctuate greatly. Prices for premium wine grapes are more constant and usually go up, especially with *Vitis vinifera* varieties.

Others simply love it. Some growers don't expect to get rich from their vineyards, but they love their work. In parts of California, where 90 percent of wine is produced, some grape growers can and do get rich.

Before you make an agreement to buy grapes, you ought to know the reasons the grower sells them. It will give you a leg up on what to expect from the quality of the grapes and the quality of the experience of dealing with that grower.

Even when you plan ahead, even when everything goes as planned, even when you know what you're doing, something might come your way to challenge the decisions you've made and the decisions you are about to make according to plans. For instance, the decision to rely only on your grapes for the wine you produce could be challenged, and you'll have reason to change your plans, to buy grapes to augment your crop, to make up for a bad vintage, or to add a new varietal wine to your product line.

To Augment Your Crop

In the best case, you underestimated your success rate, grew too fast in your wine sales, and find yourself needing more grapes to produce the volume of wine your forecasts say you can sell in the coming year.

In the worst case, you simply didn't buy enough land to begin with or you couldn't raise the money for planting the size vineyard you had in mind.

Master of Wine _____

Constantly review your forecasts against actual sales. Your forecasts may have to be revised so you can plant a vineyard in time to meet the growing demand for your wine.

When You Had a Bad Year

If your vineyard suffers from a bad year, odds are that other grape growers in your region will, too. But that won't necessarily mean you'll have no local sources for grapes. Remember those microclimates I discussed in Chapter 10? A microclimate can be the source of seeming miracles:

Miracle 1: All around the region, a nasty winter kill devastated crops, but in some special places, and thanks to careful tending by farmers who know their land well, the damage was mild or not at all.

Miracle 2: A sudden hailstorm ripped through a small patch of the region, wiping out grape crops, but only in a narrow path.

Miracle 3: One grape-growing region in your state 300 miles away happened to have a good year when you had a bad one.

In addition, the weather across the United States varies greatly. Wineries can buy grapes from anywhere in the country provided they follow the guidelines set down by federal and state regulations. (I get to those later in this chapter.) It's likely that when you have a bad vintage year, someone else in another part of the country might not.

The Winepress _____

In most of New York State, the winter of 2003–2004 nearly wiped out the 2004 vintage, but on Long Island, where the winter was also harsh, its maritime climate helped avoid a wipeout.

When You Can't Grow That Variety

You did your homework and selected a region for your business that you were assured could support growing the grapes you wanted to grow. You're doing okay with what you have, but you also notice that certain wines you don't produce—and can't grow in your region—are picking up in demand. If you'd like to compete with those wines, what do you do?

You can buy the grapes you want from anywhere across the United States, but as you'll see later in the chapter, when you buy grapes from outside your region, you may need to adjust your marketing plans.

Know Your Supplier

No matter the reasons that cause you to buy grapes when you hadn't planned on it in advance, you'll need to establish good business relationships with grape growers. Don't just go out and buy grapes from anyone. Interview grape growers and buy from the ones who impress you. You want to know the following:

How much experience does the grower have? It is, of course, good to have experience, but experience can also produce an entrenched mentality. How did the grower start out, and what changes has he or she made since then?

Does the grape grower have wine knowledge? Someone with no knowledge or who doesn't like wine may have difficulty understanding your standards.

Does the grower have a viticulture philosophy? Find out what the grower thinks about conventional, organic, and biodynamic methods (remember those from Chapter 11?). Also, find out what the grower thinks about grape ripeness and maturity.

Who else buys the grapes? The best recommendation may be to identify the grower's other customers. But you need also to evaluate the level of competition that would mean between you and them, and the grower's allegiances. In a bad year, when crops are reduced, you want to know where you stand when the grower must choose who gets how many tons of grapes. If the grower is also a wine producer, I bet you can guess who comes first.

What kind of contract does the grower expect? It's best to be clear up front on what the grower expects of you. Like any other contract, a grape purchase agreement is based on many conditions.

When you interview grape growers, walk their vineyards. Be extra alert for the following:

- The general condition of the posts and trellis system
- Weed control
- Overall grape cluster health
- Sun exposure of the vines
- Air drainage
- Soil and microclimate conditions
- The general condition of the person and his surroundings

How to Buy Grapes

If you suddenly discover in the middle of autumn that you need to buy some grapes, you'll be in for a shock. You can't just pick up the phone and place an order for grapes as if it were a take-out food delivery. You can, but you may have to make quite a number of calls before you get anywhere.

It's best to start the grape-buying contract process for that year's crop soon after you forecast your production for the coming vintage. If you have a long-standing relationship with a grower or growers, of course approach them first.

You know the style of wine you want to produce, and you know what condition the grapes must be in to produce that wine. You need to tell the grape grower how much sugar and acid you aim for in the grapes, or the pH you seek. In other words, you need to establish harvesting parameters for the grapes you buy. You need to also spell out the length of the contract, trucking arrangements, and winery input into viticultural decisions.

Barring a tremendously unforeseen disaster, an experienced grower often knows midway through the growing season how it might end and can make a reasonable guess at the expected harvest date for each variety. But you need to monitor the growing season, too, and evaluate whether or not the grower will be able to meet your grape maturity parameters at the time of harvest.

> **The Winepress**
>
> Entering into a grape contract is like any other business contract, except that growing grapes is farming and producing wine is subject to excise taxes. Federal and local regulations might apply to some of the terms and conditions. Take a look at existing grower and winery contracts to guide you.

There will be times, however, when you'll be forced to buy grapes from someone you don't know or someone in another state. Even in these cases, seek recommendations or references from others, and be sure to have a written agreement that spells out the conditions under which you will accept delivery of the grapes and what and when you will pay for them.

Federal Appellation Rules

Under the U.S. Treasury Department Tax and Trade Bureau (TTB) rules, you can't claim certain things on a wine label unless you meet certain requirements. One of the most important of those requirements is to identify your grape crop's growing location, its appellation of origin or American Viticultural Area, or AVA (TTB regulation 27 CFR Part 9).

The Winepress _____

According to TTB regulation 27 CFR Part 4, when used on a wine label, *estate bottled* specifically tells consumers that the grapes were grown and fermented, and the wine was aged and bottled, on the producer's property within a certain appellation of origin. The words *produced and bottled by* tells consumers that you fermented, aged, and bottled the wine on your property but you either grew none or some of the grapes that went into making the wine.

If your business plan is to produce and label wine from grapes grown only on your property, you can't buy grapes from anyone else and use them for that wine. You can't do it because harvested grapes are accompanied by a paper trail. Where they were grown and harvested, the weight of the crop, and the price paid for them must be invoiced. After those grapes are fermented into wine, a paper trail must be established to prove which wine they wound up becoming.

Also, if your business plan is to include wine in your portfolio that's produced within one regional appellation, you can't buy grapes outside the appellation unless you meet certain grape-blending percentage requirements governed by four separate appellation configurations, which are further broken down into 14 subrules. Again, the proof is in the paper trail.

If your business plan is to produce wine without identifying an appellation on your label, you can buy grapes from anywhere in the United States and blend in any percentage. What you probably won't be able to do is get that wine into the *ultra-premium* price class, as people who spend money on those wines often want to know the appellation of origin or AVA.

def•i•ni•tion

Ultra-premium wine is a marketing term that refers to wines exceeding $25 a bottle. It's a wide spread, as wines can reach as high as hundreds of dollars a bottle, which are called *luxury wines*.

State Agricultural Rules

Generally, states recognize the federal appellation of origin rules with a few exceptions concerning blending percentages. Your state permit, however, may still limit your ability to blend.

In individual states, the so-called farm winery license may come with a requirement that limits grape purchases for wine to crops grown only in that state. Remember that bad winter in New York that I mentioned earlier? In order for most farm wineries to produce wine that year, the State Liquor Authority had to change the regulations to allow them to buy grapes from outside New York State. Now, New York farm wineries can automatically include grapes from other states in their products, but only when state authorities acknowledge a crop emergency.

In many states, the Department of Agriculture and Markets (A&M) generally governs farming within the state, including grape crop pesticide and fungicide use and disposal, plus grape pricing policy. A&M has its own set of rules for grape farming, and the rules may make an impact on how you buy and when you must pay for grapes. In some states, grape buyers must be bonded to ensure that growers are paid for their crops based on the agreed-upon contract.

A&M can, and does in some states, mandate that you must post the prices you'll pay for grapes on a prescribed date before the start of the official harvest season, making it a must that you forecast your grape needs well in advance.

It's in the Contract

You can wing it and make a verbal deal with your grape suppliers and then post the price as required with your state A&M. But that's sure to get you into a scrape or two. The best way to buy grapes is under contract. The contract you draw up with grape growers should specify your target crop yield, the type of growing techniques, specific harvest and delivery parameters (handpicked, mechanical picked at night, delivery before a certain hour, etc.), and price.

Because the grape harvest is based on the weather, the harvest parameters are an important measure to both sides and also a contentious condition in the contract—in certain years, it may be impossible to meet the parameters.

The prices agreed upon are contingent on meeting the other conditions, which leaves you with another potential contentious issue. You can offer a price for grapes based either on the tons per acre harvested or a flat per acre rate not tied to tonnage picked. When you make the decision to offer what you'll pay, consider this: prices based on tons per acre harvested give growers a negative incentive to produce more grapes per acre and potentially dilute quality; prices based on the acre harvested give growers a positive incentive to produce lower yield and potentially higher quality.

> **Master of Wine**
>
> You must resolve any contractual disagreement over the price well in advance of the deadline to post prices.

It's About Quality

If you follow most of the preceding suggestions for locating a grape grower and establishing a contract, you'll have established the quality parameters important to you. But business dealings don't always go as smoothly as planned. Disagreements among you and one or more grape growers can surface, especially during an unusual or potentially disastrous growing season.

For a farmer, the loss of expected income from a crop might mean the difference between paying and not paying the mortgage for the coming year. If a grower cannot meet your parameters for whatever reason, it's a sure thing the grower will seek a way either to get you to change them or get around them. It's your business to stay on top of the growing season and keep up a good relationship with grape growers so disagreements or problems beyond either the grower's control or yours still get you the best-quality crop possible.

A Weighty Issue: Tonnage

When you buy grapes, you're invoiced based on the weight by the ton. The volume of wine you can produce is based on the grape tonnage you press. The volume of wine your winery sales can support is based on your forecasts.

Be careful when you make your grape-buying calculations. Obviously, if you come up short you can't produce the volume of wine you expected to produce. If you have an oversupply of grapes, you may be forced to sell them off at a loss. Looked at that way, an under- or oversupply of grape tonnage can potentially lose you money.

The Winepress

It takes approximately 1 ton of grapes to produce in the neighborhood of 150 gallons of finished wine.

Timing Is Everything

You may not run a large enough winery to hire a traffic manager, but at harvest time, you may need someone to fill a similar role. Depending on how many different grape varieties you buy, your deliveries can flow smoothly, or they can step all over one another.

As harvest intensifies, growers can sometimes become frenetic if a spurt of bad weather is on the horizon—this is where contract disputes often arise. It's not uncommon for growers to start picking before the date they had agreed they would start. If you don't know their plans, you could be faced with trucks you didn't know were coming driving in behind trucks you had already scheduled.

Harvest timing is critical but so is the time between harvest and press or fermentation. A few tons of grapes sitting in their bins waiting hours for their place on the crush pad can start to deteriorate. And the weight of the grapes on top bear down on the grapes at the bottom and juice begins to flow—juice that can start fermenting.

Costing Grapes into the Price of Wine

In Chapter 7, you learned how grape costs get into the wine price. Like all stories, there's more to this one, too.

After you've figured what the grapes cost, you then have to figure what they're worth as wine. In Chapter 10, you learned about the hierarchy of grape varieties, their demand, and their prices. To price your wine, you generally start from the name of the grape variety, as some wine varietals command more money than others. Next, you might think about the style of wine you intend to produce.

Master of Wine _____

Costing wine also includes the cost of fermentation, aging (wood barrels are expensive), bottling, packaging, marketing, and sales.

In addition to the overall "what the market commands," after you buy grapes, you'll add costs to produce the wine—time being one of them. Generally, if the cost of grapes exceeds 50 percent of the retail price of the finished wine, you'll probably lose money on that wine. (Pricing wine is covered in more detail in Chapter 18.)

The Least You Need to Know

◆ You can always buy grapes. Be sure to establish relationships with grape growers *before* you make a deal to buy.

◆ Federal appellation regulations have an effect on your grape-buying decisions.

◆ State agriculture regulations have an effect on the timing of and the price you pay for grape purchases.

◆ Signing contracts for grapes is the best way to ensure the grape quantity *and* the quality you seek.

◆ Don't allow the cost of grapes to exceed 50 percent of the retail price of the wine.

Chapter **13**

Designing Your Winery

In This Chapter

- ◆ Laying out your winery
- ◆ Tips for creating smooth traffic flow
- ◆ The importance of a good laboratory
- ◆ The visitor center
- ◆ When to seek a contractor

There's nothing so necessary to the bottom line in manufacturing than efficient production methods. Logistically, producing wine is as much a challenge as any other production line. Plus, wine is governed by the same health standards of food production and requires the same diligence the food industry gives to quality control.

The critical employee in any winery is the winemaker. Of course, a well-rounded winemaker needs an understanding of the chemistry connected to wine, but he or she also needs to understand the government regulations, some statistics, and a little logistics.

In this chapter, you lay the foundation for your winery and begin to understand just how the business of wine flows. It all starts with a floor plan or, as the U.S. Treasury Department Tax and Trade Bureau (TTB) requires with the application for a permit, the *plat*, a drawing of your planned winery layout.

How large and how expensive your winery layout will be is of course determined by your winemaking plans and your growth forecasts.

The Logistics

The TTB's requirement for the plat is so it can assess rules compliance on your part and ensure that you understand the excise tax requirements, which is reflected in the section of your plat called the bonded warehouse, the location in your winery where bulk and bottled wine is stored and is subject to excise taxes.

The TTB requirement is a blessing, because it forces you to think about the art of managing the flow of goods as you lay out your winery floor plan. Your plat will become the basis for directions you give your architect. You may not lay things out perfectly at first, but you'll at least have everything down that your architect will need to understand and to come up with better ideas if necessary.

Before any wine flows in your winery, you have to consider the flow of two important utilities: water and electricity.

Water Power

It takes multiple gallons of water to make one gallon of wine. You read that right. Your water needs might start in the vineyard as irrigation, but in the winery, water needs really kick in. You have to rinse before you start the crush and press, and you have to clean them after you use them. You have to rinse before you fill tanks, and you have to clean them after their use.

It's the same throughout every wine production function, with barrels, filters, pumps, bottling equipment, and laboratory analysis: rinse before, clean afterward. Then, unless you have an exceptional staff who can perform without touching anything around them—or spilling anything—you have to clean the winery.

If you produce wine as many in California are, from extremely sweet grapes that help raise alcohol levels, you'll even add water to your wine. But when you do that, you actually increase the volume of wine, too (more about that in Chapter 15).

In addition to all your production water needs, you have to clean up the visitor center and tasting room. Plus, you have all those plumbing needs. You should consider tapping a water source for the visitor center and office space that's separate from the production line.

Unless your source is an aboveground tank that gravity-feeds water to the winery, you need electricity to move it through the winery.

Electric Power

Even if your winery is solar powered, it might astound you how much electric power a winery can burn up, and that power isn't accessed from your garden-variety three-prong electric wall outlet. Much of the electrical use in your winery will be to pump water and wine and maintain temperature control over the wine. But these are not small items.

In general, a single-phase 120-volt electrical service can take care of heating and lighting. But the wine production requires an electrical system that carries more power. Much of your winery equipment consumes a heavy load with three-phase wiring and either 480-volt capacity to carry that load or 220- to 240-volt if you can get away with lower capacity..

Depending on where you're located, electric and water service have the potential to be among the costliest overhead expenses. In some West Coast areas, water is a scarce resource, and in the Northeast, electricity rates can be quite high.

From Grapes to Wine

To keep costs in check, you need an efficient layout for your winery so redundancies and extra loads on equipment are at a minimum. In the winery, the grape crush pad and press, fermentation area, tank and barrel storage area, bottling line, and bonded warehouse all require special logistical consideration.

Check out the following figure that shows a sample winery floor plan. You can put together something similar for your permit application, and it can also guide your architect.

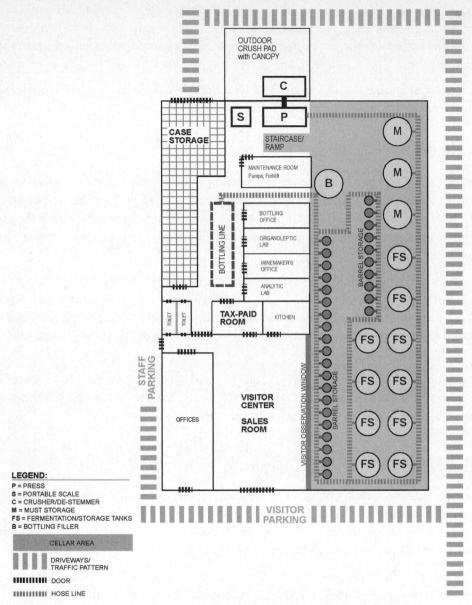

Your winery design could look something like this.

Crushing and Pressing

Think of a winery as an industrial production line, with raw materials going in at the beginning and finished products coming out at the end of the line. In the winery, the beginning is the crush pad, which is often outdoors. That's where the large tubs that hold about a ton of harvested grapes each go from the vineyard.

Handling fresh fruit on a large scale is all about timing and space. Get the logistics wrong, and your wine—and your bottom line—suffers. Grapes begin to deteriorate right after they're picked. Delivery vehicles must get in and out of the crush pad area quickly and efficiently.

The crusher splits and de-stems grapes. The stems are removed and disposed of in accordance with your state's Department of Environmental Conservation (DEC) standards, and the split grapes are moved to their next destination with a must pump (defined in Chapter 14).

Having no need to draw color from skins, white grapes go to the press right after crushing so they can be fermented as juice—some whites are pressed without ever being crushed. The press is often right nearby the crush pad, and it can be inside or outside. Red grapes go into large fermenting tanks to draw color from the skins while they ferment; red grapes are pressed after fermentation. The fermentation tanks should be situated close to the press.

The Winepress _____

Grape skins are very resistant. Only brute force can split them, and only perfect application of the pressure can prevent obliterating the pulp inside. If you don't believe it, squeeze a grape with your thumb and index finger and feel its resistance.

The area that contains the crush, press, and fermentation tanks must be planned and mapped out for ease of entry first for trucks laden with grapes coming into and leaving the area and then for tractors and forklifts moving grape bins around. Pumping lines between locations should be easily accessed. If your winery is in one building, the crush and press should be situated at the back of the building, with the visitor center and office at the front.

Fermentation

The food-processing end of winemaking starts at the crush pad but kicks into high gear the moment grapes begin to ferment. The simple formula of yeast dining on sugar can go wrong in so many ways, not the least of which is in temperature control. Some wines need cool fermentation and some need warm, but fermentation's natural tendency is to become hot.

The Winepress _____

To minimize potential violent stirring from pumping wine, some wineries are designed as multi-level facilities and use the force of gravity instead of pumps to move wine from tank to tank.

It's not only possible to ferment in tanks outdoors in certain climates, it's sometimes desirable. Otherwise, for optimum control, indoor tanks may need to be wrapped with insulation or with a cooling device.

When they're in place, you don't want to go moving around your wine tanks. Be sure you've consulted with the right people before deciding on the size of your tanks and the most efficient spacing between them.

Storage

After fermentation, wines are headed either for tank or barrel storage. The tank storage area will be larger than the fermenting area to accommodate blending, wines going into smaller tanks, and wines from past vintages that remain in storage. Barrel storage usually gets its own area. In smaller wineries, fermenting tanks often double as storage tanks.

The Winepress _____

Wines being transferred from one tank to another and to bottling may be filtered. Filtration units are usually mobile, so you need an area to store them when they're not in use.

Temperature control remains critical throughout winemaking. This is when the wine rests, ages, and develops its overall character. This also is where good preplanning for winery insulation pays off. Still, some tanks may need to be refrigerated.

Bottling

The bottling line is where the wine runs through its final filtration, the bottles are filled and capped, and the labels are applied. It's the last stop before your wine is packed in boxes and stacked in the warehouse ready for delivery or removal for the tasting room. The bottling area should be located as close to the case storage warehouse as possible. Many wineries hire companies that bring in a mobile bottling line often set up on the crush pad.

The scariest thing that can happen in a winery is product contamination—little airborne critters that can infect wine and spoil it or make it re-ferment in the bottle. Some wineries protect themselves from such invasions with a *sterile bottling line*.

A sterile bottling line is an enclosed sanitized room. The people working in the room wear sanitized garments, gloves, and even masks. You could perform surgery in this room. The wine is sterile filtered and then enters the bottling line in as pure a state as it can be. It's processed through sanitized equipment and into sanitized bottles and then moved out to the room where the bottles are packaged in boxes.

There's a cost to creating and maintaining a sterile bottling line, but some say there's a cost to *not* having a sterile line. Speak with a consultant and assess the cost-to-risk ratio.

Warehousing

Before wine makes it to our *palates*, a lot of it sits and waits on *pallets*.

After you bottle and package your wines, they need to be warehoused. This area is exactly what it sounds like it should be—large enough to hold your bottled inventory on pallet racks.

I mentioned a *bonded warehouse* earlier in the chapter. It's called "bonded" because your federal permit to produce wine requires that your winery be protected with an insurance bond large enough to cover the cost of inventory lost to damage or theft. As long as the wines rest in the bonded portion of your facility, you don't have to pay a tax to the federal government. But as soon as you move the wine out of the warehouse, the federal

The Winepress

First in, first out, or *FIFO,* and *first in, last out,* or *FILO,* are inventory and logistics control methods. The warehouse is where you apply such methods so you know where and when your boxes of wine are in inventory.

and local taxes that apply to the volume you moved must be recorded and paid during the next reporting cycle. (You learn about reporting cycles in Chapter 22.)

The Tax-Paid Room

When you move bottled wine off its pallets in the warehouse, it's headed either to the loading dock for delivery to your distributor, to a restaurant, or to a retailer. Or it can be going to your tasting room storage area, which is known as the *tax-paid room.*

Even though the wines are still on your premises, after they're removed from the bonded warehouse, the tax on them is due. The tax-paid room is a small storage area to hold a few days' worth of wine to supply the visitor center tasting room. It's not part of the bonded facility.

In the Lab: Solving Winemaking Problems

You might get away with not having a sterile bottling line, but every winery needs a laboratory. The laboratory's size and capacity to evaluate wine samples depends on production volume and the winemaker's level of expertise. It also depends on the winery's isolation or proximity to an external laboratory.

The laboratory may be divided into two rooms: one for *organaleptic* analysis, where chemistry is practiced, and one for tasting wines, where blending and other decisions are made.

In the organaleptic lab, the winemaker takes wine samples to check for overall makeup—which includes alcohol, acidity, pH, and residual sweetness—and for stability, potential infection from spoilage organisms, and the general health of the wine. When a problem is discovered, the winemaker determines how to fix it and then checks again later to see if the fix worked.

If you set up a laboratory, it should be in a separate room sealed off from the rest of the winery to reduce the threat of contamination. It should still be close to the production and bottling line, which are the areas the winemaker goes to draw samples.

Many wine regions include an external laboratory, perhaps at the cooperative extension office, for those times when neither your basic lab nor your winemaker is equipped to handle a diagnosis.

The Visitor Center Tasting Room

In Chapter 19, you learn the reasons for having a visitor center tasting room and how best to use it. For now, take my word for it: you need and want to build a tasting room.

Master of Wine

A glass wall to the wine cellar gives visitors the opportunity to see what's going on in there. It also prevents the potential liability of having tourists traipse through the wine cellar.

In Chapter 6, you were told to be a sleuth, to check out the competition. Your mission was to visit wineries in the area you selected for your business to see how things are done. If you spaced out your visits so you arrived when business was at its most brisk as well as when it was at its least, you'll have noticed the size of local tasting rooms and whether they efficiently accommodated increased traffic at busy times. With this information in hand, you are that much more equipped to design your own tasting room.

Your tasting room should be sectioned off from everything else—from the office, from the warehouse, and from the production facility. But because this is a winery, and making wine interests your customers, you might want to give them access to the production facility from the visitor center—if not physically, then emotionally.

Designing the Floor Plan

The same effort that you put into designing the floor plan for the production, bottling, and storage facility goes into designing the tasting room and for the same reason—logistics—but this time you're moving people instead of wine.

The tasting room is your high-volume sales office, so you want to make buying fun and also smooth. Before you have an architect blueprint the tasting room area, have a talk with a designer experienced in retail store design.

When designing your floor plan, one of the first things you need to think about is where to put the bar. The number of people you expect to host determines the size of the tasting bar. Its placement is also utilitarian (near the water pipes, for sinks) and aesthetic (how it fits into the space and how traffic is handled to and away from it).

You also need to include display areas. After all, the tasting room is your retail salesroom, and people like to browse through retail product displays. Your wine is the most important product, but don't rule out accessory items. The display area needs to be mapped out carefully for smooth traffic flow that leads directly to the cash register. And the cash register should be placed where people can't avoid it on their way out, but it shouldn't be placed so people standing in line are in the way of people coming in or people shopping.

> **Sour Grapes**
>
> Before you go ordering seats for your bar, read this: many wineries have discovered that having seats at a tasting bar hinders customer traffic and wine sales, as some visitors are forced to stand while others who sit may turn out not to be customers.

Speaking of people coming in, ill-placed entryways and exits can cause traffic bottlenecks and may be in violation of local fire and building codes. Check to see where they need to be placed and how many you must have, and fit them into your plan so people can get in and out easily.

Finally, a business that serves the public must provide restrooms. Inconveniently or ill-placed restrooms can both annoy customers and hurt sales. But restrooms right in plain sight in the midst of the display take some of the fun out of the visitor center, especially on a busy day when a line forms. Restrooms should be situated discretely yet easily accessible.

Allow Extra Space for Events

The practice in many regions is for wineries within a certain radius of influence to join together to create timed wine festivals that increase the daily traffic to their tasting rooms over a few selected weekends. In one day during an event, a winery might host as much as four times as many people than over a normal tourist season weekend.

The Winepress _____

In wine regions of the U.S. Northeast, Columbus Day weekend and the weekend following it produce the largest number of visitors over any other weekend.

Heavy as the traffic is on these weekends, wineries often complain that cash flow is good during the events but bottle sales per customer falls. It could be because of traffic jams. Proper ingress and egress, and location of the restrooms and the cash register can help minimize traffic jams. A tasting room floor plan, coupled with a well-thought-out wine tasting plan, of course, should accommodate the overcrowding. The same is true for special holiday traffic.

Your Building Contractor

The plat is an initial drawing that will likely be changed, but not by much. To give you motivation not to make too many changes, TTB awards a permit based on knowing that you understand what's important: the area that is bonded. Any changes to your bonded winery will require securing permission from government bureaucrats and another plat drawing.

If you've talked with a variety of consultants and other winery owners, your plat should be thought out well enough for an architect to begin blueprints. The time to start looking for a contractor has arrived.

Master of Wine _____

Odds are that the best sources for contractor recommendation are other winery owners and local businesses. Still, try online at the Associated General Contractors of America at www.agc.org/index.ww.

When you decide on a contractor and agree on a price, you should also agree on a payment and construction schedule that includes punishment for missed deadlines. The punishments are financial; the terms must be agreed to by contract.

Your contractor may find that changes need to be made to the design, but those changes should never be made without consulting you, the architect, and the TTB, if they impact the bonded facility.

Your contractor is responsible for ensuring the building is within code regulations. The building and fire department may send inspectors to the construction site periodically to be sure code issues are properly addressed. Staying on top of the construction is the best way to avoid finding out too late that there are code problems.

Once your layout of the full-production winery is complete and submitted to the TTB for approval, you can start looking at equipment. In Chapter 14, you learn how to stock your new barn, and what it might cost you to do so.

The Least You Need to Know

- To produce wine, you may need as much as three to five times its volume in water and a three-phase electrical wiring.

- Producing wine successfully requires efficient logistics.

- You separate production and storage areas to reduce contamination and to comply with federal bonding requirements.

- Logistics is equally important in your visitor center and tasting room as it is in production.

- The simple drawing that you submit for your federal permit to produce wine is the basis for architectural design and construction.

Part 4

Getting It All in Place

Now that you know what it takes, what it costs, and how you'll supply grapes for your wine, it's time to equip you for success. Part 4 is your shopping cart to produce wine. After that, you'll decide what you want your wine to be like. You'll build your staff and train them to create a company built on good people and good products. You'll also get to take a deep breath and consider one more option before you move on. As you turn to Part 5, you'll be watching your plan nearing its final shape.

Chapter 14

Stocking the Barn

In This Chapter

- ◆ The equipment you need for your winery
- ◆ The singular importance of the tractor
- ◆ The importance of a backup system
- ◆ How to buy equipment

Unless your winery is really, really small, every step of the winemaking process, from putting the first vineyard post into the ground to slapping a label on the bottle, will be mechanized. Even if your winery is tiny, most of the operations will be semimechanized—unless you're ready to fill 1,000 cases of wine bottles with a funnel and a measuring cup.

The nature of the equipment needed—stainless steel, oak barrels, powerful pumps, mechanized production lines, motorized vehicles, and so on—dictates that the cost of equipping a winery is steep. Appendix B includes a chart of potential equipment prices, and equipment suppliers can be found in the wine industry supplier directory listed in Appendix C.

In this chapter, you learn the basic necessity of the production equipment, plus a few of the ancillary add-ons often connected to a winemaking style or marketing philosophy.

The Basic Equipment List

To produce wine, you need the following:

- One or more tractors (if you operate a vineyard)
- A few gadgets to latch onto the tractors (I explain in a bit.)
- One or more forklifts
- A scale
- A crusher/de-stemmer
- A wine press
- A few must and fermentation tanks
- A few pumps of various sizes to move pomace, wine, and water (plus a lot of hosing with fittings)
- Temperature control units
- Large and small stainless-steel storage tanks
- Oak barrels
- A steam generator and cleaner
- A wine bottling and labeling system
- A mobile filter system
- A variety of ancillary equipment to meet your special needs (I explain a few of these coming up.)
- Computers
- A gas or diesel-powered electric generator

Whether you're buying an existing winery or building from scratch, talk with your consultant winemaker to create a checklist of what equipment you need. Your winemaker may have different ideas about the winemaking process than either you or the owner of the facility you plan to buy. At the very least, your architect needs to know your equipment plans to be sure to fit what you want into the space you have, especially the tank storage.

Certainly, the items on the list have an influence on the cost of starting your business, and they may also have an influence on the size of the business, at least for the first few years.

The All-Important Tractor

Unless you plant grapes on a 75-degree slope, you can't grow them without the help of a tractor. (And if you do have such a steep slope for a vineyard, you may need equipment not mentioned in this chapter—a gondola and tramway, for starters.)

Do you remember the PTO (power take-off) from Chapter 4? A tractor with a PTO is among the most versatile pieces of equipment you will ever see. It helps you get the vineyard posts into the ground—you do it by first attaching a posthole drill to the PTO; it spins and drills the holes. After you make the holes, you attach a hydraulic-operated post-pounder and pound the posts into the holes. Then you attach the machine that enables you to unwind, run, and tighten the wires to the posts that will support your vine tendrils as they grow and reach into the world.

After you plant the vines, the tractor is even more indispensable in the vineyard. Attach large spraying machines to the PTO and you can apply fertilizer or weed killer to the ground or pest and disease control to the vines. You can even prune the vines with a hydraulic generator attachment to your handheld vine pruning sheers and save yourself from the pain you might get in your hand from repetitive cutting motions.

You may not own a grape-picking machine, but you may need one. If you do, you also need your tractor to ride alongside the harvester and pick out from the bins any debris that gets into the picked grape clusters during the vine shaking. The tractor, fitted with fork tines, might carry the bins to the crush deck, or, if you pick by hand, it might pull the wagon that's loaded with boxes filled with grapes.

The Winepress

Vineyard posts (preferably locust) keep the wires that you staple to them taut. You can bang the staples into the hardwood posts by hand if you think you need the exercise, but it's more fun—and faster—to attach a generator to the PTO that runs a hydraulic-powered hammering machine.

If you're farming only a few acres, you can get by with one tractor for the vineyard. Just be aware that tractors have a mind of their own, and they seem to like to wreak havoc at the most inopportune times.

If you go the organic or biodynamic grape-growing route, you may not reduce your tractor needs—after all, you still have to get the posts and vines into the ground. The spray material you use will be different, but the sprayer may be the same.

Mechanical Grape Harvester

Not too long ago, mechanical grape harvesting was relegated to large producers making mass-market wines. The machines violently shook the vines, often splitting grapes and threatening to crack branches or split trunks. Premium wines were produced from handpicked grapes. Handpicking is still the preferred method in many premium vineyards worldwide, but *mechanical grape harvesters* have been perfected to be gentler on vines and grapes, which is handy when the weather doesn't provide the time to handpick.

def•i•ni•tion

A **mechanical grape harvester** is a tractor on a high pedestal that controls a machine that shakes grapevines. The grape clusters fall onto a conveyor that's part of the harvester and then into 1-ton bins situated at the bottom of the conveyor. Harvesters come with lights, so you can pick at night, when the cooler air temperature creates optimum picking conditions.

A mechanical harvester is quite an expense for a small winery, so usually these machines are shared. The harvesters often belong to grape growers who do not produce wine but who hire themselves out as pickers for the area.

More Necessary Vineyard Equipment

Much of the other vineyard equipment is based on your grape-growing methods, which is guided by your farming philosophy, the topography, and the weather in your location. The following partial list gives you an idea of what I mean:

Take out   In the fall, you attach this to the tractor to push soil from the rows over the roots to protect the roots from severe winters. In the spring, you push the soil back into the rows.

Hay spreading   If you plan to mulch vineyard rows with hay bales, you need an attachment that spreads the hay.

Hoes and discs   You may need to hoe land you prepare for planting, and you may need to disc land to aerate the soil around the vines.

Specialized mixing machines Biodynamic methods require mixing and stirring you can do with attachments to the tractor PTO.

During the course of your grape-growing career, you'll surely find need for more specialized equipment. This list gets you through start-up.

Forklift

The forklift is second to the tractor in indispensability. You have three types of forklifts at your disposal.

First is a gas-powered forklift (with a reasonably comfortable seat) to lift the 1-ton grape bins and move them from vineyard to winery. It's also used to unload pallets of supply items like bottles or small equipment. The forklift has a sharp turning radius to get you in and out of tight spaces.

You can also opt for a compact electric forklift for indoor use to stock and remove pallets from racks in tight spaces. It has a step-stand and no seat.

Or you can go with hydraulic tines connected to your tractor to move the 1-ton grape tubs during harvest, to get the grapes either to a holding area or into the crusher/de-stemmer, and to lift pallets of supplies.

Scale

In many wine regions, the larger wineries have scales for weighing harvested grapes. The scale is built into the ground, usually right near the crush pad. A truck with empty containers is weighed on its way to pick up grapes, and when it's weighed again, with grapes in the containers when it returns, the empty weight is deducted from the total weight. This enables you to create an invoice for the tonnage being bought or sold. Some small wineries use a small movable scale for weighing smaller lots, which they put into macro bins, smaller than the usual grape-picking tubs or bins.

Wineries with their own vineyards can weigh with a large moveable, portable scale.

The Winepress

Remember from Chapter 12 that the volume of wine you produce must have a traceable paper trail back to the grape tonnage that was crushed and pressed to produce it.

Crusher and Press

Gentle is the operative word when processing grapes for wine, and your splitting, crushing, and pressing machines must be as gentle as possible. The crusher/de-stemmer is a necessary machine, if only because it mechanizes what once was done by feet. Its other purpose is to remove the stems so they don't adversely affect the juice's flavor.

The machine comes with a hopper at the top to accept grapes. At the center of the unit, a drum houses a blade with many perforations that rotates at high speed to split grapes and remove them from their stems to make it easier to extract their juice. It's done so fast and efficiently you almost can't see it happening.

For white wine, the crushed and de-stemmed grapes are sent to the press with a *must pump*, a heavy-duty pump designed to push through great amounts of solids. The exception is when white grapes are pressed as whole clusters (skins not crushed).

One of the most common presses in use is called the bladder press. (Other types of presses are available; their use depends on the type of wine and the volume produced.) The stainless-steel bladder press has an opening and closing mesh shell that surrounds a rubber bladder. When the bladder is full with split grapes, the shell is closed and pressure is slowly applied so the bladder squeezes the grapes to release juice through the mesh and into a holding tank at the bottom. A human being often controls the bladder press with hands on the switches, but computers are increasingly used to set and apply slow pressing timers.

The juice at the bottom is pumped with a juice pump either into stainless-steel fermenting tanks or into large wooden vats or smaller oak barrels, depending on wine style. Because red wine is fermented with skins intact to extract color, the split grapes are pumped from the crusher with a must pump directly into an open fermentation vat or tank.

Fermentation and Other Tanks

The volume of grapes and wine you process determines the sizes and number of tanks you need. You don't fill fermentation tanks to the brim—unless you want more cleanup in the winery! Your fermentation tanks need to be at least 30 percent larger than the volume of must or juice you intend to ferment.

To hold back the residue at the bottom of the tank when racking after fermentation (see Chapter 15), racking doors on fermentation tanks need to be placed higher than racking doors on storage tanks. Some companies provide dual racking doors for multiple-tank use.

Generally, stainless-steel tanks are preferred for cleanliness and ease of use. But when you want to produce a wine with certain qualities that are extracted from wood, you can ferment in large wooden vats or in small wooden barrels, although cleaning the latter after fermentation is quite a task.

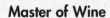

Master of Wine

For every storage vessel that's full, you'll need an empty one on hand when you're ready to rack the wine. It doesn't mean you need double capacity, but you do need the right number of vessels to accommodate the movement of the volume of wine you produce.

Temperature Control

Controlling temperature is the single most important thing you do for wine during fermentation and when in storage afterward. For this task, devices are available to wrap tanks with an insulation material that holds the temperature. Piping with chilling fluid is also used to cool down tanks. Tanks can be bought already wrapped.

Temperature-control devices are set with thermostats either by hand or by computer. The computer method monitors radiant room temperature to make effective use of the transfer of heat and cold through super-conductive stainless steel.

Barrels

I may sound like a broken record, but your wine style dictates your barrel needs. Using oak barrels in winemaking is not a necessity. Oak barrels are expensive; they come from a variety of countries and in a few sizes, which is a refinement of stylistic decisions.

The last time I checked, oak was still wood; wood is porous; porous can be problematic, especially when it's not thoroughly cleaned or sanitized. Using oak creates a lot of work in the cellar.

The Winepress

Many winemakers have turned to oak alternatives. Some use stainless-steel tanks lined with oak staves that release flavoring into the wine. Others use oak dust or oak chips wrapped in large teabaglike containers that are dipped into a stainless-steel tank for a certain amount of time to release flavoring into the wine. Tank suppliers offer these products.

Part of the appeal of oak barrel storage is that it subjects wine to an oxidative process that creates complexity. Wineries that forego oak barrels but want to simulate the aging process for their wines use equipment attached to tanks that releases tiny amounts of oxygen into the wine over a short period of time to simulate the oxygen transfer of aging wine in oak—they call the technique *micro-oxygenation*.

Steam Generator and Cleaner

An essential cellar rat function is to sterilize the equipment. One of the best devices for that is the high-pressure steam cleaner. It's used to wash off the crush and the press decks, but it's really effective for cleaning stainless-steel equipment and storage vessels. (I highly recommend you regularly steam clean the walls, floors, and other equipment, too.) The steamer literally sterilizes the metal—and does so very quickly.

The steam cleaner is an indispensable piece of winery equipment, and on a sunny day, you can use it to clean your car, too. Some wineries also use an ozone generator to ensure that the newly cleaned equipment isn't infected with airborne mold and mildew.

Bottling

Whether your wine production is small enough for you to bottle by hand or large enough to warrant a mechanical system, you need to somehow get your wine into a bottling line holding tank directly from its storage vessel. In wineries that filter, the wine is pumped through its final filtration stage just before it makes its way to the bottling filler.

The Winepress

Connected to the mechanical bottling line is equipment that adds inert gas like nitrogen to displace the oxygen in empty bottles as the wine flows into them from the holding tank. The process is called *sparging*.

A mechanical line moves the bottles along on a conveyor at a set pace as each bottle is filled and capped. (You must decide which type of bottle closure you want to use before you decide on your bottling line.) Some bottling lines fill 3 to 5 bottles a minute; others go as fast as 30 bottles a minute.

The final stop is at the labeler. Generally, the bottles go into the case boxes by hand.

Because wine is food, whether or not you bottle it in an enclosed, sterile environment—which is recommended—workers must wear a combination of protective clothing for their safety plus gloves, hats, boot protectors, and even masks to protect the wine from contamination.

Other Winery Equipment

Here's a short list of a few other pieces of winery equipment:

Centrifuge/separator   Some wineries use a centrifuge or other device to separate solids from juice before fermentation, but this equipment is fast going out of favor.

Filter devices   Wineries filter their wines through a variety of filtering devices. Filtering is an important process and usually requires two to three passes through an increasingly tighter filtration medium to remove the smallest particles and microorganisms. Filter equipment is mobile so it can be used right at the storage tank location.

Spinning cone and reverse osmosis   The latest winemaking technology includes methods of adding back or extracting water to reduce alcohol by volume or increase intensity of the wine. These machines do the work, but they cost an awful lot of money.

In the Laboratory

A winery laboratory is all about chemistry. You'll need things like burners, a microwave oven, a sink, a refrigerator, and a freezer. You'll also want to plan for lots of counter space and a desktop computer.

The computer has become an indispensable device not only in the office but also in all winemaking processes. In the lab, the computer is used for calculations, record keeping, charting, and grafting; in research for chemical reference guides; and a source of reaching out for help through e-mail.

In the Tasting Room

It's a tasting room, so you'll obviously need a tasting bar. You can buy or build one, to the size and shape you need.

Go over your tasting room ideas with either an architect or a consultant; you'll be surprised how many small details you can miss. A tasting room is not only about serving wine, it's also about traffic management and hospitality, not to mention providing entertainment.

You'll also need to install sinks, some refrigeration, a dishwasher or two, some glass racks, wine racks, gift item racks, and a counter for the cash register(s), and of course, don't forget the restrooms.

Delivery and Pick-Up Vehicles

If you deal directly with retailers and restaurants, you may need a small delivery truck or a van fitted to handle increased weight. And if you plan to buy grapes or juice, you may need a truck for picking them up.

A winery is generally not allowed to make direct deliveries to consumers, so forget that.

Electric Generator

Wouldn't it be a shame if all your equipment were in place, sterilized to perfection, and you were ready to process your first 5,000 gallons of premium wine ... and the electric power goes out?

If you have a gas- or diesel-powered electric generator large enough to provide the power you need for at least one eight-hour workday on one tank of gasoline, this isn't a problem. You can rent a generator, but how do you know in advance when you'll need it?

Where Does All This Equipment Come From?

Some of the best winemaking equipment comes from Italy and Germany. Many U.S. suppliers also exist. For a partial list of suppliers that deal in foreign and domestic equipment, check out *Wines and Vines* magazine's wine industry supplier directory in Appendix C.

> **Master of Wine**
>
> With such specialized equipment, you should always compare prices. If there is a wide gap between the price from one supplier and a second supplier, picking the cheapest may be more trouble than it's worth. Some equipment, especially storage tanks, can be custom built.

There's nothing wrong with buying used equipment. In fact, you can get great deals at auctions. (Many wineries start out equipped with stainless-steel tanks that once served the dairy industry.) If you do buy used equipment, be sure to check out the dealer carefully or, if you buy at auction, bring along someone with the knowledge to inspect the equipment.

Equipment breaks down. Many times, your staff will become familiar enough with the idiosyncrasies of individual equipment that they can devise quick fixes until the machine can be repaired. When repairs are necessary, you want to know the dealer can help, so, before you make equipment buying decisions, talk to other winery owners and your extension service for recommendations.

Keeping Track of Costs

You need to build all equipment costs into the financial and forecasting sections of your business plan. The total equipment cost in the hypothetical winery in Chapter 7 was $205,000 (for a breakdown, by equipment, see the chart to equip a small winery in Appendix B).

Prices for stainless steel fluctuate greatly, and if you buy European-built equipment, the cost you pay can fluctuate widely with the performance of the U.S. dollar in world markets.

The Office and Staff Kitchen

Your front office needs equipment, too. Here's a brief list of the items you might need:

◆ Telephones, of course!

◆ Fax machine

◆ A mailing machine

◆ A photocopier

◆ A desktop computer

◆ Coffee maker, stove or microwave, and refrigerator

◆ Furniture

◆ Don't forget the water cooler!

Not-So-Incidental Incidentals

In your daily operation, you'll need a variety of little machines or equipment to run the business efficiently. Here are a few ideas you might want to have on hand:

◆ A handcart or two

◆ A small conveyor and small pallet jack

◆ Box wrapping and taping machines

◆ Your own gasoline storage tank

◆ A shed to store chemicals

◆ A shower and lockers for employees

This chapter is by no means the complete list of equipment to fit your exact needs. It is a list of essentials to get you started.

Throughout this and other chapters I've said "depending on your wine style …." The time has come to pin down what I mean by that phrase, which I do in Chapter 15.

The Least You Need to Know

◆ When you operate a vineyard, the tractor is the one piece of indispensable equipment you should have.

◆ Your wine styles and the size of your winery facility dictate your equipment needs.

◆ Include your winemaker in equipment decisions.

◆ Get equipment dealer recommendations.

◆ Consider buying a gas- or diesel-powered electric generator.

◆ Make equipment checklists for you and for the business plan.

Chapter 15

What's Your Wine Style?

In This Chapter

- The right and the wrong way to make wine
- The old way and the new way to make wine
- Chemistry—a blessing and a curse
- Getting closure

In France and Italy—two of the oldest European wine cultures—there's no word like the English *winemaker* to describe the caretaker who oversees wine. There's a reason for that. In Chapter 1, you learned that if left alone, wine makes itself. A quick refresher: wine is the result of fruit that hasn't yet rotted. When it does rot, the fruit aims to become vinegar. After fermentation but before it goes to vinegar, wine enters a middle state, and that's where the winemaker tries to keep it for as long as possible.

This chapter is an introduction to the grape-growing and winemaking techniques you need to consider for the health of your wine and for the viability of your business.

Tradition, Schmadition!

In the dictionary, the definition of *tradition* includes phrases like "long established" or "handed down." But how long is long, and while we're on the subject, how many times must something be handed down before it becomes a tradition?

> **Master of Wine** _____
>
> Some wines live for decades in a barrel and then live further in the bottle. Some wines must be consumed quickly. Some wines need chemical coaxing to make it to the bottle. Other wines that shouldn't, somehow manage to make it into a bottle and then die on a shelf or in a consumer's wine cellar. The path you embrace for your winery will determine what happens to your wine in the bottle.

Over the centuries, new technologies have certainly influenced everything in our lives, and wine is no exception. The caretakers of old who were born into the family business have given way to today's winemakers who get at least four years of higher education to learn how to keep wine from turning into vinegar and keep the tradition alive while doing it.

Which tradition will you make yours?

The Way the Ancients Did It

The ancients didn't know what was going on in their large wine vats. They just dumped in the grapes and waited. When the wine was done fermenting, they added spices and water. The tradition of adding spices was practical—to preserve the wine. The tradition of adding water was to adjust the alcohol.

> **The Winepress** _____
>
> Louis Pasteur (of pasteurization fame) discovered the truth behind fermentation—and the friendly bacterial action that takes place in wine. He once called wine "the most healthful drink."

Preserving wine is still accomplished with additions. It's just that the additions have been changed, except that water is still added to adjust alcohol (more about that later).

The Way Our Grandfathers Did It

It wasn't until the mid- to late nineteenth century that the science of bacteria caught up with winemaking. But after the discovery of bacteria and what it was they did to make wine survive or die, wine producers clung to tradition anyway and didn't do much to change the way they made wine.

It took until the turn of the century before modernity caught up with winemaking, and even then, it was limited to a certain segment of the wine industry. The tradition always seemed to be "if it ain't broke, don't fix it"—an attitude that held even when it was, in fact, broke.

Remember John from Chapter 3? Part of what got him into the wine business was the memory of his grandfather making wine. But now that John produces commercial wine, he doesn't exactly do it the way Grandpa did. John intervenes where Grandpa might have allowed the wine to proceed on its own. John took classes and learned what can happen just by the introduction of too much air into the wine.

The Winepress

The French developed a concept that identifies wine as an expression of the land. They call it *gout de terroir*. Translated, that's "taste of the earth." It means you should be able to taste differences in wine based on where the grapes were grown, and to do that, you must intervene as little as possible in the winemaking process. The concept spread throughout the European wine world.

Grandpa's Traditional Pitfalls

Ask most winemakers in the mid- to late twentieth century if wine could be produced without sulfur dioxide (SO_2), and they would have answered no. Because it protects wine against oxidation, this one chemical is largely responsible for the health and aging ability of modern wine. But SO_2 has become one of the most controversial of the seeming modern interventions, even though its use in wine was developed in second-century Rome. (It's estimated that in Rome, as much as 10 percent of the wine produced turned to vinegar before it could be consumed. The discovery of sulfur dioxide in the second century helped fix the problem.)

Ah, that *volatile acid* smell that blew across the room when the cork was popped from grandfather's wine. That was acetic acid, the stuff necessary to begin the vinegar process and the stuff that SO_2 additions suppress.

In Europe, SO_2 has been used to protect wine for hundreds of years but many of our European grandfathers from peasant stock didn't seem to know that. In fact, many knew little about chemistry. When they didn't use SO_2, instead of producing wine, our grandfathers on this side of the pond often produced half the ingredient for vinaigrette.

Another grandfatherly thing was not to clarify or filter wine. Instead, our grandfathers let the wine rest and wait for solids floating in it to fall to the bottom of the tank. Then they siphoned off the wine (known as *racking*) to another tank, leaving behind the debris at the bottom of the previous tank.

After a few of these rackings, the wine was clear—to the naked eye. But things would happen to this seemingly clear wine later on when it would cloud or re-ferment in the bottle. The naked eye does not catch microscopic critters.

Our Traditional Solutions

The most vexing problems connected to wine are easily remedied by making SO_2 additions, clarifying, and filtering. The following paragraphs cover a few problems and their solutions.

Premature oxidation, or browning. It's called premature oxidation, but it really isn't premature—it's the natural order. Everything oxidizes; it's what makes food and drink turn brown. SO_2 molecules in wine delay oxidation. By carefully measuring SO_2 additions and then sealing the bottle, the winemaker allows wine to oxidize extremely slowly—converting what normally takes weeks into a process that takes years.

Acetobacter (and other microorganisms). You can't prevent bacteria from getting into wine, but SO_2 can keep them from ruining the wine. Most microorganisms, like the acetobacter that makes vinegar, thrive in the presence of oxygen. By delaying oxidation, SO_2 prohibits them from thriving.

The Winepress

SO_2 is naturally produced as a by-product in fermented food—cheese, bread, pickles, wine, etc.—but at levels too low to delay oxidation for any length of time. It's added to wine to increase its effectiveness. SO_2 is also added to many packaged foods, especially baked goods, to increase their shelf life.

Hazy and clouding. A lot of natural stuff floats in any liquid. In wine, fermentation creates conditions for a variety of proteins and other components to float. A wine that's not clarified may become hazy or cloudy, and some develop a white haze right down their center. Much of clarifying is accomplished by additions of egg white or certain natural animal- or earth-bound materials. These things are heavier than the stuff in the wine so they take that stuff to the bottom of the tank. Left behind in the old tank, the stuff can't cloud the wine either in its new tank or in the bottle later on.

Re-fermentation. It's virtually impossible for fermentation to remove all sugar from wine, plus some wines are purposely made sweet. If you leave sugar in wine and you don't filter before you bottle it, you leave potential yeast cells that can eat the sugar and cause a secondary fermentation in the bottle. The lingering yeast cells that can restart fermentation when conditions allow are quite tiny. Filtration is accomplished by a series of passes through tighter and tighter filters that take out the smallest materials and cells that clarifying leaves behind.

New Traditions

Today, additions or lack of additions to wine can determine the price of a bottle, not to mention the winery's reputation and the consumer's acceptance.

For example, after a few centuries of being frowned upon, it's now back in vogue to add water to wine to reduce alcohol. But although many winemakers do it, a number of consumers don't like it, for many reasons. And I mentioned that SO_2 was a second-century discovery for winemaking. But the combination of a lack in understanding on the consumer's part about what exactly the chemical is and does leaves many today unhappy over its addition to wine. And whether or not they care about what's in the wine, some people may have allergies to some of the ingredients used for clarifying wine. Also, while filtration removes the additions along with microorganisms, filtration itself is seen as an intrusion on the wine's structure.

New traditions in wine are assembled with each television or newspaper news cycle about health. They may not have all the facts, but whether or not they know what they want and why they should have it, you have to listen to the consumers to stay in business.

What About Organic?

There's a trend in the United States for wines produced by so-called noninterventionist winemakers. The theory is that the less that's done to wine, the more natural and pure it is. Again, right or wrong, it's your responsibility to respond to the customer.

On many wine-oriented websites, conversations spring up over this or that noninterventionist producer of this or that wine. Some of the talked-about wines come with an "organically produced" label; some don't. The short answer to why is that the subject of organic wine is confusing, to say the absolute least.

In Chapter 11, you learned about the biodynamic method and organic certification for grape growing. In winemaking, there's no organic certification. For a wine to use the claim "organic" on the label, the vineyard has to have been certified and the wine has to have been given no SO_2 additions.

In many cases, consumers are glad and willing to pay more for wine that comes with no added SO_2. The same customers, however, hate the idea that they paid a lot of money for a wine that they discover is oxidized, or worse. This dilemma alone causes many wineries that grow their grapes organically to add SO_2 and forgo the organic certification. It's a decision you'll face, too.

> **Sour Grapes** _____
>
> Claims are made that SO_2 causes headaches. To date, no scientific study confirms that belief. But SO_2 can cause respiratory problems in people suffering from asthma, and that's why, when SO_2 levels exceed the minuscule level set by the federal government in 1985, a wine label must include the warning "CONTAINS SULFITES."

Is Intervention for You?

The downside of what the ancients did and what our grandfathers didn't do for their wines has been fixed by chemistry and food technology.

Or has it?

Those who make wine today often hold a degree in higher education with emphasis on *microbiology* or, in a layman understanding, the stuff that can kill a wine. Many of these winemakers go the technology route and spend a lot of money on meters, machines, and chemicals to keep their wine pristine. On those same Internet websites where conversations take place over wine, these winemakers are called *interventionists*, which isn't always a compliment.

You can better understand interventionist methods, and whether they're right for your winery, by asking yourself these questions:

How mature should the grapes for my wine be? The style of wine you make is determined largely by when you pick the grapes. One stylistic version today is to allow grapes to hang on the vine well past their traditionally established harvest dates. When this is done, the flavor of the wine is more intense and the alcohol content is higher, thanks to the high sugar levels. This is when water is added during the winemaking process. The grapes were so richly intense with flavor that the wine doesn't seem to lose much from water dilution other than alcohol by volume.

Do I like oak? The French established the use of oak to replace the ancient ceramic amphora for wine storage and shipping. Over time, the oak barrel advanced from a storage and shipping container to a wine aging vessel. Soon, oak barrels became important to winemaking, which of course increased their demand and made them more expensive. Today, with deforestation on everyone's mind (and the rising cost of barrels), there's reason to turn to the oak chips and wooden oak staves I mentioned in Chapter 14.

Does making wine really need chemistry? You've already learned about SO_2, but have you heard about copper sulfate? Copper sulfate is allowed as a spray against disease in a certified organic vineyard. (Copper is a natural earth element.) It's also allowed in wine in small amounts to fix a particular aromatic problem that can develop when nutritionally deficient grapes ferment. But consuming copper, which builds in the human body, can be toxic. If they knew, consumers probably wouldn't like that wine may contain traces of copper.

The Winepress _____

You won't find water dilution intervention mentioned anywhere on a wine label, you won't find oak teabag intervention mentioned on wine labels, and until recently, copper was never mentioned on wine labels. But copper intervention will soon be mandatory information on the label, as will use of clarifying agents.

Are potential allergens right for use in wine? Peanuts, eggs, and fish can all produce sometimes-severe allergic reactions in people. These are some of the sources for clarifying agents used in wine.

The wine style you choose for your business is the product of the decisions you make after you answer these and many other questions. Answer the questions as you imagine your target market consumers would answer.

The benefits some intervention brings often outweigh the risks of leaving wine to its own devices. But the trend in the United States is for organic and for sustainability, and wine is going to have to be part of the movement. You have to decide on your winemaking methods and styles with this in mind.

To help you make your decision, the government will soon mandate that wine labels include nutritional as well as ingredient labeling, just like food. For all I know, the regulations may be in effect by the time you read this book.

Should You Go Green?

If you haven't heard of *global warming* or *global climate change*, you must be living in isolation. You can rest assured that the wine industry has heard the two phrases and is responding by going green, wherever it is reasonable to do.

The Winepress _____

California's State Assembly regulation, AB32, has perked up the Wine Institute of California (www.wineinstitute.org), which has joined in a global effort to create the first International Wine Industry Greenhouse Gas Accounting Protocol. It's in a formative stage, but the aim of the protocol is to lower greenhouse gas effects caused by winemaking and distribution.

The latest concern in the wine world is called *carbon footprint*. It refers to the level of influence that producing and distributing wine has on carbon dioxide emissions into the atmosphere. (Carbon dioxide is a by-product of fermentation.)

In a recent experiment performed by a wine writer and a sustainability engineer, calculations of an ultra-premium wine produced in Napa Valley and sent to Chicago restaurants produced twice as much carbon footprint than calculations of a wine sent to the same location from Australia and a wine sent from France.

The result of the experiment was blamed on the heavy glass bottle of the American wine, so packaging is one of the intervention methods going through changes. Packaging inventions that replace glass and are aimed at lighter-weight materials are entering the wine market as you read this.

Choose Your Closure

You might not think wine's closure method is all that important, but it is. This little necessity, which has been part of producing wine since the seventeenth century, has lately become one of the major decisions to have to make at a winery.

Cork

The cork has been stuck into the neck of wine bottles ever since a Portuguese bottle designer came up with the stackable, shouldered bottle. Before then, wine was shipped in upright, bulbous bottles with rags stuffed in or wax covering the opening. Stacking bottles made it possible to ship more wine in the same space on ships, but stacking required a tighter closure at the opening so the wine stayed in the bottle. The job went to the cork, and coincidentally, the Portuguese grew cork trees.

As an added benefit, seventeenth-century wine shippers discovered that the cork created a tight enough seal to protect the wine from spoiling as quickly as it used to spoil. Not only that, they realized that the cork seemed to let the wine age more gracefully.

So what went wrong?

In a word, *chlorine*.

Manufacturers sterilized corks with a chlorine solution. Chlorine was used to clean winery walls, floors, equipment, tanks, and barrels. In addition, *chlorphenol* compounds can be taken up in commercial trees subject to pesticide sprays and into wood molding subject to preservatives.

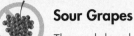

Sour Grapes

The cork has been a major part of the wine aging process as it rests in the bottle, and for that reason, cork has been a revered tradition—until the tradition of cork met with the technology of sanitation.

In the late 1980s, it was discovered that chlorphenol compounds allowed an airborne fungi that was getting into wine to flourish and ruin some of the wine. It made wine smell like wet cardboard and taste like a glass of bitters. (The offending chemical that ruins wine is *2,4,6-trichloroanisole*, or TCA. It's commonly referred to as *cork taint*.)

Plastic

By the 1990s, a plastic stopper had come on the market to replace cork. (It's still in use today.) The stopper almost looks like a cork, especially the one that's colored like cork. But most of the stoppers come in bright blues, pinks, reds, and other colors—they obviously aren't corks.

So what went wrong?

The idea behind their invention was that plastic stoppers would eliminate cork taint. Just like cork, the plastic stoppers are opened with a corkscrew. Still, the flashy colors turn off some traditionalists who love the cork.

Sour Grapes

Plastic stoppers are still in wide use but generally aren't used to cap ultra-premium wines because the market just won't accept them.

Plastic stoppers pose a few problems of their own. Sometimes they don't seal tight enough, letting wine oxidize, and sometimes they seal too tightly, making opening a bottle of wine quite a challenge.

Screwcap

One of the newest developments for sealing wine bottles, the *screwcap*, is not new at all—it's the technology of the soda pop and beer industries.

The screwcap is touted as being TCA taint free, and it is. It's easy to use, it offers a tight seal, and some of them are supposedly environmentally recyclable. Its light weight makes for a decent carbon footprint. It's perfect—right?

So what went wrong?

There's an argument over a potential negative effect that the screwcap might have on wine in the bottle. Its tight seal may in fact starve wine of oxygen completely, and that can cause the wine to reduce into sulfurous smells such as rotten eggs or burnt rubber. Plus, there's the question of biodegradability.

Glass

The absolute latest development is a glass stopper with an intricate design that its manufacturer obviously touts as the product that provides full and perfect closure.

So what went wrong?

It's too early to say. The jury is still out.

So What Do You Choose?

The TCA problem is one of the most vexing in the wine industry, and it obviously cannot be solved without some form of intervention. It's an important business decision because the closure you choose determines how much you spend for your bottling line equipment. Because it is a packaging issue, the closure speaks to tradition as well as to cost. Last, the closure you choose has an effect on the prices your wine can command.

Mounds of scientific papers and piles of remedies for or against intervention winemaking already clutter research labs and Internet websites. Your job is to pick one. Don't pass up the chance to talk over the matter of intervention and nonintervention with the local cooperative extension agent, other winery owners in your area, and experts in wine marketing. This subject comes up again in Chapter 19, when you explore marketing your wine.

The Least You Need to Know

- ◆ Tradition has no clearly identified boundaries.
- ◆ While you might see intervention as necessary, the market might see it as negative.
- ◆ Sometimes intervention in the winemaking process is your only choice.
- ◆ Sometimes the intervention you choose has a serious effect on your bottom line.
- ◆ Expect the federal government to start regulating certain environmental aspects connected to wine production soon.

16

Germinating Your Team

In This Chapter

- ◆ What to look for in an interview
- ◆ How to train your staff
- ◆ What are people worth?
- ◆ Establish responsibilities

It takes a number of employees to run a full commercial winery. Not all of them need a college degree, but you don't want to hire just anybody. It's important to establish hiring procedures that benefit you and your employees. Also, develop proper procedures for removing those workers who aren't cutting it.

Generally, quality employees won't just fall into your lap. It's your job to find them and to lead them. In this chapter, you discover how selecting employees can add value to your business.

Interview Tips

Interviewing is a skill. You have to ask the right questions—and remember the answers each of the applicants give. So take notes, before and after. After all, even a well-trained human resources manager brings notes to an interview and takes notes of the applicant's answers. You don't want to have to rely on memory when you start calling people back for a second interview or to make a job offer.

During the interview, there's one way to get a good look into a potential employee: make eye contact. You should also be cordial but be direct, and be sure you stay within the law when you're interviewing. Some questions are illegal to ask during an interview. Stay away from these questions:

◆ How old are you?

◆ Are you a native citizen?

◆ Do you have any physical disabilities?

◆ Have you ever been addicted to drugs or alcohol?

◆ Are you married?

Master of Wine

For top managers, the best place to begin your search, after recommendations, is by placing want ads in trade magazines either in print, online, or both. Check also with the local university's extension service as well as its graduating classes. If you need a certain caliber of winemaking expertise, you might find the person through universities that offer enology programs.

Some questions are perfectly legal, as long as they apply to the job and are asked in that context. For instance, if you interview for the tasting room, it's perfectly okay to ask a person's age because serving alcohol requires a minimum age that varies across the United States.

Your business is licensed and has liabilities. If you plan on drug testing new employees as well as ongoing ones, you should check with both federal and state laws governing the practice.

Training Tips

In the vineyard and wine production business, periodic training is required for many functions like handling chemicals and heavy equipment. But you also need to train staff in the ways your company operates.

Never assume people will learn how things are done at your company just by doing. People can be set in their ways, and they will bring their habits to a new job. Establish an overall training program that applies to the company as a whole and also specific training programs for certain jobs.

One of your most important training programs is for tasting room servers to deal with potentially intoxicated customers.

The Winemaker You Need

The winemaker is your most important employee. Sometimes, the winemaker is the CEO or top-level middle manager.

It helps to have a winemaker with you when you're in the building and equipment-buying phases. That consultant winemaker you've been using to get you started is a reasonable choice, but maybe the time has come to hire a staff winemaker.

To select a winemaker with the best qualifications, ask yourself the following questions:

Is this person's experience hands-on only? Some winemakers come from the bottom up—literally. They start as cellar rats, work themselves up to a position as assistant winemaker, and move into the top spot. These winemakers are likely to cost less in salary than one with a college degree, and they may offer practical experience that can help you with designing an efficient workflow throughout the winery. The trade-off to hiring an ex cellar rat may mean a winemaker that lacks a thorough understanding of food chemistry.

Does this person have an enology degree? A degreed winemaker brings chemistry to the table as well as technology. Winemaking is food production. A winemaker with thorough training in chemistry and technology will head off many potential disasters as bacterial and virus infections lie in wait, viewing each new wine as their personal prey. But someone fresh out of university could also be woefully deficient in the practicalities of winery workflow and efficiency, and of working with others.

Does this person have winemaking experience at one or more wineries? Regardless of whether the winemaker has an education or began as a cellar rat, if the person has been a winemaker at one or more wineries prior to coming to see you about a position, you may have a potentially valuable asset in front of you. A word of caution, though: a winemaker who has been popping around from winery to winery could very well be or become a problem employee. Seek comments from his or her previous employers.

The Winepress

From the Greek word for wine, *oinos*, comes *enology*, our word for studying winemaking. The preeminent U.S. enology schools include the University of California, Fresno State University, and Cornell University. Enology is also taught at various highly regarded schools across the world.

How is his or her personality? It won't be easy, but you must try to find out about the winemaker's personality. Organize more than one interview if necessary, and get as many recommendations or have as many conversations with others as you can about the person. A winemaker needs to be calm and rational in the face of seeming disaster, and he or she needs to be smart as well as resourceful.

Other Employees

Right behind the winemaker in importance are the vineyard and visitor center managers. The vineyard manager needs an understanding of farming and farm equipment. The visitor center manager needs to be sales and service oriented. Each needs good people skills.

In the Vineyard

The vineyard manager keeps farm equipment in working order and gets the grapes planted, pruned, tied to the wires, sprayed, tended, and harvested. It takes good scheduling to service that kind of workload while keeping costs down.

A vineyard manager doesn't necessarily have to come with years of vineyard experience; general farming experience can suffice. Still, it's much easier to get things going when the vineyard manager brings grape-growing experience to your new business. An experienced vineyard manager has seen what the weather or a recalcitrant tractor can do to the best of plans and has also gone through the fire of managing people. That experience will be to your advantage.

Make a walk in the vineyards part of the interviews for a vineyard manager. Be on the lookout for the following, and make notes:

- Does he or she understand the reason for the location of your vineyard rows?

- Does he or she agree or disagree with your vine-spacing program?

- Does he or she show knowledge of the equipment and workflow your vineyard will require?

- Does he or she know much about the grape varieties you want to plant?

- Did he or she offer smart or at least thoughtful suggestions?

- Does he or she drink wine? (You may be surprised, but some people apply for jobs in the wine business and don't know much about or aren't interested in the end product.)

One of the responsibilities of your vineyard manager is to hire the regular staff and the day laborers or migrant workers. Once you settle on the person you want to manage the vineyard, make your company employment policies clear to that person along with your vineyard needs and then let the manager do the interviews.

Some farm work involves special skills, but the overall work doesn't require highly technical skills or involved thinking. At the same time, farm work can be dangerous. Be sure the vineyard manager understands that you need people who display common sense.

A vineyard is an all-year operation, but it has its down time. Many farm workers pull double duty at wineries as cellar workers, specifically helping out on the bottling line, in the cellar, and even in the tasting room. Bring the winemaker in on vineyard hiring, but let the vineyard manager have a say in the final decision.

Sour Grapes

You cannot ignore the illegal immigration situation. The federal government has established reporting standards, and it's best that you take them seriously. Migrant farm workers are a hot spot, but the regulations apply for all employees. Everyone must fill out the federal IRS Form I-9, Employment Eligibility Verification.

In the Cellar

As in the vineyard, it's the cellar manager's job to staff the cellar, and the winemaker happens to be the cellar manager. Let the winemaker interview cellar rat candidates.

Remember that the cellar rat may one day become a winemaker. This is a job for a fast and eager learner with a passion for wine and perfection, not to mention cleanliness. The cellar of a winery needs to be as spotless at the end of each day as any food processing plant. Bacteria and other microorganisms are adept at finding the most hospitable porous surfaces like wood and insulation. A partially or poorly sanitized winery may float for a year or two without incident, but if your cellar rat is a slacker, one day the tiny bugs will conquer your wine.

Needless to say, this is a job for neither a slacker nor a slob.

In the Visitor Center

It's likely that for the first year or two, you'll be an ever-present force in the visitor center/tasting room. This is where the winery's image is upheld and the highest per-bottle profit is generated. Yet the day will come when you're ready to hire a visitor center manager.

When interviewing for a visitor center manager, look for the following particular backgrounds and/or talents:

- An outgoing, positive personality
- A team player
- Sales, promotion, or marketing experience
- Sales management experience
- Public speaking or education experience
- Experience in retail and/or hospitality (hotel, bed-and-breakfast, restaurant, and tour or travel agency)
- Experience in the wine industry (Don't forget to ask if he or she drinks wine!)

If you find someone with all this experience, consider yourself having just met with divine intervention! Odds are, you'll find people with a range of experience in some but not all of these areas.

After you hire and train in company policies, let the visitor center/tasting room manager interview people to staff the bar, lead tours, and run the cash register.

On the Road

Whether you sell wine through a distributor or sell direct to restaurants and retailers, you need someone on the road. A distributor has a sales staff, but generally, that army of representatives has too much to do and too little time in which to do it. If you don't stay in constant contact or work with your distributor, your sales will suffer.

Don't assume that your winemaker will be a good salesperson. In fact, assume the opposite.

In the beginning, you may be the best person to work with the distributor and make direct sales to restaurant and retail accounts. As your business becomes profitable and grows, you'll hire more people to go on the road. How many you hire depends on how much your business grows and how far and wide your wines are distributed.

Most of what you need to look for while interviewing a salesperson is obvious. You want a positive, outgoing person who expresses a can-do attitude. It's preferable that the person has a sales background, but it's also not a bad idea to find a young person fresh out of college with an interest in and a personality for sales.

When you hire your first employee for the road, you might act as the sales manager, but during the job interview phase, keep in mind that one day you'll need a sales manager, so look for someone you think can be groomed for the position. Look for hints that show whether or not the people you interview are organized, methodical, motivated, and goal oriented; these are traits you want in a sales manager.

> **Sour Grapes**
>
> An unprepared salesperson trying to motivate a distributor sales staff will quickly become ineffective, and retailers faced with the same lack of preparation will chew up and spit out your salesperson.

A salesperson who brings wine sales experience is of course a plus, but if you like someone who brings sales experience in another field, be sure the person has an interest in wine and then train the person in how to sell it. Remember that wine is a regulated business, and there are things a salesperson cannot do or say for the sake of making a wine sale.

In the Office

Staffing the office may not be as important as staffing the production and sales teams, but don't shortchange the effort. A smoothly operating office support staff can make the worklife of everyone in the company efficient and simpler.

A product business runs on supplies. It's much better for the efficiency of your business if the department managers aren't spending inordinate amounts of time on the phone chasing down supplies. So who do you think would be one of your most valuable employees?

Depending on the size and success of your business, you'll need either a purchasing agent and office manager, or an office manager who can double in the positions. This is a job for the experienced. Mistakes that obstruct the supply line can be quite costly. Also, a winery requires a lot of interconnecting record-keeping for the government—it's not the job for a novice.

When Do You Need Them?

The decision of when to hire staff is sometimes made for you, as you sit behind a pile of things to do and discover that you don't have the time to do half of them. But this isn't the best way to go about building your staff. First, you'll be desperate and likely make some poor choices. Second, if you've allowed things to go long enough, you may have also allowed your business to lose some money.

In business, time definitely is money—and so is timing. Maybe the upfront costs are high if you start to build a staff before you plant the first grapevine, but the end payoff might be equally high.

You already know you need a winemaker with you when you're buying equipment for the start-up. If the consultant winemaker interests you, that's the time to start talking about a full-time position.

The best time to hire a vineyard manager is when you're ready to start developing your new site. An experienced vineyard manager can help you iron out the potential wrinkles in your layout and plans. If you buy an existing vineyard, you might entertain keeping the existing manager on board, or you'll have to get a new one as soon as you close the deal.

Sour Grapes

Your goal is to expand the staff for your business to meet its growth without breaking the bank. Don't wait to hire new people until after you're faced with overworked, disgruntled employees.

You don't need to hire a visitor center manager until you have wine to sell or until you can afford to hire someone. The same holds true for a sales representative on the road. But if you're going to do those two jobs, then right away, get yourself one or two experienced and trustworthy people to run the office, because you'll have neither time nor energy to do all that.

What's the Going Rate?

Any business has either established or generally unwritten salary parameters for particular jobs. At the same time, there are as many fluctuations in the pay rates as there are people who receive them.

It takes a little research on your part to feel comfortable that the salaries you offer are within the range of the going rate.

Talk, Talk, Talk to Your Competition

Obviously, you have to pay people at or above the legal minimum wage. Equally obvious, some jobs are worth more than others. One way to determine wine industry pay scales is to talk to the competition. For general pay rates for office staff, talk to other business people. Set a salary budget for each position and try to stick with it.

Trade magazines are a good source of pay rates; among the best is the periodic *Wines and Vines* magazine survey of winemaker and other salaries in the industry.

Your top-paid employee is likely the wine-maker, followed perhaps by the vineyard manager. The office manager and visitor center manager make up the second tier. As management, this group of employees receives pay based on an annual salary, which is not tied to the number of hours they work. Cellar rat, vineyard laborers, and office and tasting room clerks are paid by the hour and are subject to all legal requirements for overtime pay.

> **Master of Wine**
>
> When you're putting to-gether salary budgets, don't forget you'll have to add your portion of employee payroll taxes to every employee's pay. Depending on the state you're in, the cost can exceed 20 percent in excess of the payroll.

If your winery has seasonal ups and downs, you may need part-time employees. Local universities often are a good source for interns, especially when the interns are enrolled in enology, horticulture, or business schools.

The sales staff may be paid in one of a number of ways. You can pay them a straight annual salary. Some organizations find it best to offer a salary to a new sales staff for a year or two, while they build sales and territories. After the established period ends, and the sales territories are active, a commission system goes into effect.

Draw against commission is another option. In an already established sales territory, it's common to offer a new hire an annual sales goal. A commission rate is agreed to and paid in installments, in advance. When sales exceed the goal, the salesperson receives additional commissions on future sales for the year.

Salary plus commission is yet another option. A salary is set, but when sales reach a certain level, the person is paid commissions beyond salary. The drawback of this system is that a less-motivated salesperson happy with the salary can rest on it.

Finally, you can pay a straight commission. For the truly motivated salesperson, a straight commission based on sales can become the most rewarding pay system. But it's risky, too. This system usually is a good deal for the business, except when an over-zealous performer trying to increase commissions does things that can be illegal or unethical.

The Benefits

Providing employees with health insurance benefits is a powerful way to draw top-notch people. It's also among the costliest ways to do it. The cost of health insurance plans averages a 10 percent rise each year.

The Winepress

Small businesses often find it difficult to join in group insurance plans. In many localities, the local chamber of commerce or other business associations is a large enough pool for insurers to provide group policies.

If you can't provide full health insurance benefits, you might be able to provide half or some other portion of the cost of insurance.

Retirement plan benefits also draw good employees. The most widely offered benefit is the so-called 401(k) or similar plan, where the employee has money withdrawn from payroll to go into a retirement account of his or her choice, and the employer matches the amount.

Other benefits programs can include the following:

◆ A creative vacation pay formula that rises in value for every year or so an employee is with the company

◆ Sick pay that accumulates when unused

◆ Day care services

◆ On-premise gym facility

◆ Lunch provided

◆ Annual sales bonus or profit sharing plans

◆ Annual picnic, holiday parties, or special recognition events

Who's Responsible for What?

A small business is like a family, and we all know what happens in the family. Just like the head of the household, as a business owner you are the leader, the chief executive, and the psychologist. What you don't want to be is the day care attendant. Your operation needs not only a hierarchy but well-defined job responsibilities.

The old saying that wine is made in the vineyard doesn't mean the winemaker does the vineyard manager's job. When the vineyard manager wants to harvest the grapes on Tuesday because the weather threatens but the winemaker wants the grapes to hang on the vines another two weeks for what he or she perceives will provide optimum maturity, someone is going to have to make the decision.

The same holds true throughout the employee chain. Although each employee has a job to do, the job often relies on or is relied upon by another employee. Managers make the decisions, but not for someone else's department.

The best solution is to hire people to run departments who get along with other people and who never seem to want what others cannot or will not provide. For that experience, instead of a business owner, you'd be better off becoming a monk. In the real world, it's important to establish individual employee responsibilities, but it's equally important to have employees that can bend a little because they will have to at some point.

A regularly scheduled managers meeting can help head off friction, and special meetings to solve special problems are even better. It doesn't hurt for managers to hold regular sessions with their staff, too.

Company Policies

At the meetings and in daily operation of their departments, managers must work within the framework of company policies. You set the policies, and you build them from a combination of experience and government mandates. Managers are not doing a good job when they circumvent or ignore policies—it sets a bad example and creates problems for the business down the road.

When you hire employees, you'll be handing out a bunch of forms for them to fill out for the government and for your files. Hand out written company policies, too. And when one of your favorite employees comes to you to ask for a favor that's against company policy, try with all your might to resist bending your own rules.

> **Sour Grapes**
>
> Business owners should be on the lookout for managers who don't take seriously the sensitive subjects of ethnicity or any form of discrimination.

Company Politics

For a business book I worked on, my co-author and I interviewed a number of corporate CEOs and middle managers. One of the questions was about company politics. Almost without exception, the people we interviewed had trouble talking about the subject—some refused to admit that company politics even exists.

As long as you have people working for you and not robots, company politics will exist at your company. People have feelings that can be hurt. Someone convinced that his or her work is the best in the world won't understand why someone else gets a promotion or why the one who gets everything wrong even has a job.

Master of Wine _____

Many times, politics stems from poor communication. Having regular meetings is one way to address political maneuverings; being fair and showing no favoritism is another way.

When you find that a person's political shenanigan affects morale, you may have to act. You can have the manager do it or you can do it, but there will come a time when you'll have to fire an employee. Don't be cruel; be efficient and businesslike.

Now that you have the winery staff, can I interest you in another way to start and run a winery, with minimal staff? Read all about it in Chapter 17.

The Least You Need to Know

♦ Seek extra talents in the people you interview for a position, for yours and for their future growth.

♦ Train your managers and then delegate responsibilities to them.

♦ Set payroll budgets and pay people what they are worth.

♦ A good employee benefits package can attract top people.

♦ Hold managers responsible for their decisions and for maintaining company policies.

♦ Face and deal with company politics.

17

Let Someone Else Do It: Custom Crush

In This Chapter

- ◆ How to keep your day job
- ◆ Learning the business on your time
- ◆ Be in the wine industry but not in a vineyard (or a winery)
- ◆ The minimum legality of your permit
- ◆ Deciding when to take the next plunge

This is the right moment to tell you an open secret: you don't need either a vineyard or a production facility to run a wine business. You can have your wines produced, stored, bottled, and packaged for you by someone else. It's called *custom crush*, and it's a concept that has wings. By taking the custom crush route, you may be able to fulfill your dream without having to meet a banker or a venture capitalist.

There are reasons for and against the custom crush method. In this chapter, you discover what they are.

Custom Crush on the Web

Here's a quote from an online custom crush business called Crushpad (www. crushpadwine.com): "… Crushpad Commerce hides the underlying complexities of operating a wine brand and enables you to focus on the areas where you can provide the most value—styling and promoting your wines. We take care of the rest." And they certainly do take care of the rest. An online custom crush company lets you start a wine business with as little as 50 cases of wine. The company does all the work necessary to get your wine into the bottle.

In this method of establishing your wine business, you let someone else do it for you. But there's more than one way to custom crush. You can probably find a custom crush method that suits what you want from and what you can give to your business.

Keep Your Day Job

You've read 16 chapters, so you've already figured out that starting and running a winery is not something you can do in your spare time. But if you really, really want to get into the wine business and keep your day job, too, custom crush online could be the answer.

Among the most important reasons for choosing custom crush is money—not enough of it, and an unwillingness to try to raise a lot of money because of the risk. Custom crush online reduces the risk to almost nothing, and you can select the size of wine business you want, as well as the pace at which you can make it grow—all while keeping your day job.

This is what an online custom crush company can do for you commercially:

- Help with legal and licensing functions
- Source and select grapes
- Crush and press grapes
- Ferment, analyze, store, and bottle your wine
- Register your label, package, store, and take orders for your wine
- Make deliveries and shipments
- Help with the bookkeeping and accounting functions
- Help with government reporting compliance
- Help meet the taxes due

Here are the things you would do:

- Pay an upfront fee to join

- Promote and sell your brands

- Accept payment of the net profit on sales of your wines from the custom crush company

This custom crush model leverages economy of scale to spread capital investments among members of the online community. Usually, there's a fixed upfront membership fee and the company takes a commission on the sale of your wine.

> **Sour Grapes**
>
> The online custom crush method gives you neither the feel of the earth nor the adrenaline rush running a production business can provide. For some, that's a drawback.

Plow Profits into the Business

When you keep your day job, and the wine business is not your sole source of income, you have the freedom to use sales revenue to put back toward building the business for the day when you're ready to strike out on your own.

With the online custom crush system, you don't have to know much about the wine business or do much to learn about it, except promotion and sales. A major plus is that there are no employee payrolls, no fixed time schedules, and no bureaucrats to deal with on a regular basis.

Focus on Ultra-Premium

The online business model's focus is usually on ultra-premium brands (more than $25 per bottle). The company selects the grapes and the winemaking process for you, bottles and warehouses your wine, makes distribution and delivery arrangements, and even handles the online orders for your wine.

As with any other business, going the online custom crush way is a decision you should weigh carefully. Ask yourself these two questions:

Does this method truly create individuality for my brand? Some in the wine business say that this business model is essentially a private labeling system with the same wines under a variety of labels. You'll need to find out exactly what you're buying into when you sign up with an online custom crush company.

Does the online business model offer me the experience I seek? If your motivation to get into the wine business stops at seeing your name on a wine label, this business model may work for you.

> ### Master of Wine
> The ultra-premium wine consumer market is extremely open to Internet buying. E-mail lists have fast replaced snail-mail newsletters.

You have to be honest about whether or not you'll like running an essentially digital wine business. You'll be involved in making decisions for your brand—you'll have to identify the market; design your brand's image; and then market, promote, and make the sales contacts. But you'll do most of this by e-mail, telephone, or Internet.

Brick-and-Mortar Custom Crush

These versions of custom crush come in two models. You can choose to merge your custom crush product into your own physical location, or you can choose to be part of a cooperative custom crush brick-and-mortar facility.

Custom Crush at Your Place

If you have some money but not enough to start a vineyard and production facility, you can get into the wine business with an investment of a couple hundred thousand dollars. With your own building, you can enter the wine business *à la carte*, through a model where you select which parts of the winemaking process suits you best.

> ### The Winepress
> Using an external custom crush facility does not exempt your business from a federal and state permit to produce, distribute, and sell wine, but it will reduce the time you spend with bureaucracy.

Let's do some supposing. Suppose you're a grape grower and you'd like to produce a little wine to sell from a small building on your farm that you can make into a tasting room. You can make a deal with a local winery to accept your grapes for crushing and pressing and then ferment, store, and bottle the wine for you, under your label.

Or suppose you're a winery seeking to add to your product line without increasing equipment costs. You can make the same deal as the grape grower, and you can use your grapes, the other winery's grapes, or someone else's grapes.

Or suppose you want to start a wine brand but not a winery. You have just enough money to build a slick-looking visitor center and tasting room. Your plan is to build a wine business slowly so the day you retire from your day job, you can move into the business and expand it. All you need is bottled wine under your label. You can make the same deal with a winery that either of the preceding two makes.

Or suppose you want to make your own wine but you don't have the resources to set up a large facility with crush and fermentation capacity. You can have grapes crushed, pressed, and fermented and then transferred to you for storage and bottling, which can be done by a mobile bottling company that comes to your door when you need it.

In any of these cases, you have to be licensed just as any other winery is licensed, because you take possession of the wine and sell it.

Going the brick-and-mortar custom crush route not only allows you to learn the business, it gives you the freedom to build the business at your pace. And if you use your own investment money, you won't have to service major land, building, and equipment debt load.

Co-Op Custom Crush

Suppose you graduated from a premier university with an enology degree. You want to start a winery, but all you really have is a massive college loan debt and some savings. There are others like you, maybe everyone in your graduation class. One night, while sitting around wallowing with a few of your classmates over some wine, one of your friends mentions a new deal he heard about.

Each winemaker can source grapes wherever he or she wants and send them to a cooperative custom crush facility the winemakers pay a fee to join. After fermentation, the wine goes into cooperatively owned storage equipment. Throughout the wine-making process, each winemaker is responsible for his or her wine, but they help one another.

When the time comes to bottle the wine, a mobile bottling unit arrives and bottles for a fee. The bottled and packaged wine is shipped, under individual labels, to each winemaker's offsite tasting room, which may or may not be located in the wine region. (Many wineries and tasting rooms are going up in heavily trafficked areas of cities. They are called "urban wineries.")

In California, where the climate offers an abundance and sometimes surplus of grape crops, custom crush is fast becoming the normal way for people to enter the wine business. The trend is picking up in other states, but custom crush methods require a fairly consistent grape crop source, which isn't always available from year to year across the United States and Canada.

The Proper Bondage

In Chapter 13, your winery plat showed the tax-paid room sealed off from the bonded production and warehousing areas. When you remove wine in bulk or in bottles from one bonded area, you can move it either to another bonded area or to a tax-paid area.

Sour Grapes _____

If you have no production facility of your own, the U.S. Treasury Department Tax and Trade Bureau (TTB) issues you a permit for an "alternative premise." This kind of bonded transfer may be under tighter scrutiny or not allowed at all in some states.

With custom crush, the wine is in bond under the custom crush facility's federal permit. When the wine is transferred to you, it is in bond under your federal permit until you remove it to sell for wholesale distribution or for direct retail.

Crush Under Contract

Like all business arrangements, establishing a custom crush relationship is best done under contract. The contract should specify the scope and description of services the custom crush will deliver. It's best not to face "he said, she said" surprises after you've committed to a large volume of grapes or wine.

The contract should also explain the custom crush invoicing procedure. It should clearly spell out not only when invoices are processed but also for which services. This adds the value of serving as a checklist of the services agreed to. It is especially necessary when you use the à la carte method and select parts of, rather than all available services, and when you need to extend storage time for any particular reason.

The fees, charges, and terms of release are also to be clearly outlined. If you owe the custom crush money, you may not get your wine when you want it, or you may not get it at all.

The contract should also specify the critical time frame in which the custom crush facility processes the grapes.

Winemaking consulting should also be addressed in the contract. You have to pay an additional fee for the custom crush winemaker's services.

A statement of liabilities and indemnity should be included. This absolves the custom crush facility of marketing and sales responsibilities. It also spells out its liability for damages to your product. You'll need to consider insurance coverage, too.

Look for a statement of your responsibilities. This is where you determine which services you want and what you must do on your part. For example, if you will deliver grapes, that is one of your listed responsibilities. In some arrangements, you may decide to buy the bottles, corks, etc. directly from suppliers rather than pay a markup on materials to the custom crush facility.

Other conditions or provisions might be necessary, for example, for the two parties to spell out additional services required by either.

Finally, you'll want an overall legal statement of the entire agreement and the process for changing or even canceling the contract.

The letter of agreement should be accompanied by a list of all the services available. This document spells out the complete winemaking process from grapes to finished wine in bottles as well as the costs to you for each individual service you choose. It also comes with a timeline of responsibilities.

> **Master of Wine**
>
> Once you've made the decision to start your business in one of the custom crush methods, marketing and sales remain major responsibilities, and they need to be forecasted and planned. You still should create a business plan.

The Importance of Creativity and Flexibility

Sure, if you go the custom crush route, you probably won't have to work much if at all with architects, contractors, bureaucrats, employees, and all the others I've been discussing, and you may not run a vineyard either. But you'll still need to be creative, especially when establishing your image.

You'll still have to come up with a name and logo for your business that catches attention, and, as I've mentioned, your greatest effort will be in marketing your wine. This is where you'll need to be both creative and flexible.

> **The Winepress**
>
> The market for wine shifts from product to product and style to style. Those with no investment in a slow-to-respond vineyard and expensive, possibly outdated wine-processing equipment have greater flexibility.

You may have been involved in the winemaking decisions, but what you have in the bottle is not your own doing. There's nothing wrong with that; it's done every day in every wine region in the world. But you don't have to shout about it. If you believe in the wine and the wine is good quality, you can take full ownership of it … but you'll have to be creative.

On the Label

TTB rules clearly state that the identification and address of the production facility must appear on the wine label. This means where the grapes were processed and fermented and where the wine was stored and bottled.

Even though you hold a permit, if you received the wine already bottled, you cannot claim ownership on the label. Under the words *Produced and bottled by* will appear either the name or the bonded winery license number and the address of the custom crush facility.

If the wine was delivered to you in bulk, and you stored and bottled it at your address, you can claim partial ownership. Your business name and address will appear under the words *Cellared and bottled by.*

Your Image

The image you create is the most important part of the reason behind the success of the custom crush route.

Most consumers don't know the fine distinction between the words *produced* and *cellared*. Many wineries offer products at the ultra-premium price point with *cellared by* on their labels. They can do so because they've established an image to go with their prices, whether that image is in the packaging, in the awards they've won, in the tasting room surroundings, in their marketing as an exclusive wine producer, or in a combination of these things.

Your Staff

Other than winemakers with desire but no funding, many people who take the custom crush way come from other professions. They may be money managers, marketing experts, promotion and publicist powerhouses, or celebrities. They often are perfectly situated to establish a niche in the marketplace by virtue of their experiences and connections.

You may not be a celebrity, but you may be someone with talent, someone who has a vision of your business niche. Maybe all you need are two or three professional consultants to get that packaging down or to identify that premium market. You might need a consultant to design your building or your road sign, or both. But when it comes down to the day-to-day running of the business, it may take only you and a couple family members, or you and two employees.

The Winepress

It's possible for 2,500 cases of wine at ultra-premium prices to bring in enough money to support two or three people, and if the location is good, the tasting room might not have to be open all 12 months of the year.

How Much Money Do You Really Need?

The cheapest custom crush choice is the online version. Here, you pay a setup fee and your portion of production costs. Depending, of course, on the size of membership and production capacity, this version should bring costs down considerably, and you can choose the production volume, starting at only 50 cases.

The Crushpad company advertises gross margins of 50 to 100 percent, before marketing expenses and taxes.

The estimated cost to enter a brick-and-mortar custom crush business is from 10 to 30 percent of the cost of building a complete winery facility without a vineyard—from $1 million down to $100,000 to $300,000.

The End of the Line (It's a Good Thing!)

When you go brick-and-mortar custom crush, you take possession of the finished wine. You can take the wine in bulk for storage and bottling at your facility, or you can take the wine bottled.

Suppose you start out small, maybe a few thousand gallons of wine, and you decide to store and bottle it yourself. A building the size of a two-car garage can easily store 2,000 gallons of wine, provided you can set up a water line for cleaning and have enough height for the tanks. Double the size of the garage, and you'll have room for a case box warehouse.

Master of Wine

You'll need a truck to pick up your bulk wine, or you can pay the custom crush facility to make the delivery. The vehicle used to transfer the wine must also be bonded.

When you're ready to bottle your wine, you can call the local mobile bottling company to come by. They'll back into your storage facility and filter, bottle, and label your wine while you stack the finished cases in your warehouse.

Whether or not you store the wine in bulk and bottle it or you take already bottled wine from the custom crush company, if you aren't already an operating winery with other products, you'll need a tasting room. This will be your front, your image and appearance to the customers, so make it a good one. Build it rustic or modern, large or small, brick or wood. But whatever its size or material, be sure it's tasteful.

If you don't operate a vineyard, consider establishing a small one around the property. Visitors like to see vineyards as they drive into your driveway—and make the driveway welcoming, too. Landscape around the property, but keep the atmosphere in line with your product placement: if the wine is ultra-premium, the tasting room experience should be ultra-premium as well. (You'll find out more about pricing your product in Chapter 18.)

The Least You Need to Know

♦ You can get into the wine business on a small scale, part-time or full-time.

♦ Custom crush wine production lets you learn the business at your own pace.

♦ Online wine marketing and shopping is a growing segment of the wine industry.

♦ The custom crush route gives you greater flexibility at the lowest cost.

♦ Put most of what money you save with custom crush back into your marketing and image.

Part 5

The Fruit of Your Labor

Like plants, businesses grow, and for plants—or businesses—to grow, they need cultivation, care, and a proper diet before their fruits can be sent to market. You've laid much of the groundwork, and you've produced that first bottle of wine. Now you have to get it out there.

Part 5 explains how to establish your pricing, cultivate your customers, and get the word out. You learn how to introduce your business and keep people talking about it. After these chapters, you'll be ready to set the stage to project your business into its future success.

18

Value Your Crop

In This Chapter

- ◆ Establish the value of your wine
- ◆ Place your business in its proper class
- ◆ Easy ways to keep down costs
- ◆ Limit unwanted surprises
- ◆ Keeping the market supplied

Remember from Chapter 1 that the wine industry serves three consumer markets. Your challenge is to identify the wines that each market wants, choose which market or markets appeals to you, and find out how to service that market at the lowest cost and the highest profit to you. And you're going to have to price your wine. This chapter shows you how to do that.

What Will Your Market Bear?

Lesson number one: determine what your market will bear. Make your determination after doing some research into the three major consumer wine markets:

- The affluent

- The middle class

- The next generation

The market segments often overlap, but you can generally get a picture of the market and decide which part or parts of it you want to service. To get started, look at wine-buying trends in the following important categories:

- Regular compared with organic wines

- Most popular wines

- Type of wines that bring in more profits

- The latest per capita wine consumption

- Demographic spending on wine by age groups

- Sales in restaurants

If you're starting out as a local winery with no or little national distribution, you'll need statistics from your state to compare with national trends. That may be more difficult to locate, but you can start with informed local promotional and informational organizations like the chamber of commerce, the local university cooperative extension service marketing and economics curriculum, and your state office that gathers and stores census records.

The Winepress _____

You can get the latest national statistics from a combination of private services like the *Gomberg-Fredrikson Report* (231 Ware Road, Suite 823, Woodside, CA 94062), Roy Morgon Research (www.roymorgan.com.au), DemographicsNow (www. demographicsnow.com), and the U.S. Census Bureau (www.census.gov).

After you gather general demographic statistics and buying patterns, compare your potential market with the three major characteristics of the overall basic wine market. Look for how many are available to your winery from each market segment.

Determining Your Market

There's nothing wrong with trying to service the whole market. But a decision like that needs to be made carefully. Ask yourself these questions:

Based on your business model—national or local winery—is the complete wine consumption market available to you? In some locations, a local winery might have a wider reach to certain segments of the market than to other segments. For instance, if you're located near a college community, you might have quality access to two of the markets: the affluent and the next generation. But you may not have access to a middle class market.

Based on your intended production volume, can you supply the size of the complete market within your reach? If you plan to produce a few thousand cases of wine, and you're located in the Northeast with access to 54 million potential wine buyers, you may run out of wine selling to one segment of the market before you try to service a second segment.

Based on your planned wine style, will your products appeal to everyone? This may be the most important question of all. Trying to be all things to all people can create an image problem. One way to handle this is to create more than one brand or label, each aimed at a particular segment of the market. That kind of marketing usually requires large production, not to mention a large staff and a national marketing reach.

It won't help you much if you intend to be a mail-order-only business and you find that the segment of the market you want to reach doesn't buy wine that way. After you decide on your intended customer base, refine your demographics into submarkets.

> **Master of Wine**
>
> Don't worry if you find that you can't, or if you don't want to, service the complete potential wine market—many wineries don't even try. Select the segment that's right for your business and do all you can to service that market. You can always change course as your business grows.

Priority Customers

Let's say you've identified that you want to focus your wine sales on the middle class, because you've found that it represents the largest group of wine consumers and you want to go after that group. Look into how middle-class wine shoppers break down—what do they eat and drink, where do they live, what is their income, etc. Try to pinpoint the middle-class consumers who will bring you the best return on your marketing and promotion investment.

For example, according to Roy Morgan Research (www.roymorgan.com.au), in an average four-week period in 2004, 30 percent of adult citizens across the United States consumed about 10 glasses of wine each. Given that information, it would be nice to know which market segment they represent, and also how and where they consumed the wine. Did they consume most of it or none of it in restaurants? Did they buy most of it or all of it at a local retail shop? Did they buy a large portion of the wine they consumed from winery tasting rooms?

The answers to these questions will build a consumer list. If your business model is to sell the majority of wine in your tasting room, then after you identify the consumers who bought the majority of their wine from tasting rooms, they are your priority customers.

Secondary Customers

Now let's say that the balance of your target market consumed more wine in restaurants than from other sales outlets. Based on that information, to reach that secondary market, you might allocate a portion of your production either through the distribution network or through your own direct sales to restaurants.

The Winepress _____

In many states, the percent of markup by wholesalers is mandated by the legislature, and the percent of markup in retail outlets may also be mandated. Having that information enables you to forecast a price for your wine in the tasting room that competes with its marketplace price.

Because selling wine through a middle business (a wine distributor) reduces your per-bottle profit, while you service the secondary customer base, you should also try to persuade them, through marketing, to become priority customers.

New Customers

Someday, some people in the middle class may become affluent and many in the next generation will become the middle class. Until a group of consumers enters into the market segment you've targeted, you should view them as potential new customers.

Find out what your potential market seeks. You might have to create new products for them, or you might have to simply create a marketing program that places your existing product in their hands. For example, if they dine in Asian restaurants, maybe your wine would pair well with Asian food. Or if they spend a great amount of time on the Internet, maybe you need to consider creating a winery blog (more about blogs in Chapter 20).

Pricing Your Product

You've identified and located your target market, so the time has come to price your wine. Do you understand the basic wine pricing formula? Not the formula that says "get whatever you can get for it," but the one that starts at the crush pad.

Basic Wine Pricing Formula

Every consumer product starts its retail pricing by looking at the cost of raw materials. In this case, grapes are the raw materials, so the cost of grapes is the first item in the basic wine pricing formula. You can't sell wine without packaging it, so bottling, capping, labeling, and boxing are the next most important costs. After grapes and packaging comes direct labor and overhead costs, including materials, advertising, etc.

Remember that CPA consultant you hired? Get him or her to determine the labor and overhead cost for every bottle of wine you produce. That number comes from your forecasted production volume divided into your forecasted labor and overhead costs.

> **Master of Wine**
>
> The formula for establishing the cost of a consumer product is nicely explained online at www.referenceforbusiness.com/encyclopedia/Con-Cos/Cost-Accounting.html#TYPES_OF_COST_SYSTEMS.

Let's say the CPA tells you the labor and overhead cost per bottle is $1. The basic cost formula now looks like this: cost of grapes + cost of packaging + $1.00 = cost to produce a bottle of any particular wine.

One wine produced from grapes that cost, say, $10 a gallon of finished wine would mean that the grapes represent about $1.70 per bottle (12 bottles = 2+ gallons); add about $2.50 per bottle for packaging, plus $1.00 for the labor and overhead, and that particular bottle of wine costs you $5.20 to produce.

You're now ready to price your wine.

What Can You Live With?

The first thing to ask yourself when deciding on a price for your wine is *What percentage do I want for my bottom line profit?*

Assume that to meet your bottom line profit, you need a 30 percent return from each wine you sell to distributors. For the bottle of wine that costs you $5.20 to produce, you'd charge the distributor about $6.70. The distributor would charge the retailer

$6.70 plus, say, 20 percent, or $8.05. The retailer markup is 30 percent, which means, in the end, the list price to the consumer is $10.50 (the totals have been rounded). You can charge $10.50 at the tasting room for the wine, too, giving you a full 100 percent markup of $5.30 over cost.

Simple isn't it? You can get rich!

Not so fast. Selling wine is not like selling a specialized widget with limited competition.

Eyeing the Competition

In Chapter 1, I told you about the many wineries that have grown up over the past 30 years, and about projections for the future. The wine business is extremely competitive. You and every other winery compete for the consumers' dollars.

If you simply priced your wine using the uncomplicated calculation, cost + markup = retail price, you might lose out to the competition.

Their Pricing

Odds are that the wineries near yours offer generally the same wine list you offer. If they sell a wine comparable to your $10.50 bottle, but because of their *economy of scale* they can sell it at $9.75, how are you going to get the money you ask for your wine?

def•i•ni•tion

The phrase **economy of scale** generally refers to lowering per-unit overhead costs by increasing production volume.

Before you price your wine, you need to check out the going rate for that style of wine. You may find out that your price is just a little high, and so you lower it to compete. You can make up the difference in your profit margin by lessening how much of it you sell through the distribution network and increasing how much you sell at the tasting room.

Their Discounting

No sooner do you finish your reconnaissance of the competition than you discover they have instituted a new program both at wholesale and at the tasting room that reduces the price of their wine based on certain volume buying. Is it worth changing your pricing structure or meeting their discount program with one of your own? Maybe, but maybe not.

If your marketing and promotion was good, and you've placed your product in an almost exclusive position, you may not even have to worry about what other wineries charge for comparable products. This concept is called "perceived value"; it means that the consumer expects your product to cost a little more, and believes it's worth the money.

The Winepress _____

In most states, wineries must post their wholesale prices with the state's liquor control authority at least 30 days in advance of release of the wine, including discount schedules. In many states, the winery cannot change its price until the next 30-day cycle report is due.

Build In Your Profits

In the end, what you charge for a bottle of wine reflects what it costs to produce, plus the goodwill of your customers that allows you to earn the profit you seek. You instill the goodwill by studying and then meeting your market's requirements.

Study Consumption Patterns

One of the well-known patterns in wine sales is the November-December buying rush. Conversely, January is probably the worst month for wine sales. Knowing the best and worst wine sales months gives you the chance to target your promotional efforts. Knowing everything in between gives you the chance to spread your pricing over the rest of the year to cover the cost of discounting—because there is a cost connected to it.

In addition to knowing when customers buy, you need to know what they buy on those occasions. If you produce a wine that pairs well with turkey, it's a no-brainer that you should promote that wine for Thanksgiving. If you have a wine that pairs with chocolate, promote it around Valentine's Day. If you produce a sparkling wine, guess which holiday to target!

The Winepress _____

Many retailers in New York City, one of the largest wine markets in the United States, say that their single highest wine sales day is the Wednesday before Thanksgiving.

Supply and Inventory Flowchart

One of the worse things to have happen is to be unable to supply your product to an eager market. Take a good look at the buying patterns you uncover so you can establish your supply chain to the market. Create a flowchart, if you will. Keep close track of how the wine moves through inventory, and make adjustments as you need to make them.

Scheduling Special Buys

When you need to slow down sales so your priority customers don't lose out, there's probably no need to apply discounts. Instead, you might put your wine on allocation to the distribution network. This cuts back on how much wine you send into the pipeline, and it may also help keep the price stable.

> **Master of Wine**
>
> Wineries with a cultlike following allocate, or hold back, wine as a regular plan of business. They create demand by selling less but at high prices—sour grapes for consumers, maybe, but profits for the wineries.

When you see a need to speed up sales because inventory is building, you may want to consider discounting. Sometimes, you can raise the perceived value by raising the price to speed up sales!

Cash Flow

Good cash flow is good, but it can also fool you. Although it is a measure of success, it isn't *the* measure. It's not uncommon for businesses with what seems like healthy cash flow to fail in spite of it—they miss the hidden costs.

Hidden Costs

The prices you charge for your products may generate good sales, but if misapplied, they may be too low to generate profit. Also, when your prices are fine and your sales look good but aren't good enough to support the constancy of your fixed costs, your cash flow may not show the problem until it's too late.

Dig deeply into what it costs to keep things running. Look especially for the costs that don't show up in accounting lessons: wasted payroll hours, wasted power use, wasted storage space, wasted packaging costs, wasted marketing and promotion costs, wasted staffing, and so on. Wasted moments and wasted expenses eat up profits.

Tangible Worth

Boxes of empty bottles are worth something only when they're being filled. Until then, they're an unnecessary expense, so why have them sitting around in inventory?

Everything you own in your winery has tangible value, including what's in inventory. Inventory eats up the book value of your business, and it can eat up profits by creating false assets. Be sure every one of your assets is worth holding for the period of time you hold it.

Intangible Worth

Employees have both tangible and intangible value. Their tangible value is obvious: the winemaker makes the wine, the vineyard manager keeps a good vineyard, the cellar rat is a neat freak, and the office manager runs a tight and efficient ship. But their intangible value may not be so obvious.

Employees think about your business, and they do it from their perspective rather than from yours. They can generate profits or cost savings simply with good ideas. Listen to the intangible value of your employees by holding regular meetings with the specific aim to talk about increasing company profits. You'd be surprised how much employees have to offer.

> **Master of Wine**
>
> Employees provide an intangible value in the visitor center and tasting room when they exude the contentment of working for your company.

Finally, Your Pricing

Remember lesson number one: determine what your market will bear. Yes, you compete with other wineries, but that's not the only reason behind your pricing policy.

You may subjectively believe that you produce better wine. You know great wine is produced in the vineyard—that's why your grape costs are much greater than the competition. You're confident that your wine should cost more.

The Winepress _____

In the United States, consumers can buy Cabernet Sauvignon wine from as low as $6 per bottle to as high as $600. Quality, image, and service are the deciding factors.

If you've done the marketing and promotion well, then what you believe about your wine is what your customers will come to believe about it. That's called goodwill, and you may be able to add another few percentage points to your price to cover that valuable intangible.

How do you build that intangible value? By cultivating your customers, which is the subject of Chapter 19.

The Least You Need to Know

♦ Research the market and then decide who your consumer customers are.

♦ Know when consumers buy wine and when you have it to sell to them.

♦ Don't assume that a good cash flow means your profits are automatically good, too.

♦ Your wine price reflects your costs as well as the intangible worth of your customer's goodwill.

19

Cultivate Your Customers

In This Chapter

- Count the customers you have
- Get to know your customers inside out
- Communicate with your customers
- Invite your customers home
- Go out and meet and eat with your customers

When you open the doors to your business, you should already know who's going to come visit—that's what the demographic research and business planning you did was all about. But consumers may not be your only customers. A winery may service three customer categories: wholesale, retail, and consumer markets, and each needs to be cultivated.

Cultivating customers means enticing them into your domain, staying close friends with them, and inviting yourself into their lives. In this chapter, you discover what you need to touch on for each category of customer.

The Wholesale Market

Suppose you sell your wine only at retail in your tasting room, but as your business grows, visitors to your tasting room wonder why they can't get your wine at the local shop or restaurant. You can get on the road and sell the wine yourself to shops and restaurants, but what if many of those visitors live in another state, or what if you simply have neither time nor resources to get on the road?

The Three Tiers

In 1933, the 21st amendment to the U.S. Constitution marked the end of the national prohibition of the distribution and sale of alcohol. But it was also the beginning of *localized* prohibition, as the states were given the right to control and regulate sale and distribution according to their desires.

The Winepress

State legislators generally allow localities to decide whether or not they will be "dry" or "wet," or whether or not they'll practice prohibition locally. In dry localities, no wine is distributed, but oddly, some allow wine production in the locality.

Most states developed rules to make it expensive and difficult to distribute and sell wine. Some states opted to take full control of alcohol commerce, leaving little room for private distributors and retailers to do business. These states are called "control states." The remaining states allowed private business to distribute and retail alcohol but under a strictly regulated regime known as the three-tier system. Simply put, the system mandates how wine makes it to consumers: from producer, to distributor/wholesaler, to retailer/restaurant, to consumers.

Wine Distributors

In some states, wineries can apply for a permit that allows them to distribute direct to retailers and restaurants, and even to consumers. Usually, the permits are based on volume produced. Larger wineries generally can't distribute direct to consumers.

Distributors hold a permit to warehouse, solicit sales for, and deliver wine. Distributors are supposedly working for their winery customers, but because of the competitiveness of the wine business, only the truly large corporate wineries are the distributor's bosses. Small wineries must treat distributors as if they are *their* customers.

Before you sign your winery with a distributor, ask yourself what you hope to get from the relationship. Do you want to expand into restaurants? Do you want to open a retail market? Do you want to grow your sales through distribution over a particular length of time? If you don't know what you want, the distributor certainly won't be able to figure it out for you.

Take a close look at the distributor's portfolio. Is it top heavy with conglomerate wine companies or with exclusive, smaller producers? Are the wines in or out of the pricing class of your wines? Is the book filled with drastic discounting? Not all distributors are for all wineries. You need the right fit for yours.

Sour Grapes

Depending on the state you're in, you may have a wide choice of distributors from which to choose; you may have a limited choice; or, in a control state, you may have to use the one you're *told* to use: the state.

Solicitors

Here's how distribution works: you produce the wine, you sell a portion or all of your wine to the distributor, and the distributor lists your wine in its portfolio and sends solicitors out to sell your wine to restaurants and retailers.

Why should a solicitor sell your wine over someone else's?

The answer to that question is like the proverb about the squeaky wheel that gets the oil. If the only time you make contact with your distributor is to send a shipment of wine and then make a phone call two months later seeking payment for it, you probably won't get much out of the relationship. After you settle on a distributor, you need to work with the staff that is, as they say in the business, "on the street."

Distributor solicitors may or may not hold extensive wine and wine sales knowledge, but they do understand when the producer of a product is on their side. Let's say you want the distributor to get your wine only into restaurants, and for that you allocate 500 cases of wine and hope to see all of them in restaurants within six weeks. That's a tall order from a winery that has no restaurant market yet.

The first thing the distributor staff will want to know is what you're going to do to help them sell the wine. Here are some things you can do:

◆ Give them enough samples so they can taste your wine with restaurant buyers.

◆ Advertise your wines in the market.

◆ Set up a series of wine dinners with restaurants in the market.

◆ Organize an incentive contest for the solicitors; the one who sells the most wins something.

To introduce your program to the distributor, you must go to one of the normally scheduled weekly meetings distributors hold with staff and make a presentation. Better still: offer to host their meeting at your winery. There's nothing more powerful than personal contact to motivate a sales team—that and a chance to win a trip to Bermuda!

Wine Exporters

Generally, you have to operate a large winery to make it in the export business, but there's always room for a well-placed marketing project to get a certain number of cases overseas. If it's worth your effort to export a little wine, you'll need to hook up with a licensed exporter/broker.

The Winepress _____

Dealing with a wine exporter is much like dealing with a distributor solicitor, except that the exporter already has contacts lined up. You fire up the exporter's interest, and he or she does the rest.

In your search for an exporter, first decide which country interests you. Most exporters specialize in one or a small number of countries, and some countries are more open to wine from the United States than others. For instance, Denmark is an extremely good market for wine the world over, in part because it produces so little of its own. On the other hand, you'd probably have a hard time selling your American wine in Italy.

The Retail Market

Whether you sell wine to the retail market yourself or do it through your distributor, wine bars, restaurants, and wine shops are also customers, and they need your attention.

Wine Bars

Wine bars can be among your best sales representatives. Their customers frequent the wine bar mainly to try out new wines. The bar generally cycles products, pouring a few wines by the glass for a few days or a week straight before moving on to other products.

Because the idea behind the wine bar is to pour wine by the glass, you have to provide samples for the buyer to select. Be sure you can supply as much wine as the buyer wants, and be sure the wine bar is included in your promotional materials and activities.

Restaurants

You'll do the same for restaurants as you would for wine bars, but you might have to go an extra mile.

Restaurants are high-traffic, high-volume businesses. They operate at quite a pace. With exceptions, turning over tables is a restaurant's bread and butter. If the diners don't know which wine they want, the ones they hear about will often be the ones that have the momentum in the marketplace and at each particular restaurant. Your wine should be among them.

Work with the restaurant staff. Offer the manager your time to train the staff not only about your wine, but about wine service in general, and about the wine region where your wine is produced. Motivate the restaurant staff the same way you motivate distributor solicitors—hold a contest to reward the waiter who sells more of your wine.

If you've eaten in a restaurant lately, you're sure to have noticed the markup on wine—anywhere from three to four times the retail price. Your wine would benefit from better sales in a restaurant if its price at the table wasn't so high. Work with restaurant management to address the markup on your wines.

> **Sour Grapes**
>
> It takes a dedicated wine buyer and staff to move wine in a restaurant. Other than in high-end restaurants, too often, wine is treated as a passive commodity that's supposed to sell itself.

Wine Retailers

You know those notes on retail wine shelves that tell you about the bottle of wine in that shelf space? These are called *shelf talkers*, and guess who provides them? You provide them! And be sure to do this because they help sell your wine.

In many states, wine retailers are allowed to hold special in-store wine tastings. Be a part of them. All the discounting in the world is unlikely to achieve goodwill between you and the retailer better than when you show your support by providing a person and some wine for the tasting.

The retailer's customers appreciate your effort as well, and just like by-the-glass pours at a wine bar, the in-store wine tasting is a great way to introduce new releases or new products.

> **The Winepress**
>
> State alcohol control boards have rules for and against in-store wine tastings. The ones that are for it also have permit rules.

The Consumer Market

The consumer is where you can earn the most profit on your product sales simply by selling wine to them directly, in your retail outlet: your visitor center tasting room or by mail/Internet order.

Why a Visitor Center Tasting Room?

Surely, the reason to have a tasting room is for customers to sample your product and take some home with them. But is that all?

A tasting room is the face of your winery. On a daily basis, it is how new customers are introduced to your business. You not only want to make a good impression, but you want your tasting room to be memorable and a source of good times.

Treating Tourists Right

Tourists may be the largest group of customers you'll cultivate. Spare no effort. Here are some ideas for making tourists feel more welcome:

◆ Get the best people you can to staff the visitor center, and train them well.

◆ Make your winery tour an engaging, inventive program tourists will remember; most winery tours are alike.

◆ Design an inviting, warm tasting room environment, but don't forget that its intent is to sell wine, not to play host to people for hours.

◆ Don't withhold your top wines. Pour everything that's for sale.

◆ Use glasses, not plastic cups.

◆ Serve snacks that are salt free, sugar free, and without flavorings.

> **Master of Wine**
>
> Popcorn makes a fine tasting room snack, but don't use any salt, butter, or oil because these foods interfere with wine taste. Place a few hot air popcorn machines around the tasting bar. When the popcorn cooks, the sound of the machines creates a festive atmosphere.

In some states, you are allowed to charge a fee for the wines you pour at the tasting room. A small winery located in a heavily trafficked region can find itself pouring quite a volume of wine, and the pours can eat into profits. Plus, a fee reduces the traffic of those people who just want to drink. But when you charge for tastings, make the experience worth the fee.

When you do your job well, your tasting room becomes home for repeat customers. By keeping track of your customers and their buying patterns, you can determine in advance whether repeat customers warrant that you waive their tasting fee. Some wineries give back the tasting fee in the form of a credit on wine purchases. Keeping a mailing or e-mail list also allows you to inform customers about special events.

Special Tasting Room Events

Your chamber of commerce can give you a picture of when tourist traffic peaks in your region. In between the peaks, consider creating your own special tasting room events, geared toward bringing in local traffic and repeat customers. Find a reason to celebrate, and give your customers a reason to celebrate with you. You can also develop special events in conjunction with other wineries.

In addition to special events, open your tasting room in the evening for special dinners that pair your wine with gourmet courses. Organize an art gallery event staged at your tasting room, a charity event, or a regular night of music. Turn your tasting room into a place where local groups can meet.

Special tasting room events are a fine way to cultivate repeat customers. More importantly, they cultivate potential new customers. Still, on overcrowded days, your sales per person might be lower than on quieter days. As the traffic rises and the sales decrease, your staff can become disheartened, and it can reflect how they treat customers. Give them frequent breaks from the crowds.

Mail Order/Internet Sales

The computer age leaves no excuse for businesses not to stay in touch with their customers' buying patterns. It's an especially important tool to track customers from other states. So many people are online nowadays that it would be a monumental oversight on your part to let customers get out of your tasting room without leaving behind their e-mail address at the very least. One particularly good way to get e-mail addresses is to set up a keyboard in your tasting room and let the customers sign directly into a database. Creating a wine club online is all the rage these days.

Sour Grapes _____

In 2005, the Supreme Court ruled that it's unconstitutional to allow in-state wineries direct access to consumers while barring out-of-state wineries. Most states have reacted by opening up direct shipping, but also by making it expensive and with time-consuming reporting rules. Before you ship out of state, check out your state's rules.

Develop a newsletter and send it regularly to your customers, not just whenever you think of it (e-mail is by far the preferred method for sending newsletters). Don't give the writing to an intern or just anyone on staff who is free to do it. It's amazing what a good writer can do to make your business memorable. You'll find ideas to promote your winery in Chapter 20.

Taking Your Show on the Road

The tasting room is the entertainment center of your business, but the entertainment doesn't end there. Sometimes, you should take your show on the road.

Off-Site Tasting Rooms

In some states, wineries are allowed a certain number of off-site tasting rooms and visitor centers they can own and develop anywhere in the state, provided it's a "wet" locale. Generally, you can do everything at an off-site tasting room and visitor center that you can do at your main tasting room, so why not do it?

Your biggest decision concerning the off-site tasting room or visitor center will be whether to build or to rent space—a decision that you'll base on plenty of research into the market both for wine and for real estate.

> **Master of Wine** _____
>
> Before you set up an off-site tasting room and visitor center, do the same kind of demographic research you did to get your business started. This time, you may have much of the information already in your computer files.

Wine Festivals

Many wine regions across the country hold an annual wine festival. This is a great place to sell wine and meet both old and new customers. The best of the festivals make shopping easy for attendees with well-thought-out systems that make use of ticketing and tracking purchases.

The festivals offer many other attractions that include wine education and wine dinners, each of which offers your business an opportunity to reach customers by serving your wine in the program.

Restaurant Dinners

Few opportunities to wow your customers are better than you or your winemaker making a special dinner and wine presentation at a restaurant. The idea is a win-win-win situation: good for the restaurant, good for the customers, and good for your business. But don't go blindly into the night to your nearest restaurant.

Be sure the restaurant manager is interested in your wine dinner. Some will offer only off nights for a wine dinner, so they don't have to give up tables. Others will offer only the poorest locations in the restaurant. These are signs that you may not get good support, or even the best serving staff.

Select a restaurant that lets you work with the chef to establish a special menu to pair with your wines. Get the restaurant to offer your wine both by the glass and by the bottle for at least a week, beginning on the night of the dinner. The increased wine sales will please the manager.

> **Sour Grapes**
>
> Before you create programs to cultivate customers, you need to be crystal-clear about the regulations in your state regarding what you can and cannot do to promote wine consumption.

In Chapter 20, you discover the best ways to get the message out that you exist and want to cultivate your customers.

The Least You Need to Know

- A winery serves three customer groups—wholesale, retail, and consumer—and each needs special cultivating.

- Educating your customers about your wine is one of the most important steps you can take to increase your sales.

- Give your customers incentives to buy wine from you and to be loyal to your products.

- Your winery tasting room is not just a bar, it is also an entertainment and wine retail sales outlet.

- Some of your best opportunities for sales may be to cultivate customers on the road.

Chapter 20

Let People Know You Exist

In This Chapter

♦ Giving customers directions to your door

♦ Using technology as advertising

♦ The lingering value of visuals

♦ Drawing customers to your wine at retail outlets

Let's face it: consumers are fickle—and they're even more so when you're one of thousands of wineries vying for their attention. No matter how loyal customers become, things happen, people change, and people vanish. Your business must actively look for new customers. You must advertise the fact that your winery exists and that consumers can buy your products.

In this chapter, you discover the many ways available to you to capture consumers' attention and stimulate their buying genes.

Print Advertising

Who doesn't like to see their name—or their winery's name—in print? Print advertising is a good place to start to get your name out there.

They may not be read in the numbers that they once were, but local newspapers still have a following. As for the consumer magazine world, one of the healthy segments of it is lifestyle, and that includes food and wine.

Newspapers and Magazines

Unless you're a global conglomerate, or an extremely wealthy entrepreneur who can burn up cash, forget advertising in the big newspapers. First, they're truly expensive, and second, if your wines aren't nationally distributed, you're really wasting money.

On the other hand, local newspapers may be just the right fit. They offer two major benefits: they can attract locals as well as visitors in the area, and they're generally inexpensive.

Like newspapers, magazines need advertising revenue to function. They use readership demographics to lure advertisers, so that's the first thing you need to know when deciding whether or not to place an ad in a magazine. But don't be drawn in by wine consumption demographics only.

The Winepress

In many wine regions, organized groups of wineries join in cooperative advertising campaigns. These can be quite effective at bringing people into a region.

If your winery is located in a touring region, and if you don't have national distribution, an ad in a travel magazine might produce better results than an ad placed in a national magazine dedicated to wine consumers. Still, ads in wine magazines can also pay off, especially if the demographics fit your target market.

Ad space in consumer magazines can be quite expensive and generally aren't reasonable for a start-up winery. For a magazine segment that might prove less expensive and equally valuable, look to the airlines. More and more, airlines are looking at wine as a profit center during flights, and more and more articles about wine appear in their magazines.

Your Print Ad Strategy

Advertising is a passive activity. You place an ad, you hope consumers see it, and you wait for them to flock to your door and more than pay for your ad. An ad has to be really good to produce those results.

Sour Grapes

Many small businesses place ads in local newspapers that offer coupons and special discounts. Before you place such ads, ask yourself if your business needs bargain shoppers and what the bargains might do to the overall image of your winery.

When you start, print ads may not bring you an immediate dollar-for-dollar return on investment. But the general idea is for ads to generate enough sales to pay for themselves.

If you don't have a professional print layout artist/designer on staff, hire one. Newspapers and magazines offer in-house design and layout, but they don't have the image of your company in their heads.

Radio and TV

There was a time, long ago and far away, when a business chose among three or four national or local network affiliates to place an ad over the airwaves. In modern times, it isn't certain who owns which radio station, and television is a field of hundreds.

The rules that apply to print also apply to radio and television ads, but the money involved can be a rude awakening. Your best bet may be to stay local, and after you decide that, your better bet may be to sponsor public television programs. But first obtain the local network's demographics. If your target market is the next generation, public radio and television may not be the place for your ad dollars.

It pays to talk to a local advertising agency about radio and television. Agencies specialize in buying media for specific advertising needs. They probably know more about the demographics than the networks.

Free Money!

It's not exactly free money, but some states provide funds to wineries and winery organizations to use for advertising and promotions. Based on the percentage of matching funds provided by the state, you may be able to reduce your advertising budget considerably.

In most cases, state funds are distributed through the state's agriculture programs, and the money goes either to an industry-wide organization or a bureaucratic office, or both. In some states, the state sets up an office to administer funds and to provide promotion and advertising expertise.

Your Winery Online

The Internet is no longer the future; it is the here-and-now technology. If your business doesn't have an Internet presence, you are losing market share. I'm not talking about your winery's website for promotion and sales here (although I do talk about that in Chapter 21). For now, I'm talking about advertising your winery on other websites.

Master of Wine

As with print ads, don't let the website holder design your ad. When you talk to an Internet designer, don't easily accept the bells-and-whistles approach. Always remember your winery's image.

Two avenues for advertising are open to you online: websites and blogs.

When you're thinking of websites, don't limit yourself to wine-related websites. Look for lifestyle business sites that will present your ad to your target market. One of the good things about advertising on the Internet is that you can surf and select the websites that appeal to you free of charge and in your spare time.

Blogs, short for *web logs*, are a growing Internet phenomenon. What started as individuals making their thoughts known has developed into a place for columnists and others to promote their thoughts but with a major magazine behind them. Like websites, blogs sell ad space. Use the same general selection process you would use for advertising on websites.

The Winepress

Some of the top wine magazines now have websites: *Wine Spectator* (www.winespectator.com/Wine/Home), *Wine Enthusiast* (www.winemag.com/homepage/index.asp), *Food and Wine* (www.foodandwine.com), and *Decanter* (www.decanter.com). Some offer columnists' blogs as well.

The combination website and blog could very well become your least expensive form of advertising, and if you operate a website and can take wine orders, the dollar return may be quicker than it is with conventional advertising.

That's a Good Sign

In Chapter 9, you discovered what to expect from a logo designer. One extremely important use for your logo is on those large stationary advertising devices: road signs.

Road Sign Design

It seems obvious that a road sign should be readable, yet some are impossible to read. An effective sign should have a reasonably large area of *white space*—unused space—to call attention to the information that the space surrounds. The sign must be cleanly designed, in bright colors, and large enough to read as drivers approach it from a few hundred feet away.

Most advertising messages should be as brief and informational as possible. Special consideration goes to a road sign. C'mon, people are traveling at quite a clip when they approach a sign. You can't get away with long, narrative pieces that explain your whole philosophy. You must be brief and to the point.

The important advertising message on a road sign includes the following:

+ *Who you are*   Your company name

+ *What you do*   A brief message such as "Distinctive Wines for Distinctive Tastes"

+ *Where you are*   The road number and town name of your location

+ *How to get there*   Quick, brief directions from the sign's location to you

The Winepress

The size of a road sign depends on the scale of the road, the speed limit on the road, and local zoning ordinance.

Where to Put a Sign

Of course you want a sign in front of your driveway. Other strategic locations for a road sign include the following:

+ On highways as drivers approach your area

+ At highway exits

+ At approaches to your town, village, or city

+ Near shopping districts

+ On the local wine trail or route

You can only put up a road sign where it's allowed, and each locality has its own set of roadside sign rules. You may face sign restrictions in some areas. Check with the local authorities before you pay for a sign.

Sign Material

You want your sign to be around for a while, so talk to a professional sign maker. Express the purpose and duration you have in mind for your sign. Some materials are better than others in certain climates, and some painting methods are more durable than others. Sandblasted signs may be a great alternative.

Your Label Is Your Ambassador

Your wine label is far and above the best ambassador you've got, and one of your best advertising devices. Consumers often remember labels before they remember wine producer names.

Label Design

In Chapter 9, I talked about the difference between a fine artist and a commercial artist. Label design is commercial art—its job is to draw the attention of your target market.

The Winepress

Animals sell wine. According to Nielsen's Beverage Alcohol Team, "The sales generated by new brands featuring a critter outperform other new table wines by more than two to one ...." (www.nielsen.com)

Just like a road sign, a wine label needs to make good use of blank space so it underlines the information it surrounds. Colors and spacing are key elements. (Raised gold lettering on a black background is a bad idea.) A label should sport a clean, readable type style and font.

Also, like a road sign, a wine label needs to be readable from a distance, at least from a few feet away in the aisle of a wine shop. But unlike a road sign, a wine label needs to direct the consumer's eye to it amidst an array of dozens of competitive labels that surround it.

TTB Regulations

Many label designers wrestle with integrating a beautiful company logo and image with the U.S. Treasury Department Tax and Trade Bureau (TTB)–regulated information. Designers with wine label experience have the edge over others.

Before you start your label design, read the federal regulations. You can't say certain things on a wine label, and you must say certain other things. The stuff you must say, you have to say in a certain type font and at a certain point size. Plus, you must say them in a certain spot on the label and in a certain order.

Government label regulations are becoming more stringent. Soon, designing a wine label for its informational as well as its advertising value will take on new importance, as nutritional and ingredient lists will take up more space on wine labels.

> **Sour Grapes** _____
>
> You can't use the word *vibrant* to describe a still table wine, because the TTB says the word could be confused with sparkling wine bubbles. You can't cite health claims or studies on a wine label, or use words like *healthful,* but you must include a health warning (TTB regulations 27 CFR 4).

Label Material and Adhesion

Novice wine producers must have wasted a lot of money on wine labels that curled when damp, tore easily, didn't take colors well, or ran beautiful color drips that obliterated the message. Labels must endure the rough handling of transport to and shelving in stores. They must be able to withstand being submerged in ice buckets and then warmed. They must hold up—and stay on the bottle—when stored in damp cellars.

Talk to other winery owners about label material and glue. Your wine label can't advertise for you if the colors run, the paper curls or disintegrates, or the label vanishes into the bottom of the ice bucket. Labels that act that way also give your winery a cheap image. That's advertising you don't want.

Speaking of advertising, in Chapter 21, you learn the difference between advertising and promotion, and how to capitalize on the latter.

The Least You Need to Know

- After your winery is up and running, it's your job to let others know you exist.

- Letting people know about your business requires a blend of various forms of advertising.

- The Internet may fast become the most important advertising tool for the money.

- If you or your staff can't design websites, signs, or labels, hire professionals who can.

- Your wine label is among the most important advertising tool you have.

21

Keep People Thinking About You

In This Chapter

- ◆ Keeping your company name alive
- ◆ Doing good things
- ◆ Getting the media on your side
- ◆ Working with the competition

Good advertising is good communicating. Still, advertising in the media is a passive function. There's another way to get the message out, and it's proactive: promotion. Promotion is either going out and doing things or having someone else do things in your name—while they say good things about you, too. A good promotion or publicity campaign stays around much longer than an ad in the Sunday newspaper or 30 seconds on the airwaves.

The line between advertising and promotion is thin. Both are intended to increase sales, but promotion also supports your products while it keeps your business name in circulation.

In this chapter, you explore the ways available to you to keep interest alive in your wine region, and in your wine, far into the future.

You Can't Beat a Brochure

In North America, touring wineries has become a regular part of vacationing. In some regions, the wineries are the main tourist attraction. When you're located in a wider wine region, you're part of a family. Just as it sometimes pays to advertise cooperatively, it also pays to print a cooperative brochure, to show that the family is close knit and works together—visitors like that.

There's a difference between placing an ad in a magazine and creating a brochure. The ad allows you a tight space in which to present your case. It can be an expensive couple inches of exposure, so you focus on directly selling a product or products. A brochure is like a little book; it tells your story, and it stays in the consumer's possession for a longer period of time.

A brochure sitting in a rack with dozens of other brochures at a tourist center needs to use space efficiently and effectively so it's eye-catching. That calls for a good design. After a tourist picks up the brochure, good writing with good photography draws them to you. A brochure is less about specific wines and more about promoting a feeling. You should mention your wines, of course, but don't talk wine prices in a brochure—you're generating long-term interest, not immediate sales.

When deciding what style and material to use for your brochure, remember this: it's your image, so don't be cheap about it. At a minimum, go for a two-color brochure. But keep in mind that a four-color, glossy paper stock, with high-quality photographs is sure to impress. And remember that people are or will be on vacation in your region. They look at brochures for ideas and to plan their itinerary. Don't bog them down with too many pages—four foldout panels are enough.

Master of Wine

Your business will benefit from having its own brochure as well as the cooperative one. Design it well, and don't forget the important stuff like location, map, hours, and contact information. Send your brochure to people on your mailing list.

Unlike target advertising, a brochure uses the shotgun method. The unit cost of printing a brochure drops steadily as you increase the number of brochures you have printed, so there's a reason to print a greater number and distribute them widely.

You can distribute your brochure yourself, but why should you? Busy as wineries are during tourist season, you don't need to make a commitment you'll regret later for lack of time. In most tourist regions, you can find an inexpensive and reliable brochure distribution service. A good distribution service should issue periodic reports, and give you advance estimates on the number of brochures it needs to service the market.

"In This Month's Newsletter ..."

Yes, we are in the computer information age, yet there's still that tactile sensation of feeling paper, and there's still that segment of the population who either likes receiving or likes producing printed material. If you are one of them, print and mail a newsletter to your like-minded consumers.

The newsletter is a conversation with customers—keep it simple and, except for the price list and mail-order form that you include, it's not sales oriented. It's a chance for you to talk about what's been going on at your winery and what will be going on soon. Use the newsletter to promote any innovations in your vineyard or winemaking, experiments you may be conducting, or new wine styles you're exploring.

When designing your promotional material like brochures and newsletters, keep the design consistent across all pieces so each piece immediately brings your business to consumers' minds.

Master of Wine

One of the most effective ways to support your products is to establish a wine club. The club gives customers the sense that they're special by offering them early discounts on wines or special bottlings of rare wines. Some wineries sell individual barrels of wine to customers in advance, allowing them to feel they take part in the wine's aging process and bottling.

Your Winery's Website

In Chapter 9, I suggested that you register your business for an Internet domain name. Now you get to put the name to use with a website.

You can get a website going in one of two ways: hire a website designer, or do it yourself. If you aren't good at website design, and no one on your staff is either, don't try to design a site from a cheap template. Your business is too important for it to look like other websites. Plus, your site should also become a place to take wine orders, which is more complicated to build into the design.

Seek a web designer who can also help you get your domain name into the top tier of Internet search engines so when someone types in your name or other key words, your website appears in the top 10 to 25 sites that come up in the search.

Sour Grapes

Some web designers also offer to host your website online. Generally, that costs more money and leaves you with weaker service than if you went with a known web hosting company or even your local phone company if it offers digital subscriber line (DSL) capability.

A good website needs to look smart and be easy to navigate. Your website should include basic information about your business and how consumers can contact it directly. Tell the story of your company's mission, its wines, and its place in the community of wineries in your region.

Invest in a quality online sales software so you can make shopping on your website as easy as possible for your customers. You can find information about software you can use at www.inertiabev.com and www.ewinerysolutions.com.

Because you're selling alcohol, your site needs to include a warning and a consent paragraph, but don't think that's enough to remove liability. If you plan to sell wine online and ship across state lines, you must check the regulations for online buying and selling wine, sales tax collection, and shipping rules in each state.

Your Winery's Blog

If you think of your website as your brochure, a blog is your newsletter. A blog is easier than a website for posting quick notices, and it gives consumers a chance to comment, so you can have online chats about your wine with customers and, more importantly, with would-be customers, too.

The Winepress

You can set up a blog yourself with software your Internet host server might offer or with software you download. Your Internet server may also provide hosting of your blog as well as your website.

A blog can provide you with testimony-type advertising. You don't have to confine the blog to talking about your wine or winery. General wine industry news and happenings is interesting to readers. You can tie your winery into the news.

Once you establish a blog, stay with it. It takes time for blogs to generate traffic. Make regularly scheduled entries so consumers can get into a routine. One way to get people to come to your blog is for someone at your company to visit other blogs and make comments. Also, have your website designer install an area to click on that takes people to your blog.

Wine Competitions

Turn on a television any Sunday or Monday, and you're almost certain to run into sports programming. Americans love competitions.

Although some small wineries don't bother with them, wine competitions are also a fact of American life. The right award in the right competition or the highest rating in a wine critic's periodical has made many wineries profitable. But when you choose to compete, how best to go about it?

Be a Good Sport

The first thing to understand about wine competitions is that their purpose for you is to gain promotion. You or your winemaker cannot take the results of competitions personally. Winning top awards can heighten your reputation, but mouthing off for not winning can hurt your reputation. Besides, the consumer hears only about the winners!

Winning in competitions or receiving high review ratings is cause for some chest pounding. Talk about it in your newsletter and brochure—in print and online—and create shelf talkers for the wine that include its accolades.

You can refer to your winery as "award winning" or "highly rated," because it is true. But be sure you always refer to the correct vintage. Get caught mixing vintages by assigning a high rating or award to the wrong one, and your reputation could suffer.

> **Sour Grapes**
>
> Wine competitions are not science. Enter competitions strictly as an investment in promotion. If you don't do well in a competition after a number of entries, try another competition. Your wines may not fit those judges.

Choose the Best Competition for You

Some wineries cast their lot with dozens of competitions and wine reviewers, figuring that a wide net is bound to catch some fish. That's one tactic, but it can also backfire. Not all wine competitions and not all wine critics are created equal; some may even have a bad reputation.

Follow competitions and reviewers. For example, if you find that most winning wines in a particular competition are sweet and you don't produce a dessert wine, that competition may not be for you. Taste the wines that win awards or high ratings. Compare the style of winning wines to your wine style. Give your wines a fighting chance by entering them in competitions or for reviews where their style may fit well.

Finally, talk to consumers. Find out from them which competitions and which wine reviewers they trust.

Choose Your Best Wine for the Competition

Of course, you should enter a wine competition or submit your wines for review when they're called for. But you should only submit them after they're ready to drink. Only a rare competition or reviewer evaluates and assigns high marks for the potential future of a wine—mostly, they aren't supposed to do it that way.

The Winepress

In a competition, a wine critic evaluates to please his or her palate; a wine judge evaluates the wine on its technical merits.

Some wine competitions demand a minimum production volume; plus, the wines entered should be released to the market by the time of the competition. The general idea behind wine judging is to award wines that are or are about to be on the market. Consumers become annoyed when they can't buy wines that have received high marks. It can hurt rather than help the promotion of your winery.

Wine Tastings

Presenting your wine at special wine tasting events has promotional value, provided you know exactly the nature of the event and you plan for it ahead of time.

There are three common areas to offer wine tastings (I'm sure you can get creative and think of others):

- In-store
- Ballrooms
- Through your distributor

In-Store Tastings

I've talked about in-store tastings as a way to support retail shops. The in-store tastings also give you direct access to consumers, and that's promotion you want.

Another form of promotion connected to in-store tastings is when consumers who taste your wine in one retail shop then ask for it at another retail shop or in a restaurant. They become your personal solicitors!

Ballroom Tastings

By far, the largest and most prevalent wine event is the hotel ballroom tasting. Sponsors of these tastings include wine regions, wine organizations, charity events, and special conventions or festivals for consumers.

After you send in your entry form, don't stop there. Create a small environment for your booth or table that invites tasters to your wines:

- Hand out personal invitations to your winery (with a brochure).

- Pour your best wines or wines for the occasion.

- Answer questions but don't let consumers in the front of the line crowd out other consumers by lingering too long.

- Offer bread or dry crackers.

- Offer a dump bucket for tasters who don't want to finish too much wine.

The promotion value of a large tasting can be powerful, and it can be a small investment to generate future sales.

> **Sour Grapes**
>
> Don't accept just any invitation to pour wine. Check out the group and purpose of the tasting. Pouring wine at what essentially is a large party generally doesn't pay.

Tastings for the Trade

Your distributor may host one or more wine tastings throughout the year to present its portfolio to retailers in various regions. It's a good way to meet the retailers and also to take on-the-spot orders for your wine.

Offer to present an educational program to retailers. Your distributor will appreciate the effort, and it will show in retailer loyalty as the solicitors are sent out to follow up on the orders placed at the tasting.

Charitable Donations

In our personal lives, we give to charity out of a desire to help. A business can give to charity with the same motivation, and building a reputation for such charity is good for promotions. But the sad truth is that a winery is approached almost daily to donate wine for a variety of reasons. You must draw a line.

When you receive requests for donations, don't blindly accept the sentence that promises your product marvelous exposure to the market. If you want to give to a charity, that sentence shouldn't carry much weight.

Find out if participating really is promotional exposure or if the event is just another party to raise money. Not that the latter is a bad charity event, but you might want to send no wine or send wine only and forget about sending a staff member and an elaborate booth setup.

One way to support charity is to offer an auction, but make it more than just wine: auction off a dinner at the winery or some other item that might bring customers to your door.

If you feel that you're too weak to turn down charities in general, don't open your mail. Otherwise, when the donation isn't right for you, simply politely decline to participate. Maybe you'll offer a personal financial donation instead.

Make Friends with the Press

Have you heard that all press is good press? It may be true for Hollywood celebrities, but it isn't true for wine sales. Good press is your best friend.

Stay in touch with members of the press. Send them press releases about your winery, your new wine releases, your latest innovations, your staff changes, and just about anything else that can be printed and will keep your winery name out there.

Add your own ideas to the following:

- Put press members on your regular mailing list so they receive your newsletter and invitations to events you sponsor.
- Invite the press to your winery for special tastings or other events.
- If you're presenting a promotional class at a wine tasting, let the press know.
- Line up some members of the press for a conference call. Send them wine in advance, and on the day of the conference call, have the writers and you open the wine, taste, and discuss. You can also do this online through your blog.

When you woo the press, don't forget that food, travel, and general lifestyle writers are as valuable to you as wine writers, but they often won't take freebies from you so plan accordingly.

If your press release sparks interest, you may receive a request for a press interview. Before you start the interview, practice these five words: *this is off the record*. Any journalist worth anything won't print what he or she agrees is off the record. It's smart to watch what you say in public, but it's just as dangerous to say things in private to someone in the press. Better yet, don't say things you'll regret.

Master of Wine

Make a press release no longer than one page. Get the story down in the first paragraph. In the second paragraph, elaborate a little. In the final part of the press release, include the particulars about your winery and contact information for the press to reach you. Take good photographs and send them with your press releases.

Partnering for Publicity

Earlier in the chapter, I suggested that you join other wineries in a joint brochure. Consumers appreciate knowing that wineries in a tourist region work together to make their visit a better experience. Join the winery association in your region and participate in joint events on the wine "trail." The more you work together, the more goodwill you and your friendly competitors build in the marketplace.

One last thought on publicity before we leave this chapter: should you hire a publicist? A professional publicist has media and celebrity contacts, which is a plus. But publicists cost money. Carefully weigh how your promotional efforts stack up against theirs.

In fact, all promotional efforts cost money. In Chapter 22, you discover how to account for everything—financially.

The Least You Need to Know

◆ Advertising is passive; promotion is proactive.

◆ Presenting your business with other wineries has promotional value.

◆ Submitting your wines in competitions and for review is strictly for promotional reasons.

- Anytime you present your wines to the public, you have a promotional opportunity.

- Keeping the press informed can provide you with free promotion.

Part 6

Making Wine into Success

You've made it nearly to the end of the book, and now it's time for a new beginning. Part 6 takes you through the paces of running the business efficiently. The time to handle the money and the day-to-day operations has arrived. You'll learn what to expect from the government and from your customers, as well as what each expects from you. You'll bolster your company's image and its reputation. When you finish reading the last chapter, you'll be at the threshold of your future.

Chapter 22

It's About the Money

In This Chapter

- ◆ Your accounting system
- ◆ Reporting to the government
- ◆ Marrying point of sale to inventory
- ◆ Keeping tabs on everything
- ◆ Paying the tax man

Counting the coins in your pocket is a tangible way to determine personal wealth. A more accurate way is to add the tangible cash to the tangible assets, subtract the liabilities, and throw in the intangible value. That's called accounting.

At its basics, an accounting system is a picture of money coming in and money going out. But like any picture, there's more than what meets the eye.

In this chapter, you explore the types of accounting systems to choose from, plus look at accounting methods that may work best for your business. You'll also discover the value of an accounting system for required government reports.

Choosing an Accounting System

In the computer age, you don't have to be either a star bookkeeper or an accountant. You can just buy accounting software, go through the "read me" file, and plug in your numbers. (Find software online at www.pcmag.com/products/0,,qn= Accounting+Software,00.asp.)

Still, the software will be much more valuable to you if you understand why it does what it does, because there's more than one way to count your money, your assets, and the taxes you owe to the government. Also, you may want to explore a full system that can handle your accounting, your wine reports to the government, and your inventory control.

Understanding Assets and Liabilities

As soon as you establish your business, you begin to build assets and liabilities. In some cases, the things you buy will be both assets and liabilities: the portion that you pay for is an asset to you; the portion that you owe against it to a lending institution is a liability. Cash is an asset and bills are a liability. Understanding that simple formula gets you to *double-entry bookkeeping*, which is halfway to knowing all about accounting.

def•i•ni•tion

> **Double-entry bookkeeping** simply means everything of value is positive (a credit) and has a corresponding negative (a debit).

A financial accounting of your business is a listing of your asset accounts (credit accounts) against your liability accounts (debit accounts). In the end, if you're left with more assets than liabilities, that's your profit. Because inventory is a tangible asset, it's possible for a company to make a profit and be cash poor at the same time. That's called a paper profit, and it's something to strive against.

Some assets such as equipment and fixtures, for example, lose value over time, and some, like inventory, keep or gain value. An accounting system tracks the assets, and an accountant needs to know when, how, and how much to depreciate or appreciate their value. A winery is inventory- and asset-heavy. You want an accountant to augment your accounting software.

Perfecting Payroll

An important function of an accounting system is to accurately track payroll and all tax deductions.

The payroll is subject to a variety of withholding taxes and rules that, depending on the size of your business, can become a time-consuming headache—and more so because of its frequency. In addition, a payroll tax liability exceeding $2,500 a month must be deposited in a bank tax account.

Many companies hire out their payroll accounting to a payroll company that does all the calculating, withholding, tax deposits, and check cutting. You can locate a payroll company at www.buyerzone.com/personnel/payroll/buyers_guide4.html.

To Accrue: Accounts Receivable and Accounts Payable

A business may need to select whether it will operate on a cash or accrual basis. Cash-basis accounting counts assets after they're sold, as cash, and debts are counted after they're paid. Accrual-basis accounting counts inventory and invoices to others as taxable assets and counts your unpaid bills as liabilities.

A business such as a winery with extensive inventory that maintains client accounts uses the accrual basis of accounting.

For example, you sell wine to a distributor or retailer, and you invoice for it. The name of the customer and the amount of the invoice becomes a receivable. You don't have the inventory any longer, and you don't have payment for it. But you still have an asset, and you've increased its value through your markup. You're also going to buy supplies—bottles, closures, capsules, boxes,

Sour Grapes

It's generally not legal to sell wine on credit to consumers. Wine sold in your tasting room is a cash transaction, whether or not you're on the cash or accrual basis.

and so on. After you establish your credentials, you'll be billed for what you purchase. The bill comes with the name of the seller and the amount due, but of course, it's the reverse of a receivable; it is a payable, a liability.

An invoice is a transfer of asset accounts: the asset inventory becomes the asset receivable, which awaits the asset cash. A bill for supplies creates an inventory asset plus a liability accounts payable. When you pay the bill, you remove the payable liability, reduce your cash asset, and maintain the inventory asset account until you sell the supplies as part of the wine package.

Your accounts payable generally applies to ongoing business accounts. Payroll is a separate payable liability.

If your business is a C corporation (see Chapter 5), you can elect to set up an accounting system on any 12-month fiscal rather than a calendar-year basis.

Unpaid Bills

In some states, farmers are protected from buyers who don't pay their bills. Besides being overall bad business not to pay your bills, you can get into serious trouble if you don't write a check for grape purchase payables. The state has the power to collect the money from you, and it has your wine permit in its control.

If you come to a contractual disagreement with a grape farmer, don't simply withhold payment. Try to resolve the problem. Make a payment while you work it out, or call in the government agency that oversees farm payment issues—usually it's the state's agriculture and markets team.

Which Government Reporting System Is for You?

Before you shop for accounting software, you should think seriously about integrating government reporting functions into your accounting system.

The beauty of the computer age is the ease of file storage and cross-referencing. By integrating the accounting and government reporting functions into one system, all your files are in one place and all your reports are produced as one entity, so you don't have to transfer complicated data from one place to another.

TTB Form 5120.17

It's called the Report of Wine Premises Operations, and you'll get to know it well (go to www.ttb.gov/wine/new_guide.shtml). This is how you report all juice and wine movements in the cellar. You submit the report to the U.S. Treasury Department Tax and Trade Bureau (TTB) monthly, quarterly, or annually, depending on the size of your winery.

The primary reason for the form is to report juice and wine movements for excise tax purposes. During wine production, some volume is lost due to evaporation and settling at the bottom of tanks. The report shows these losses, which are then deducted from the taxes due.

The secondary reason for this report is to maintain a record of blending percentages so the TTB is assured that you are following regulated labeling guidelines that cover what you can and cannot say on a label about your wine.

The "Wine Premises" report you submit must match the excise tax return you file with the federal government on form 5000.24.

The *Wines and Vines Directory/Buyer's Guide* lists a number of companies that provide software for winery processing control. Some provide processing controls plus a business accounting system in one package; some provide separate packages.

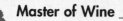

Master of Wine

The TTB encourages wineries to register with its free online filing program called "Pay. Gov." Contact the Pay.Gov office toll free at (877) 882-3277 or by e-mail at pay.gov@ttb.gov.

Whether or not you use computer software to keep track of your wine and excise tax liability, you are required to maintain a clear paper trail of every movement of wine—including accounting for its evaporation while in storage—until it's out of your hands.

State Forms

Like the federal government, states apply excise taxes to wine as it's sold. The forms and their frequency vary from state to state. Some states require accounting for wine volume in liters while the federal government requires wine volume by gallons.

You're unlikely to find one software package perfect for all your state wine reporting systems.

The Point-of-Sale System

Point of sale applies to retail sales in your tasting room. You have two options when you set up a cash register at your point of sale: you can run the cash register exclusive of your overall accounting system, adding it in manually, or you can integrate the cash register into your accounting system.

Good Old Cash Registers

The cash register was a great invention. It was both an adding machine and a control device. Mainly, it told you how much money you started with, how much you took in, and how much you gave back in change. At the end of the sales day, you "cashed out," closing out the cash register and listing your tally of sales for the day. You counted the money and compared it to what the tally told you.

Then one day someone realized the cash register could also keep track of inventory. You can still use a cash register to keep a record of sales and inventory, but now you can do even more with it.

Scanning the Scene

You know that bar code you see on product packaging? That's a computerized system called a uniform product code (UPC). When your cash register scans for a product's UPC bar code, it keeps track of inventory and pricing. (Your label designer will need to have your UPC information to include in the label.)

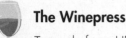

The Winepress

To apply for a UPC for your products, you'll pay a membership and setup fee. You'll receive a unique producer identity code plus instructions on how to add your individual products to your producer code. Get the process started at www.uc-council. org.

The latest cash register scanning systems enable you to create a variety of databases and create printouts for your customers that tell them all about the products they buy. The systems also make it simple to create varying discount levels.

Companies like NCR and Microsoft offer point-of-sale software that operates on a computer with a cash register box. In fact, they're no longer called cash registers—call them *terminals*.

Stay on Top of Your Goals

A point-of-sale terminal can show you on a daily, weekly, monthly, and yearly basis whether or not you are meeting your tasting room sales goals. When you close out the terminal at the end of each day, that day's figures are stored and you can turn them into a number of separate reports.

The terminal easily tracks your point of sale and inventory, but it doesn't track expenses. For that, you'll import the data into your overall accounting system. You should do this on a regularly scheduled basis to keep up with forecasts.

To track general wine market trends, become a member of one or more wine market-tracking firms and compare your wine sales data with the overall market to see how you stack up or differ from trends. This can help you identify where you need to place more promotional effort.

Paying Sales Tax

In the wine business, retailers fear four times a year most—the quarters when sales tax payments are due. That's because too many retailers don't know how to manage their sales taxes. Don't let this happen in your tasting room.

Imagine at the end of each quarter you look at your sales figures and realize that you have an extra 8 percent cash on hand. What a joy that would be! Now imagine how you'd feel if it were the other way round and you were short that 8 percent. When the time comes to pay the state and local government the money due, you don't want to be caught short.

In most states, sales tax payments are due monthly or quarterly, based on dollar amount. With each trip you make to the bank to deposit your sales receipts, separate the sales tax portion, and put that money into a separate bank account to use when sales tax payments are due.

Even when you maintain a separate sales tax account, you can get yourself into trouble by filing the tax return late. States don't take kindly a retailer that runs off with their money. Don't pay the taxes due, and the state soon will knock at your door, with a big padlock in hand. The state might not really send someone to your door, but the penalties and interest the state charges mounts quickly and steeply.

The Winepress

Because sales tax is applied at retail, that makes it the retailer's responsibility to collect sales tax and report and pay it to the state. In some states, retailers are allowed to keep a small percentage of the tax to compensate them for their time.

The same holds for taxes due to the federal government. But the fact that sales taxes are usually in the form of cash seems to get more people into trouble.

And because getting into trouble is something I want to help you avoid, continue on to Chapter 23, where you learn how to keep your customers happy.

The Least You Need to Know

- It's important that you develop a basic understanding of accounting procedures.
- Whether manual or by computer, choose the accounting system that best suits your needs.
- Integrate your accounting, government reporting, and point-of-sale systems.
- Separate sales tax receipts from general sales receipts, and whatever you do, don't be late with tax payments!

Chapter 23

It's About Customer Relations

In This Chapter

- How to keep everyone happy
- What to do when things go wrong
- People are talking about you

The customer is always right. When you get right down to it, that's an absurd notion. No one can always be right. But that isn't at all what the cliché means when it comes to your business.

After you've successfully cultivated customers, keeping them is often the more difficult task. Things happen, and not always happily. How you handle what happens is what determines the duration of your relationship with your customers.

In this chapter, you explore how bad things can happen and how you can make solutions work for both your customers and for your business. In short, you learn how to make the customer feel he or she is, indeed, right.

Taking Care of Your Customers

Every single customer you encounter must be made to feel like your favorite. Remember, you're in a consumer product and entertainment business. Your customer policies are top priority.

Just as you train your employees to take care of problems that pop up in the grape-growing and winemaking process, you must train them to take care of problems that pop up in the wine-selling process. Let's go over your customer base one more time and talk about what can go wrong between them and your business.

First up, your wholesale wine distributors. Consolidation in the wine distribution industry has created fewer distribution outlets for wineries and a bulging portfolio for distributors. Along the way, the wineries with the softest voice—and less sales volume—lose the solicitors' attention. If you happen to be in a state that allows producers to sell direct to retailers, you can decide to send your own sales representative into the market, but a better choice is to set a meeting with the distributor to find out how you can help its solicitors sell your wine. You have an agreement, and each party to an agreement is expected to live up to its responsibilities.

The Winepress

In the 1980s, 2,400 wine wholesale distributors were in operation in the United States. About 250 remain today. One national wine distribution company, Southern Wine and Spirits, operates in 30 states.

After your distributors, look to your retailers and restaurants. Whether or not you service them directly or through a distributor, stock outages, price increases, missed deliveries, and a feeling that their competitors receive more of your attention can turn relationships with retailers sour. It's always your responsibility to provide solutions. First, find out why the problems exist and then talk to retailers and restaurants about the solutions you propose.

Next up, tourists. A bad experience in your tasting room can definitely leave a lasting impression. Tourists can often be demanding and, let's face it, some people can be insensitive. Your staff must be trained to let things roll off their backs, but if a matter seems to be getting out of hand, either you or your visitor center manager needs to take over. Let the tourists know that you want to resolve the issue on their behalf.

Some of the same issues with retailers can spill over to your regular customers. Keeping constant contact with customers may get you accolades, but you'll also wind up fielding complaints. When the accolades come in, be gracious; when the complaints come your way, be proactive. Do what it takes to show the consumer that you want to keep him or her as your customer. Often this can be done by asking a simple question: *What can I do to make this right?*

The worst thing you can do when a customer complains is to hear without listening. Listen and ask, too. Try to get to the bottom of the matter. If you hear similar complaints over and over, you could have identified a problem that exists on your end.

Customer complaints can often make you wonder that after all you've done to service them, how can they be so disloyal over one failure? But remember this: if you don't address the complaint properly, you're being disloyal to your bottom line.

When Bad Things Happen

Things do happen. Here are some of the biggest problems you might face in your winery:

 ◆ Returned wine because of a bad cork or spoiled wine

 ◆ Returned wine because the customer just doesn't like it or thinks it's spoiled

 ◆ Erroneous deliveries

 ◆ Consumer complaints about treatment in the tasting room

 ◆ Drunk consumers

Let's take a closer look at each of these problems.

Returned Wine

In Chapter 15, you read about TCA cork taint. Consumers don't all understand TCA taint, and frighteningly, they blame the wine producer for the wine having gone bad and may not buy the wine again. If you choose to stay with cork over alternative closures, returned wine may be among the most vexing problems your business faces.

Those consumers who do return bottles of TCA-tainted wine should receive an immediate replacement, no questions asked. Retailers and distributors will want replacement wine, too, and of course, they should receive it immediately as well.

The same is true for wine that's spoiled for whatever reason, unless the spoilage has to do with either distributor or retailer mishandling. Then you need to work it out amicably with your wholesaler and retailer customers.

> **Sour Grapes**
>
> Wine industry estimates of loss to cork taint ranges between 3 and 8 percent. Even at the lowest percentage, that's quite a chunk in losses.

What do you do when a customer returns wine that's perfectly fine but insists that it isn't? If it's a rare occasion with that customer, accept the loss and replace the wine with something comparable. If it's a consistent problem with a customer, you may have to set a policy of no returns unless the wine is spoiled. Sometimes a customer must be led to the concept that he or she isn't *always* right!

Erroneous Deliveries

Incorrect item deliveries to your distributor or to retailers and restaurants are easily fixed, although they may cause inconvenience. When they do, you need to be pro-active to keep irritation from growing.

Incorrect deliveries to consumers are more problematic, especially when the consumers are in other states. It's costly to have a shipment returned and re-sent. This is when the question *What can I do to make things right?* becomes important. Once you ask the question, be prepared to accept the answer. Otherwise, have a policy in place for returns and reshipment that makes the customer happy.

Problems in the Tasting Room

Serving wine to tourists day in and day out is probably among the most difficult jobs in the world. Your staff has to be smiling and nice through every situation. They must endure comments and complaints on a regular basis.

Train your staff to be courteous, polite, and efficient. If a particularly irate consumer wants to see the manager, let the consumer see the manager.

You're in the business of serving alcohol, and you obviously can't afford consumers getting drunk in your tasting room. But consumers who have visited other wineries before yours may come into your tasting room on the verge. Serve them one or two tastes that tips them over the edge, and you can have a problem on your hands.

Your staff should be trained to handle not only ways to prevent consumers from becoming intoxicated but also ways to catch those who may already be there or close to it.

> **Sour Grapes**
>
> Whether or not you have dram insurance to cover liability should someone leave your facility inebriated and have an accident, no insurance prevents others from suing you in civil court.

Refusing to serve an adult a few tastes of wine is a delicate matter but one that needs to be enforced. It may be time to bring out all your charm, to make a potentially bad thing into a good thing merely by an offer of some sort of compensation like maybe some grape juice to taste.

In some wine regions, other wineries on the route call their competition to warn that drunken customers were not served at their tasting room and may be on their way to yours. This is a great way for wineries to protect one another.

Fixing Problems

Fixing bad things after they happen demands a great degree of flexibility on your part. For instance, if you have one drunken consumer, but the rest of the group is fine, following a blanket policy to refuse to serve all of them may be your worst option. Finding a way to quiet the problem consumer while serving the others may be the better option.

The same holds for business-to-business problems. For instance, a rigid policy that prevents you from providing replacement wine for whatever reason will work against you.

When a problem remains unsolved, either one or both parties to the problem go away angry and the relationship suffers. The health of your business depends on making as few customers angry as possible. Always seek a resolution to a problem. View all problems as one side of a two-sided story and then try to meet in the middle.

The Winepress

Conflict resolution doesn't necessarily mean you assume you're always wrong and the customer is always right. It means only that you need to find ways to keep customers happy.

Your Reputation Is Your Strength

You establish a reputation as a wine producer by offering quality products. How you handle everyday business decisions affects how you build a long-term reputable image. The second most important reputation builder is good customer relations.

People Talk

Talk may be cheap at times, but it can also be expensive. When angry people talk, they elaborate, expand, and maybe even make up things to get back at a company. Enough spreading around of a story, and you can find your reputation in the dumps.

But it's not all bad news. People also talk when they feel good. They talk about how well they were treated, about how you came through when others often do not, about how important your policy makes them feel. This is the talk you want going around, and when it does get back to you, use it in your promotions.

Reporters Talk

If an angry customer writes a letter to your local newspaper and a reporter calls to get your side of the story, resist the urge to hang up the phone. Refuse to talk, and you'll seem like you're either arrogant or hiding something. The best thing you can do is to cooperate and talk about all the positive things about the issue.

By reasonably and patiently telling your side of the story, you may not help the situation completely, but your reputation may be saved. In the process, you may make a friend in the media.

Your Competition Talks

You share customers with your competition, and it's nice to work together. But don't talk about the competition in front of your customers. If you discover that the competition is talking about you to customers, work it out with the competition, not with the customers.

> **Sour Grapes**
>
> Everything your staff says in front of consumers in your tasting room can travel to the next tasting room. Don't let consumers establish your relationship with the competition.

Unless you're a publicly traded corporation, you have no obligation to spread information around about your business. If you have a financial crisis, a problem with production, or a problem with your distributor, it's best to work it out in private. Spread around only stories that keep your reputation aloft.

Let Your Staff Talk

You've trained your staff in the company policy toward conflict resolution with customers. Now you should let your staff have a say in the results.

Reserve time in your regular meetings to go over the various situations that popped up since your last meeting that required keeping customers happy. Find out why the problems existed. If there are product failures, find out who or what was responsible for them. If there are policy failures, find out what the staff sees as the problem.

If what you discover at the meetings means you have to make changes either between you and suppliers or in your internal policies, do it.

In the next chapter, you get some ideas about handling other day-to-day matters that may not be essential to promoting sales, but certainly are essential to opening your doors each day, ready for business.

The Least You Need to Know

- ◆ Plan for problems by having resolution policies in place.

- ◆ Assume that bad things will happen, and be ready to make things right for your customers.

- ◆ Maintain a good reputation by staying silent when you should and by talking when you should.

- ◆ Monitor your conflict resolution policies and change them quickly if need be.

- ◆ Customers may not always be right, but it helps to make them feel as if they are.

Chapter **24**

It's About the Day-to-Day

In This Chapter

- ◆ Your day-to-day to-do list
- ◆ Securing things
- ◆ Keeping it clean
- ◆ Keeping everything going

Thanksgiving, Christmas, and New Year's may be the only days of the year when your lights are turned off. It's difficult enough keeping any business environment fresh and bright, but throughout the course of the year, your business will host the public and be under government scrutiny. It needs to be as fresh and bright as it is operational.

In this chapter, you discover how best to keep your place of business open, on time, clean, and in working order. Keeping the business looking good and staying functional is good for business and also builds morale.

Turning On the Lights

Even in the middle of a bright and sunny summer day, to do business, the lights must be turned on. I suppose that just like a computer-controlled heating and cooling thermostat, you could install a timer that turns the lights on and off, and maybe you should, but then, what will you do if a power outage takes place in the night and your timer is out of synchronization?

There's no getting around it; every day that your business is open, someone must be held responsible for turning on the lights and opening the doors.

Scheduling

If Type A personalities don't sleep at their place of business, they probably ought to, because odds are they're at their desk before anyone else arrives and after everyone else goes home. Luckily, you aren't one of them. You're smart enough to know that you can't—and shouldn't—do it all. You've created an employee schedule.

The Winepress _____

Obviously, to open and close the business requires keys and alarm system codes. Generally, opening and closing a small business is management's job.

Your vineyard manager and winemaker will schedule harvest, and your winemaker will schedule wine rackings, bottling, and release. But neither can do anything if you haven't scheduled when the lights are turned on and the doors are open, and by whom. Scheduling clearly emphasizes who's responsible for what, and it maps out how and when things are done.

Work with your staff to create a schedule everyone can live with. Try not to make anyone, especially a salaried person, feel that the responsibility to open or close the business is too much extra work. Schedule a separate person to open and another to close each day.

Security

The best kind of security may be a human being patrolling the facility throughout the night. But that can become a major expense.

The next best security is a computerized alarm system with a control function should the alarm be breached. In addition to knowing the code to set and turn off the alarm, those responsible for opening and closing the business should memorize a password. When an alarm is breached, someone at the alarm company immediately phones your business main line. The person who picks up is asked the password; if the answer is incorrect, the alarm monitor notifies both the police and the managers, whose names are on the "to-call" list.

Have Alternative Plans in Place

If all goes well in the morning, the doors are opened, the alarm is turned off, and the lights are turned on. But what if all doesn't go well?

For every manager scheduled to open the business, a backup manager should be on call. If something truly goes wrong, and the manager responsible to open had good intentions but just didn't get there on time (maybe a speeding ticket?), a responsible someone needs to know and then act.

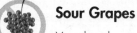

Sour Grapes _____

Your hourly employees are scheduled to arrive for work, and when they get there, you don't want them wasting your money standing around waiting to be let in.

Maintenance Resources

When the person opening the doors walks into a flood or electrical problem, the plumber's or the electrician's phone number should be readily available. Maintain a list of important phone numbers, and keep it near the alarm so the manager doesn't have to take another step after shutting off the alarm to make that phone call.

Repair work can disrupt a busy wine cellar's and visitor center's regular daily schedule. If at all possible, schedule repair work when the business is closed.

Keeping Up Appearances

The first thing your visitors see is the ground around you. That should be the first thing you look at each morning. Be sure the place is inviting.

The Vineyard

A vineyard can look as if it was planned or as if it was left to run wild. The planned one is more inviting.

If you've got vineyard posts that have had their day, replace them. If the weeds have suddenly spurted upward, mow or pull them. These and other problems are not only bad for your crop, they're unsightly and bad for your image. A vineyard should look like a brushed, clean, perfect row of soldiers on a parade ground.

Sour Grapes _____

Rules and regulations require signs and notification whenever you spray chemicals in your vineyard within a certain number of feet from public access like a driveway and parking lot. Know the rules.

The Driveway

Crushed stone appears rustic; it keeps that countrylike image alive. Crushed stone also makes a fine driveway material, as long as you keep up with it.

It's frightening to see what winter can do to the earth. Check out the driveway after each winter. Be sure any earth-heaving that takes place when frozen ground thaws hasn't created craters the crushed driveway stone has sunk into. You may need to grade the driveway and dump some more stone before the new tourist season begins. It's worth it: it will protect your visitor's new Rolls Royce!

You can blacktop the driveway for a cleaner, smoother surface, but you'll still have to check for damage and potholes after each winter.

The Parking Lot

Your parking lot is an extension of your driveway, so take care of the grounds as you would the driveway. The parking area screams out whether you care or you don't care about your visitors.

Separate employee parking from visitor parking: it's better not to have employees take up valuable space, and visitor parking should be as close to the tasting room as possible. And be sure to set up a few parking spaces for the disabled that are easily accessible to the front door. It's the law, covered by the American Disabilities Act. Get familiar with the law online at www.access-board.gov/adaag/html/adaag.htm.

Mark the parking area clearly, and use directional arrows to guide visitors. This is especially necessary to keep visitors and delivery trucks from sharing space.

Many businesses don't consider it, but customers appreciate shaded parking spaces.

Keep a supply of tools around for emergencies like flat tires, dead batteries, etc.

Visitors should leave your visitor center carrying wine. Make it easy for them to get to their cars, and you will have ended their visit on a positive note.

The Building Exterior

It might be obvious, but peeling paint, rotting wood, and graffiti on outside walls will not invite quality customers to your winery. A clean environment in good repair will. Keep your landscaping around the driveway, parking lot, and front of the building tended. Visitors like to take photographs, so give them something to remember.

And although your architect and contractor will have known the rules and the need to accommodate the disabled, remember that a ramp is useless if it's cluttered and wheelchairs can't get by. You could be subject to a fine, too.

Keep the Place Clean

A neat, clean ground around you entices customers. A neat, clean inside of the building creates good working conditions. Not to mention it's the law. After all, you are producing food. You can't be clean enough. Your wine requires that you keep pathogens at bay. Don't allow spills to go untended for a long period of time. When certain microorganisms invade certain porous materials, they dig in. Often, they don't rear their heads until much later, when you least expect an attack on your wine.

If you aren't clean enough in the wine cellar, someone else will let you know: the government inspector. Inspectors sometimes phone ahead, but sometimes they don't. When they do arrive, they look for things like mouse droppings, built-up soot, off odors, and generally poor controls.

And what about your customers? After your sparkling grounds lure them in, it would be a shame to turn them away with a sloppy, greasy visitor center and tasting room. It's also the law that whenever you serve edibles and potables to the public, you must follow the inspector's guidelines.

Generally, you need to wipe clean the tasting room and kitchen area throughout the workday, with special attention given to the floor—sticky stuff on the soles of shoes makes people uncomfortable. At closing time, you give the area a thorough going over.

> **The Winepress**
>
> Local government regulations apply to the heat in a commercial dishwasher and rinsing requirements. A winery restaurant is also subject to local regulations for cleanliness.

Remember that a clean environment is a comfortable environment. In addition to your customers, your staff will appreciate keeping the place clean and free of obstructions. It's also good for your accident rate and worker's compensation insurance costs.

The cellar rat takes care of cleanliness there, and the tasting room staff does it in that location, but a professional cleaning company that sends people in overnight to clean the office area is a good idea, especially when you have an overnight guard to keep watch.

All in Working Order

Getting the lights on, the doors open, and keeping the place and surroundings clean will please your customers, the inspectors, and your staff. But that's not all that will please your staff. Most people want their day at work to run as problem free as possible. Equipment that continually breaks down can ultimately break down employee morale, too. They lose energy, and your business loses money.

Make friends with local repair people. Ask around for recommendations, interview people, and give them small jobs to begin with to test temperament, talent, and reliability. Keep all equipment in top shape with a regular maintenance schedule.

Vineyard Equipment

Having someone on staff to do general maintenance on farm equipment goes a long way. Set up a schedule and checklist for regular maintenance on all farm equipment so you need to contact a repair shop only when necessary. The distance between you and the shop may cost you time and money.

Winemaking Equipment

Pumps and hydraulics, refrigeration units, and computers can fail, even after they appear to be in good working order. A winemaker and cellar rat with the talent and ability to keep things running are invaluable assets. Once again, maintain a maintenance schedule.

When something serious does go wrong, first contact the equipment supplier. Maintain an updated listing and phone number for all your equipment suppliers.

Tasting Room Equipment

Refrigeration and plumbing are the most serious equipment failures in a tasting room. The former can have a backup system nearby, the latter requires work and repair.

The next serious failure is the cash register. At minimum, back it up by having a calculator on hand.

Assign a staff person to be sure everything is in working order before each visitor center shift, and take care of repairs right away. Upsetting the tasting room flow can upset your best profit center.

Master of Wine _____

Take inventory frequently—a few times a week. It's a good check on your point-of-sale activity at the cash register, and it's a good habit for the times when you might need to maintain inventory manually, while awaiting the return of a repaired register.

Office Equipment

Computers, electric lights, and the coffeemaker are your greatest concerns in the office. Luckily, when any one of them fails, it's not much of a threat to the business, although the office workers might gather in mutiny if things aren't fixed soon enough!

I do want to stress that it's important that you always maintain an external backup for all your computer files. If you don't have a backup system in place already, put that at the top of your to-do list.

Keeping the business clean and everything in operational order are day-to-day necessities that rank right up there in importance alongside making wine sales. You can't make sales profitably if you aren't operating properly.

With your day-to-day operations running smoothly, it's time to look to the future. In the next chapter, you find out what you need to do to keep those profits rolling in.

The Least You Need to Know

- ◆ Assign managers the job of opening and closing the business daily, and have a backup system in place.

- ◆ Take security seriously, and determine the best method for your business, whether it's an alarm or a night guard or something else.

- ◆ Keep plumber, electrician, and other maintenance phone numbers in a conspicuous place in case of morning surprises.

- ◆ Cleanliness is tied to success.

- ◆ Keeping equipment in operating order is good for employee morale.

- ◆ Maintain an external computer backup. Put it in place now if you haven't already.

Chapter 5

It's About the Future

In This Chapter

♦ It's *still* all about adjusting

♦ Set yourself up for future success

♦ Your legacy, today and tomorrow

Congratulations! You're running a successful winery. Now you can take a long vacation, right? Before you leave for Bermuda, are your plans set for the future? More important, have you assigned someone to take your place?

Making a business successful is a mix of hard work and fun. After you reach success, it would be a disaster to see it wasted because you went away for a while or, worse, because something grave happened to you.

In this chapter, you discover how to keep the future bright for your business and keep your legacy alive.

Adjusting to Reality

You've planned, forecasted, built, equipped, staffed, and promoted your business. You've adjusted when necessary. Now that you're successful, you can't stop adjusting.

Stay on Top of Market Shifts

The consumer market is never stagnant. It bends and shifts. The products that sell well today could be yesterday's news as fast as yesterday makes the news. Before you cash in your frequent flyer credits for a ticket to the beach, ask yourself these important questions:

Is your product line solid with your customer base? You could save a lot of time and energy if you don't have to keep up with every new market trend. Constantly compare sales of your product line with general market trends.

Can my business shift quickly from one model to another? If the trends hint that you may have to develop new products, but all your wine is produced from your vineyards, the answer to the question is likely no. You'll need an alternative plan.

The Winepress

The 2005 movie *Sideways,* about a man obsessed with Pinot Noir, increased demand for that varietal wine at the expense of Merlot.

Who can I trust to take the reins when necessary? If you hadn't been grooming a successor, you should start right away.

Don't go anywhere for too long until you're comfortable with your answers to these questions.

Be Prepared to Tweak Your Goals

Many wildly successful North American companies have either changed or fallen. Mostly, the fallen failed to properly adjust their goals. You've been tracking your goals as your business grew, so now's the time to evaluate the goals you've met and develop new goals, to take the next step.

This may be a time to bring in one or two outside professionals—at minimum, at least a marketing consultant to help with meeting the evolving consumer market.

Stay Connected

Take a good look at what your neighbors and competitor wineries are doing to keep up with the market. Their ideas may very well apply to your business.

And subscribe to as many trade magazines as you can, attend or send someone to attend industry conferences and seminars. Gather all the information you can about the market.

Be Aware of Government Rule Changes

In the highly regulated wine business, the government can make a decided impact on your goals by changing the rules.

Whenever the U.S. Treasury Department Tax and Trade Bureau (TTB) proposes rules changes, the federal agency allows a period for producer and public comment. Stay on top of government rules changes, and when they affect your customers' access to wine, get the word out to them through your newsletter and blog, and also make comments on proposed changes. TTB listens.

> **Sour Grapes**
>
> When the federal government mandated warning labels on wine in 1985, a large volume of negative stories related to wine and health began to circulate in the press. Some of the stories became strong rumors that have lasted more than 30 years, like the one about sulfites causing wine headaches (see Chapter 15).

Planning for What's Next

Standard cost analysis doesn't change, but your situation surely does. You can raise prices on your products to keep up with inflation, but that tactic has its limits. As you set new goals for future growth, establishing new products may mean establishing new pricing strategies, too.

If your equipment expenses are fully depreciated, your paper profit will rise. Maybe it's time to forecast a new round of depreciation expenses into your plan to buy that newest technological advancement in winemaking equipment and upgrade for the future—is that tractor looking a little old to you?

When you started the business, you didn't have a track record, but you've got one now. Plus, your business is equity. Financing for growth and expansion should be easier, but you still need to draw up and follow the general rules of a business plan, especially financial forecasting.

Start your plan by identifying your future customers; then prove that they're waiting for your new products.

Once you aim to grow your portfolio as well as your sales, you'll likely need to grow your staff. Don't wait until your plans begin to pay off; make hiring additional staff part of your forecasted plan.

What's Your Legacy?

While you're looking into the future, take a glimpse at what you'd like your legacy to be. When you got started building your business, you were asked to answer the question *Who do you want to be?* At the time, you were still a dreamer with mounds of research and work ahead of you.

With the research completed, the hard work done, and dreams met, who are you today? What exactly can your legacy become? If the answer is that you are a successful business, that will be your legacy. If and when you leave the business, do you want to keep the legacy alive? If so, how do you propose to do it?

While you're in the mood for a new round of consultants, consider talking to a consultant about your exit from the business, planned or unplanned.

The Winepress

If your business is a sole proprietorship or an S corporation (see Chapter 5), you need an exit plan. Find a list of consultant firms that can help you at www. bizjournalsdirectory.com/washington/dm/default.aspx?DirectoryId= 125875&source=96.

If you want your business to continue as planned when you retire or die, you need an exit and succession plan in place. The plan also addresses potential tax burdens on your heirs. (Estate taxes that start at 30+ percent can fast grow to 50+ percent.)

Ask yourself these questions:

Do you want your children to take over the business, and if so, which ones? If ownership changes from you to a child, it prevents succeeding business growth from becoming part of your estate.

Do you want your children to take control of the business but want them to hire others to run it? Maybe your children or spouse haven't been close to the business, but you and your spouse want the family to retain control.

Do you want your spouse to have control of the business? Perhaps your spouse has been part of the business and wants to keep it alive.

Do you want your children to buy the business and leave your spouse to handle the capital gains? Your spouse determined that he or she wants out of the business after you're gone and is willing to sell it to the family.

Talk to your children and your spouse about their desires and create a plan. It can prevent a relative from messing up the estate plan after you're gone, and it can keep your legacy alive.

Talk with your employees, too. Be sure they understand that you've chosen a successor, whether it's an employee you're grooming within the company or a family member.

Before you make any changes in ownership, you'll need a business valuation. Who knows? Maybe after you find out what your business is worth, you may change your mind about succession and cash in on your success to make that trip to Bermuda permanent!

Building a winery business to success can and should be fun—it's the equivalent of eating your cake and having it, too. Creating a lasting legacy is the icing on that cake.

Master of Wine

When you decide to retire, and you want to divest yourself of the company, hire a financial planner to guide you through the many options available. After you hand over the reins of the company to your successor, family or no family, don't meddle; it undermines the new leader.

The Least You Need to Know

- ◆ A successful business can't rest. You must actively stay on top of the market and your competition.

- ◆ Stay current with the government, and be prepared for rule changes that affect your customers.

- ◆ Your successful business is equity you can use for financing future expansion.

- ◆ Don't assume you'll work forever or live forever. Build an exit and succession plan.

- ◆ You've made your business grow and taken it into the future—maybe it's time to take a vacation!

Appendix A

Glossary

18th amendment   *See* Volstead Act.

21st amendment   The amendment that repealed the 18th amendment to the U.S. Constitution, Prohibition. In this amendment to the Constitution, Congress gave the states the right to regulate and control alcohol production and sales within state borders.

American Viticultural Area   A federal recognition status applied to a long-standing grape-growing location within an Appellation of Origin. *See also* Appellation of Origin.

antifungal spray   A spray that prevents fungus from spreading.

Appellation of Origin   A federal recognition status applied to a unique climate and topography of a grape-growing region or locale.

bond   An annual fee for insurance as security to federal and local government on the value of wine inventory, should the business default on taxes. Inventory under bond must remain in a specified warehouse, and excise taxes must be paid when the wine is moved from the warehouse.

Bordeaux   A French wine region and viticultural appellation. As in other regions of France (Chablis, Champagne, Burgundy, etc.), wine producers in Bordeaux must adhere to local viticultural and winemaking rules that vary from region to region.

brew   To cook a mixture at a certain temperature to ferment alcohol.

Brix   A measure of sugar in fruit, named after Adolf Brix, who developed the device called a *hydrometer* that measures sugar content.

carbon dioxide (CO_2)   A gas that is a by-product of fermentation. CO_2 leaves bubbles in the wine that dissipate over the life of the wine's storage.

cellar rat   An endearment to identify the person who works in the wine cellar either as assistant winemaker or as general cellar employee.

chief executive officer (CEO)   A person who runs a company. The CEO can also double as the head of a particular department in a company such as the title Winemaker and CEO.

control states   States that operate their own wine retail outlets.

cooperative extension   A university department that works with farmers; it's generally in the horticultural division of the university.

crush   To split grapes open.

cultivate   To develop, propagate, and raise plants for farming.

custom crush   When a company or person provides a range of wine production services for another company or person.

distill   To concentrate a spirit by removing alcohol as steam.

dram insurance   Coverage for businesses that serve alcohol by the glass or sell it by the bottle.

egress   An exit door or doors from your winery and visitor centers.

ferment   The process of producing alcohol from fruits and grains by yeast consuming the sugar and producing alcohol, carbon dioxide, and heat. Fermentation also encourages the development of phenolic aromatics. *See also* phenolic compounds.

fertile crescent   Mesopotamia, in the Near East, where agriculture is believed to have originated.

French-American hybrid   A hybrid species of grapevines created throughout France in the nineteenth century by crossing European vines with Native American vines.

government-mandated warning   Health warnings issued by the federal Tax and Trade Bureau (TTB) seen on wine labels, among other alcohol products.

grapevine clonal selections   Vines developed either from rootstock crossings by purposely selecting and grafting one vine onto the roots of another to create desired characteristics or by selecting and cultivating the results of spontaneous field crossings that create variant vines within a variety that display certain characteristics.

green farming   A means of farming and agriculture that has reduced damage to the environment.

grow tubes   Plastic cylinders placed around new vines that act as individual green-houses.

growing season   The period spanning spring, summer, and fall, from six to eight months, depending on location, when the threat of winter frost is reduced and temperatures generally remain significantly above freezing.

ingress   An entry door or doors into your winery and/or visitor center.

juice pump   A pump used in winemaking that moves semi-solid liquid, clear liquid, and/or wine from tank to tank. It's commonly called a wine pump, but it can be used for other liquids, including water.

legal drink   A drink that only those over the legal age limit to purchase alcohol (usually 21 years old) may purchase.

logo   A company or product identifier that represents a company's name, initials, or an identifiable graphic image that is the exclusive property of the company.

macroclimate   The general climate of a large geographic location like a wine region.

microbiology   The study of microorganisms.

microclimate   The specific spot within your plot of land that almost produces its own special weather.

microorganisms   Friendly and unfriendly microscopic creatures that get into wine.

migrant labor   An itinerant workforce, usually from another country, but not always.

must   The grape solids that result from grapes having been pressed.

must pump   A pump that moves crushed grape solids (must) from crusher to press or fermentation vessel.

Native American grapevines   Vines indigenous to North America.

nursery   Where plants are propagated.

pathogens   Microorganisms that spoil wine.

pH (potential for Hydrogen)   A measure of alkalinity relative to acidity. On the pH scale of 0 to 14, water is neutral at 7. The lower the numbers measured below 7, the more acidic the liquid. Conversely, the higher the numbers measured above 7, the more alkaline the liquid. The generally acceptable pH of finished wine ranges from 2.8 to 5, making wine an acidic environment not conducive to the survival of many microbes.

phenolic compounds   Complex compounds found in grape juice that give off powerful aromas as well as potential health benefits. These compounds are found naturally in grape skins and pulp; their aroma, taste, and health benefits are activated and altered by fermentation and various other winemaking processes.

Phoenicians   The first seafaring culture (5,000 years ago) to make large profits from the wine trade.

phylloxera   A microorganism in the soil that attacks the roots and leaves of grapevines.

plat   The drawing of a proposed or actual winery that accompanies a federal alcohol permit application.

power take-off (PTO)   A rod at the back end of a tractor to which vineyard and other equipment is attached. When the tractor throttle is open, the rod spins and powers the equipment.

pre-bloom   An important period in vine growth when grape flowers get ready to bloom on the vines.

press   A mechanical device that flattens and mashes grapes to make must and/or juice. *See also* must.

quercetin   A compound in grape juice believed to be an antioxidant and anti-inflammatory.

rack   To move wine from one storage vessel into another with a pump. *See also* juice pump.

resveratrol   A compound found mostly in red grape skins believed to be an antioxidant.

revenue   Money derived from wine sales. Also, a word used by the government to describe *taxes*.

Saccharomyces cerevisiae   The yeast family responsible for fermenting wine.

sacramental wine   Any wine used for religious purposes only. Sacramental wine was allowed production during Prohibition as a means to maintain the constitutional separation of church from state.

shelf-talkers   Printed advertising provided by the wine producer or distributor and placed on the retail shelf to tell consumers about the wine.

suckering   Removing low-hanging vine branches that suck energy from the fruit and that may be positioned poorly.

sulfur dioxide (SO$_2$)   Either as a gas or made into powder form, this chemical is used in winemaking as an antioxidant and secondarily as an antimicrobial. SO$_2$ is formed naturally as vegetation decays and during fermentation.

table wine   A term recognized by TTB to identify wine between 7 and 14 percent alcohol by volume. When the wine's alcohol falls between those percentages, the words *table wine* can be used on the label in place of the wine's alcohol content.

tare   The weight of an empty truck before picking up and after dropping off picked grapes.

tasting room bar   The bar where wineries pour their wines for consumers to taste.

Tax and Trade Bureau (TTB)   The department within the U.S. Treasury Department that issues permits to produce wine, collects excise taxes on wine, and regulates wine production right down to labeling and packaging.

tax-paid room   The wine storage area in a winery where bottled wine has been taken out of bond for excise tax purposes. *See also* bond.

tendrils   The part of the vine branch that reaches and clings.

thin   To remove grape clusters from vines to reduce crop size.

Three-Tier System   The government-mandated distribution system for wine from producer to consumer: the wine producer is the first tier, the wine distributor is the second tier, and the wine retailer/restaurant is the third tier in the distribution network.

varietal   Wine named after a grape variety. Examples include Chardonnay, Merlot, Pinot Noir, and Riesling.

viticulture   The act of cultivating grapevines.

Vitis labrusca   A Native American grapevine species.

Vitis labruscana   An American and European field hybrid grapevine species.

Vitis riparia   Another Native American grapevine species.

Vitis rotundifolia   Yet another Native American grapevine species.

Vitis vinifera sativum   A cultivated Old World grapevine species.

Vitis vinifera sylvestris   A wild Old World grapevine species.

Volstead Act   Also called Prohibition, the 18th amendment to the U.S. Constitution prohibited manufacture, distribution, and sale of wine, with exceptions for personal and sacramental use. *See also* sacramental wine.

wine   A naturally fermented beverage produced from grapes.

wine in bulk   A federal term for wine in tanks or barrels. Also called bulk wine.

wine producers   Manufacturers of wine.

wine retailers   Those who sell wine to individual consumers. *See also* Three-Tier System.

wine wholesalers   Distributors of wine to retailers and restaurants. *See also* Three-Tier System.

yeast   A natural organism without which grape sugar cannot be converted into alcohol. *See also Saccharomyces cerevisiae.*

B

Forms and Worksheets

You can't start a winery without filling out forms. Some forms are required by the government; others are for you to use as a worksheet. This appendix includes federal Tax and Trade Bureau (TTB) forms you need to fill out to apply for a permit to produce and sell wine, plus reference to a TTB periodical that helps you avoid selecting improper brand names for your wine labels.

In addition, the business plan worksheet, plus the charts and numbers that follow the worksheet, are based on the Cornell University Small Winery Study, 2005/6, by Prof. Gerald White and Mark Pisoni.

TTB Winery Permit Application

While you're creating your business plan, you should also get your basic wine permit application form 5100.24 in to the Tax and Trade Bureau (www.ttb.gov/forms).

OMB NO. 1513-0018 (07/31/2008)

DEPARTMENT OF THE TREASURY
ALCOHOL AND TOBACCO TAX AND TRADE BUREAU (TTB)
APPLICATION FOR BASIC PERMIT UNDER THE FEDERAL ALCOHOL ADMINISTRATION ACT

1. FULL NAME AND PREMISES ADDRESS

3. EMPLOYER IDENTIFICATION NUMBER (EIN)
(Social Security number is not acceptable)

4. OPERATING NAME (DBA), if any

TELEPHONE NUMBER (   )
State in which organized for Corporations and Limited Liability Companies (LLC):

2. MAILING ADDRESS *(If different from premises address)*

5. LABELING TRADE NAME(S), if any

6. BUSINESS(ES) TO BE CONDUCTED AT PREMISES ADDRESS *(Check applicable boxes)*

a. ☐ DISTILLED SPIRITS PLANT *(BEVERAGE)*
　☐ DISTILLING
　☐ WAREHOUSING AND BOTTLING DISTILLED SPIRITS
　☐ PROCESSING *(RECTIFYING)* DISTILLED SPIRITS AND WINE

c. ☐ IMPORTING INTO THE UNITED STATES
　☐ DISTILLED SPIRITS
　☐ WINE
　☐ MALT BEVERAGES

b. ☐ BONDED WINE PREMISES
　☐ PRODUCING AND BLENDING WINE
　☐ BLENDING WINE

d. ☐ PURCHASING FOR RESALE AT WHOLESALE
　☐ DISTILLED SPIRITS
　☐ WINE
　☐ MALT BEVERAGES

or while so engaged, sell, offer, or deliver for sale, contract to sell, or ship in interstate or foreign commerce the alcoholic beverages so distilled produced, rectified, blended or bottled, warehoused and bottled, imported or purchased for resale at wholesale.

7. REASON FOR THE APPLICATION

a. ☐ NEW BUSINESS
　Anticipated start date _____

c. ☐ CHANGE IN OWNERSHIP
　Date of Change _____
　Name, address and permit number(s) of predecessor

b. CHANGE IN CONTROL *(Actual or legal)*
☐ Submit Basic Permit(s) with this application.
　Date of Change _____

8. OWNER INFORMATION *(List sole owner, all general parties, LLC members/managers, corporate officers and directors, and shareholders with more than 10% voting stock. Each listed person must also furnish the information in Item 9.)*

NAME	TITLE	% VOTING/STOCK/INTEREST *(If applicable)*	INVESTMENT IN BUSINESS *(Item 6)*	SOURCE OF FUNDS INVESTED *(savings, loans, gift or specify other)*

IF APPLICANT IS ACTUALLY OR LEGALLY CONTROLLED BY PERSONS OR BUSINESSES NOT IDENTIFIED ABOVE, PROVIDE ON A SEPARATE SHEET INFORMATION *(as specified for Item 9)* FOR EACH PERSON OR BUSINESS AND STATE THE EXTENT AND MANNER OF THE CONTROL. BUSINESSES SHOULD INCLUDE THEIR EIN.

9. COMPLETE FOR EACH PERSON LISTED IN ITEM 8.

a. FULL GIVEN NAME	b. DATE AND PLACE OF BIRTH	c. SOCIAL SECURITY OR EMPLOYER IDENTIFICATION NUMBER	d. ARE YOU A U.S. CITIZEN? ☐ YES ☐ NO

e. ☐ MALE ☐ FEMALE　　f. OTHER NAMES USED *(Maiden name, nicknames, etc.)*

g. RESIDENCE(S) OVER THE LAST FIVE YEARS

TTB F 5100.24 (5/2005)

a. FULL GIVEN NAME	b. DATE AND PLACE OF BIRTH	c. SOCIAL SECURITY OR EMPLOYER IDENTIFICATION NUMBER	d. ARE YOU A U.S. CITIZEN? ☐ YES ☐ NO

e. ☐ MALE ☐ FEMALE	f. OTHER NAMES USED *(Maiden name, nicknames, etc.)*

g. RESIDENCE(S) OVER THE LAST FIVE YEARS

a. FULL GIVEN NAME	b. DATE AND PLACE OF BIRTH	c. SOCIAL SECURITY OR EMPLOYER IDENTIFICATION NUMBER	d. ARE YOU A U.S. CITIZEN? ☐ YES ☐ NO

e. ☐ MALE ☐ FEMALE	f. OTHER NAMES USED *(Maiden name, nicknames, etc.)*

g. RESIDENCE(S) OVER THE LAST FIVE YEARS

a. FULL GIVEN NAME	b. DATE AND PLACE OF BIRTH	c. SOCIAL SECURITY OR EMPLOYER IDENTIFICATION NUMBER	d. ARE YOU A U.S. CITIZEN? ☐ YES ☐ NO

e. ☐ MALE ☐ FEMALE	f. OTHER NAMES USED *(Maiden name, nicknames, etc.)*

g. RESIDENCE(S) OVER THE LAST FIVE YEARS

a. FULL GIVEN NAME	b. DATE AND PLACE OF BIRTH	c. SOCIAL SECURITY OR EMPLOYER IDENTIFICATION NUMBER	d. ARE YOU A U.S. CITIZEN? ☐ YES ☐ NO

e. ☐ MALE ☐ FEMALE	f. OTHER NAMES USED *(Maiden name, nicknames, etc.)*

g. RESIDENCE(S) OVER THE LAST FIVE YEARS

10. HAS THE APPLICANT OR ANY PERSON LISTED FOR ITEMS 8 OR 9 EVER BEEN DENIED A PERMIT, LICENSE OR OTHER AUTHORIZA- TION TO ENGAGE IN ANY BUSINESS TO MANUFACTURE, DISTRIBUTE, IMPORT, SELL OR USE ALCOHOL PRODUCTS *(beverage or nonbeverage)* BY ANY GOVERNMENT AGENCY *(Federal, State, local or foreign)* OR HAD SUCH PERMIT, LICENSE OR OTHER AUTHORI- ZATION REVOKED, SUSPENDED OR OTHERWISE TERMINATED?

☐ YES. State details of each event on a separate sheet. ☐ NO

11. HAS THE APPLICANT OR ANY PERSON LISTED FOR ITEMS 8 OR 9 EVER BEEN ARRESTED FOR, CHARGED WITH, OR CONVICTED OF ANY CRIME UNDER FEDERAL, STATE OR FOREIGN LAWS other than traffic violations or convictions that are not felonies under Federal or State law.

☐ YES. State details of each event on a separate sheet. ☐ NO

TTB MAY REQUIRE additional information to process this application. If you are applying for a basic permit to operate a distilled spirits plant or bonded wine premises, you must also file additional forms and information required under the Internal Revenue Code. **OPERATION WITHOUT A PERMIT.** Criminal and administrative actions may be taken against persons engaged in a business listed in Item 6 of this form if it is not conducted pursuant to an FAA Act basic permit.

APPLICANT'S AFFIRMATION. Under penalties of perjury, I declare that I have examined this application, including accompanying statements, and to the best of my knowledge and belief, it is true, correct and complete. The applicant will immediately notify the TTB official with whom this applica- tion is filed of any change in ownership, management, or control of the applicant *(in the case of a corporation, any change in the officers, directors, or persons holding 10 percent or more of the corporate stock)*. The business for which this application is made does not violate the law of the State in which the business will be conducted. In addition, if this application is approved, the applicant will conduct operations within a reasonable period of time and maintain such operations in conformity with Federal law.

12. APPLICANT'S SIGNATURE *(Sole owner, partner, corporate officer, LLC member or manager, or if designated agent, submit TTB F 5000.8)*	13. TITLE OF PERSON SIGNING	14. DATE

15. E-MAIL (INTERNET) ADDRESS *(optional)*:

TTB F 5100.24 (5/2005)

INSTRUCTIONS

1. GENERAL. You must file this application if you want a permit under the Federal Alcohol Administration Act (FAA Act) to engage in the business of:

· Producing or processing distilled spirits or wine includes for nonindustrial use.
· Importing into the United States, or wholesaling, alcoholic beverages.

Nonindustrial use of distilled spirits or wines includes all beverage purposes or uses in preparing foods or drinks. Wholesaling under the FAA Act means purchasing alcoholic beverages for resale at wholesale. The FAA Act defines alcoholic beverages as distilled spirits, wine, or malt beverages including any fermented cereal beverages which have an alcohol content of not less than 1/2 percent.

2. COMPLETING AND FILING THIS APPLICATION.

· Please type or print and complete all items.
· Write "not applicable" in any item requesting information that does not apply to your business.
· Items 8 through 11: If this information is on file with TTB, state "On file under *(name and TTB permit or registry number or type of pending application)."*
· If you need additional room, use a separate sheet.
· If your producing or processing operations will be in Puerto Rico, contact the Director, Puerto Rico Operations, for additional requirements.
· Send this form in duplicate to the appropriate TTB (Alcohol and Tobacco Tax and Trade Bureau) office.

Location of Business	Send to: TTB
PUERTO RICO	Ste 310 Torre Chardon, 350 787-766-5584 Carlos Chardon Ave, San Juan, PR 00918 -21244
ALL OTHER STATES	550 Main Street, Suite 8002 1-877-882-3277 Cincinnati, OH 45202

3. LABEL APPROVALS FOR BOTTLED ALCOHOLIC BEVERAGES. Bottlers,packagers, and importers should have TTB approved label certificates (TTB F 5100.31). A label approval is required to sell, ship or deliver for sale or shipment, or to otherwise introduce in interstate or foreign commerce, alcoholic beverages. Also, a label approval allows importers to release specific imported alcoholic beverages from Customs' custody. For label approvals contact TTB, Washington, DC 20220, (202-927-8140). TTB does not approve certificates until you have the appropriate FAA Act basic permit. You can submit draft labels *(for example, mockups)* to TTB for review before printing the labels. Trade name approval on your FAA Act basic permit does not constitute approval as a brand name for labeling purposes.

4. SPECIAL TAX. If you operate a distilled spirits plant or bonded wine premises or deal in beer, wine or distilled spirits, file TTB F 5630.5, Special Tax Registration and Return, and pay an annual tax. File TTB F 5630.5 and pay this tax when you start selling, or offer for sale, alcoholic beverages. You do not file this form or pay special tax when your business only involves the importation or sale of fermented cereal beverages which have an alcoholic content of less than 1/2 percent or where your business is only in Puerto Rico.

5. EMPLOYER IDENTIFICATION NUMBER. You need to have this number for your business even if you do not have any employees. To obtain an EIN, file Form SS-4 with the Internal Revenue Service.

PRIVACY ACT INFORMATION

1. AUTHORITY. Solicitation of information on TTB F 5100.24 is made pursuant to 27 U.S.C. Section 204(c). Disclosure of this information by the applicant is mandatory if the applicant wishes to obtain a basic permit under the Federal Alcohol Administration Act.

2. PURPOSES. To identify the applicant; the location of the premises; and to determine the eligibility of the applicant to obtain a basic permit.

3. ROUTINE USES. The information will be used by TTB to make deteminations set forth in paragraph 2 above. Where such disclosure is not prohibited, TTB officers may disclose this information to other Federal, State foreign and local law enforcement and regulatory agency personnel to verify information on the application and for enforcement of the laws of such other agency. The information may be disclosed to the Justice Department if the application appears to be false or misleading. TTB officers may disclose the information to individuals to verify information on the application where such disclosure is not prohibited.

4. EFFECTS OF NOT SUPPLYING INFORMATION REQUESTED. TTB may delay or deny the issuance of the FAA Act basic permit where information is not complete or missing.

5. DISCLOSURE OF EMPLOYER IDENTIFICATION NUMBER AND SOCIAL SECURITY NUMBER. You do not have to supply these numbers. These numbers are used to identify an individual or business. If you do not supply the numbers, your application may be delayed.

PAPERWORK REDUCTION ACT NOTICE

This request is in accordance with the Paperwork Reduction of 1995. The information collection is used to determine the eligibility of the applicant to engage in certain operations, to determine the location and extent of operations, and to determine whether the operations will be in conformity with Federal laws and regulations. The information requested is required to obtain or retain a benefit and is mandatory by statute (27 U.S.C. 203 and 204 (c)).

The estimated average burden associated with this collection of information is 1 hour and 45 minutes per respondent depending on individual circumstances. Comments concerning the accuracy of this burden estimate and suggestions for reducing this burden should be addressed to Reports Management Officer, Regulations and Rulings Division, Alcohol and Tobacco Tax and Trade Bureau, Washington, DC 20220.

An agency may not conduct or sponsor , and a person is not required to respond to, a collection of information unless it displays a currently valid OMB control number.

Business Plan Worksheets

To create a solid business plan, you need to be methodical and organized. The steps to a business plan are no secret, but if you don't create a worksheet as your guide, it's easy to miss a step here and there. The business plan worksheet is also a way for you to verbalize (aloud and on paper) so you get a real feel and sense of what it means to start and run a wine business.

Your Executive Summary

The business:

_____

_____

Business strategy and competitive advantage:

_____

_____

Key operation issues:

_____

_____

Management team:

_____

_____

Market opportunity:

_____

_____

Key markets and distribution issues:

_____

_____

Key risk factors:

_____

_____

Profitability:

_____

_____

Financial request:

_____

_____

Your Business Description

Your mission statement:

_____

_____

Your business description:

History:

_____

_____

Current position:

_____

_____

Future plans:

    Goal #1: _____

Objectives	*When?*	*Who?*
1. _____	_____	_____
2. _____	_____	_____
3. _____	_____	_____
4. _____	_____	_____

Ownership structure:

_____

_____

Your Plan of Operations

Grape source:

Varietal	*Tons Needed*	*Tons Grown*	*Tons Purchased*	*Location of Purchased Grapes*
_____	_____	_____	_____	_____
_____	_____	_____	_____	_____
_____	_____	_____	_____	_____

Winery facilities:

_____

_____

Additional equipment needs:

_____

_____

Winemaking process:

_____

_____

Wine storage and shipment:

_____

_____

Sales outlets:

_____

_____

Employee needs:

_____

_____

Name in Bold, *General Manager*

_____

_____

Name in Bold, *Winemaker*

_____

_____

Name in Bold, *Sales/Tasting Room Manager*

_____

_____

Name in Bold, *Vineyard Manager*

_____

_____

Your Industry Analysis

Wine consumption trends:

_____

_____

Product mix trends:

_____

_____

Growth trends:

_____

_____

Economic trends:

_____

_____

Demographic changes:

_____

_____

lso.

Social/cultural changes:

_____

_____

Environmental regulations:

_____

_____

Legal regulations:

_____

_____

Taxation issues:

_____

_____

Permits/licenses:

_____

_____

Your Competitor Analysis

Names of competitors:

_____

_____

General characteristics of competitors:

_____

_____

Competitors' marketing strategy:

_____

_____

Competitors' financial position:

_____

_____

Competitors' strengths:

_____

_____

Competitors' weaknesses:

_____

_____

Your fit in the marketplace:

_____

_____

Your sustainable competitive advantage:

_____

_____

Your Marketing Plan

Target market:

_____

_____

Product:

_____

_____

Price:

_____

_____

Promotion:

_____

_____

Place or distribution:

_____

_____

Marketing budget:

_____

_____

Your Balance Sheet

Name of business: _____

Date: _____

Assets		Liabilities and Net Worth	
Current assets:		Current liabilities:	
Cash, checking, and savings	_____	Accounts payable	_____
Stocks and bonds	_____	Wages payable	_____
Accounts receivable	_____	Operating debt	_____
Prepaid expenses	_____	Short-term debt	_____
Production supplies	_____	Accrued interest	_____
Packaging supplies	_____	Other: _____	_____
Bottled wine inventory	_____	Other: _____	_____
Bulk wine inventory	_____		
Other: _____	_____		
Other: _____	_____		
Total current assets	_____	Total current liabilities	_____
Noncurrent assets:		Noncurrent liabilities:	
		Notes payable: real estate	_____
Machinery and equipment—owned	_____	Notes payable: machinery and equipment	_____

continues

continued

Assets		Liabilities and Net Worth	
Machinery and equipment—leased	_____	Leases payable: machinery and equipment	_____
Cooperage	_____	Other: _____	_____
Land	_____	Other: _____	_____
Buildings	_____		
Vineyards	_____		
Other: _____	_____		
Other: _____	_____		
Total long-term assets	_____	Total long-term liabilities	_____
		Total liabilities	_____
		Owner's equity (net worth)	_____
Total assets	_____	Total liabilities and owner's equity	_____

Your Income Statement

Name of business: _____

Date: _____

Revenues:

Wine sales—retail	_____
Wine sales—wholesale	_____
Wine sales—distributor	_____
Tasting room merchandise sales	_____
Grape sales	_____
Other: _____	_____
Other: _____	_____
Total revenues	_____

Expenses:

    Grapes   _____

    Labor   _____

    Packaging materials   _____

    Marketing   _____

    Utilities   _____

    Professional fees   _____

    Supplies   _____

    Gasoline, fuel, and oil   _____

    Insurance (other than health)   _____

    Interest expense   _____

    Taxes   _____

    Rental or lease expenses   _____

    Repairs and maintenance   _____

    Depreciation   _____

    Miscellaneous   _____

    Other: _____   _____

    Other: _____   _____

    Total Expenses   _____

    Gain or loss on sale of assets   _____

    Net income before taxes   _____

    Income tax expense   _____

    Net income after taxes   _____

Your Statement of Cash Flows

Name of business: _____

Date: _____

Cash flows from operating activities:

Cash winery receipts	(+)_____
Cash winery expenses	(−)_____
Income tax payments	(−)_____
Net cash operating income	_____

Cash flows from investing activities:

Cash received from sale of capital assets:

Sale of equipment and machinery	(+)_____
Sale of real estate	(+)_____
Sale of barrels	(+)_____
Sale of fermentation tanks	(+)_____
Total cash received from sale of capital assets	(+)_____

Cash paid to purchase capital assets:

Cash paid to purchase equipment and machinery	(−)_____
Cash paid to purchase real estate	(−)_____
Cash paid to purchase barrels	(−)_____
Cash paid to purchase fermentation tanks	(−)_____
Total cash paid to purchase capital assets	(−)_____

Net cash provided by investing activities	_____

Cash flows from financing activities:

    Cash received from operating loans   (+)_____

    Cash received from term loans   (+)_____

    Cash inflows from financing   (+)_____

    Cash repayment on operating loans   (−)_____

    Principle payments on term loans   (−)_____

    Principle payments on lease obligations   (−)_____

    Cash outflows from financing   (−)_____

    Net cash flows from financing activities   _____

Cash flows from equity activities:

    Cash received from equity investors   (+)_____

    Cash disbursements to equity investors   (−)_____

    Net cash flows from equity activities   _____

Cash flow from reserves:

    Beginning cash, checking, and savings account balance   (+)_____

    Ending cash, checking, and savings account balance   (−)_____

    Net provided from reserves   _____

    Imbalance (Error)   _____

Your Monthly Cash Flow Estimates

Name of business: _____

Date: _____

	January	February	March	April	May	June	July	August	September	October	November	December	Total
Cash in flows:													
Wine sales— retail													
Wine sales— wholesale													
Wine sales— distributor													
Gift shop/mer-chandise sales													
Cash received from new loans													
Cash received from sale of assets													
Cash received from investors													
Total revenues													
Cash out flows:													
Grapes													
Labor													
Packaging													
Marketing													
Utilities													

	January	February	March	April	May	June	July	August	September	October	November	December	Total
Professional fees													
Supplies													
Gasoline, fuel, oil													
Insurance													
Taxes													
Repairs and maintenance													
Depreciation													
Miscellaneous													
Rent/leases													
Term loans													
Operating loans													
Lease payments													
Total expenses													
Capital purchases:													
Barrels													
Stainless-steel tanks													
Equipment													
Other capital purchases													
Income taxes													
Net cash flow													

Your Financial Assumptions

_____

_____

Financial assumptions *(examples):*

    Interest rate on borrowed capital   _____%

    Expected rate of inflation   _____%

    Cost of capital in financial analysis   _____%

    Tax rate (state and federal)   _____%

Wine retail bottle prices:

Variety	*1st label price ($ per bottle)*	*2nd label price ($ per bottle)*
_____	_____	_____
_____	_____	_____
_____	_____	_____
_____	_____	_____

Grape prices:

Variety	*$ per ton*
_____	_____
_____	_____
_____	_____
_____	_____

Production and distribution:

	Year 1	*Year 2*	*Year 3*	*Year 4*	*Year 5+*
Annual production volume (cases)	____	____	____	____	____
Annual sales volume (cases)	____	____	____	____	____
Percentage of sales directly to consumers	____	____	____	____	____

Percentage of sales
directly to retailers   ____ ____ ____ ____ ____

Percentage of sales
to distributors   ____ ____ ____ ____ ____

Percentage of wine
not sold   ____ ____ ____ ____ ____

Premium Winery Start-Up Costs

Description of Expenses	Cost
Equipment:	
Receiving equipment	_____
Fermentation/storage equipment	_____
Cooperage	_____
Cellar equipment	_____
Lab equipment	_____
Refrigeration	_____
Remodeling costs	_____
Installation fees	_____
Fees, licenses, permits, certifications	_____
Special, one-time-only legal/accounting/consulting fees	_____
Pre-production labor/training expenses	_____
Beginning inventory	_____
Office supplies (letterhead, forms, paper)	_____
Computers, furniture, fax, phone	_____
Marketing expenses	_____
Land	_____
Buildings	_____
Vehicles	_____
Other: _____	_____
Other: _____	_____
Other: _____	_____
Total start-up expenses	_____

Break-Even Analysis

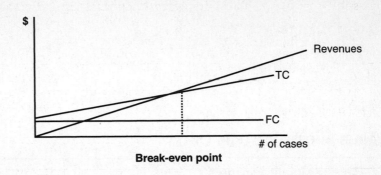

Sources and use of funds:

Source of funds:

Founders	$_____
Investors	$_____
Bank financing	$_____
Total	**$_____**

Use of funds:

Winery	$_____
Tasting room	$_____
Wine-making equipment	$_____
Grapes	$_____
Packaging supplies	$_____
Other: _____	$_____
Total	**$_____**

Sensitivity Analysis

Possible variables to adjust in the sensitivity analysis:

Initial start-up costs:

_____

_____

Operating expenses:

_____

_____

Product prices:

_____

_____

Production volume:

_____

_____

Distribution channels:

_____

_____

Exit Strategy

Most people investing in the wine industry are doing so because they enjoy the life-style and want to be a part of a winery operation. Investors realize they are making a long-term commitment to your winery and do not expect to withdraw their capital in the near future. However, investors will want to know your long-term plans for operating the winery, when they could possibly withdraw their capital, and what type of rate of return they should expect.

Your exit strategy:

_____

_____

Conclusion

The conclusion summarizes prior sections and makes final statements regarding the firm's profitability and long-run prospects. It prioritizes tasks and sets a schedule for what needs to be accomplished in the next one, three, and five years.

Use the following questions to help in writing your conclusion:

◆ Can your business be profitable?

◆ What are the keys to your business's success?

◆ What are the long-term plans of your business?

◆ What tasks must be accomplished in the next one, three, and five years?

Your conclusion:

_____

_____

Appendix

The appendix section of your worksheet should include information or documents that further explain any aspects of the business plan or the business. Entrepreneur resumés, property layouts, new product designs, credit reports, licenses and permits, and historical business records are commonly included in the appendix.

Note: The information included in the appendix will vary according to the audience.

Use the following questions to help in completing the appendix section:

◆ Who will be reading the business plan?

◆ What additional information will interest them?

◆ Do any aspects of the business plan need further explanation?

◆ Are all the necessary supporting materials included?

Your appendix:

_____

_____

Business Plan Forecasts

The following charts are based on the results of the findings of the Cornell University Small Winery Study, 2005/6, by Prof. Gerald White and Mark Pisoni.

Revenue, Capital Asset, Operating Expense, and Cash Flow Projections for a Small Premium Winery

Projected Revenues

Revenue	Year 1	Year 2	Year 3	Year 4	Year 5	Year 6	Year 7+
Direct sales to customers		$37,222	$293,954	$574,781	$808,787	$943,024	$1,171,477
Direct sales to retailers		$0	$0	$0	$59,311	$77,799	$96,647
Sales to distributors		$0	$0	$0	$0	$58,939	$73,217
Total revenue from wine sales		$37,222	$293,954	$574,781	$868,098	$1,079,763	$1,341,341

Projected Capital Asset Purchases

	Year 0	Year 1	Year 2	Year 3	Year 4	Year 5
Receiving equipment	$93,740					
Fermentation/storage	$34,231		$21,748	$22,411	$23,095	$23,799
Cooperage	$16,307		$21,855	$28,909	$35,831	$43,517
Cellar equipment	$37,358					

continues

continued

	Year 0	Year 1	Year 2	Year 3	Year 4	Year 5
Lab equipment	$11,152					
Refrigeration	$12,628		$1,272	$1,311	$1,350	$13,620
Bottling line		$122,400		$425		$451
Winery, office, and vehicles	$484,625					
Tasting room and landscaping		$331,250				
Annual investment	$690,042	$453,650	$44,874	$53,056	$60,276	$81,387

Projected Operating Costs

	Year 1	Year 2	Year 3	Year 4	Year 5	Year 6	Year 7+
Grapes	$41,488	$85,507	$132,173	$181,606	$233,931	$241,065	$248,418
Labor	$73,700	$85,635	$123,768	$160,170	$223,197	$232,096	$251,630
Packaging	$0	$30,783	$50,047	$77,360	$106,293	$135,875	$141,094
Marketing	$10,000	$2,772	$11,274	$20,293	$31,307	$39,977	$48,632
Utilities	$8,500	$10,500	$14,000	$15,000	$16,000	$16,488	$16,991
Professional fees	$6,000	$3,500	$4,061	$4,624	$5,189	$5,347	$5,510
Supplies	$1,890	$3,280	$4,970	$6,560	$7,950	$8,192	$8,442
Gasoline, fuel, oil	$750	$1,500	$1,750	$2,000	$2,250	$2,319	$2,389
Insurance	$9,000	$9,275	$12,000	$12,366	$12,743	$13,132	$13,532
Interest	$0	$0	$0	$0	$0	$0	$0
Taxes	$9,735	$10,528	$12,696	$15,053	$17,542	$19,914	$22,005
Rent/leases	$0	$0	$0	$0	$0	$0	$0
Repairs and maintenance	$11,437	$11,886	$12,416	$13,019	$13,833	$14,260	$14,705
Depreciation	$80,154	$152,595	$140,542	$136,490	$145,259	$146,175	$141,144
Miscellaneous	$4,000	$5,000	$7,000	$8,000	$9,000	$9,275	$9,557
Total	$256,655	$412,761	$526,697	$652,540	$824,493	$884,115	$924,050

Projected Cash Flows

	Year 0	Year 1	Year 2	Year 3	Year 4	Year 5	Year 6	Year 7	Year 8	Year 9	Year 10
Revenues:											
Wine sales—retail		$0	$37,222	$293,954	$574,781	$808,787	$943,024	$1,171,477	$1,207,207	$1,244,027	$1,281,970
Wine sales—wholesale		$0	$0	$0	$0	$59,311	$77,799	$96,647	$99,595	$102,632	$105,763
Wine sales—distributor		$0	$0	$0	$0	$0	$58,939	$73,217	$75,450	$77,752	$80,123
Total revenues		$0	$37,222	$293,954	$574,781	$868,098	$1,079,763	$1,341,341	$1,382,252	$1,424,411	$1,467,855
Expenses:											
Grapes		$41,488	$85,507	$132,173	$181,606	$233,931	$241,065	$248,418	$255,995	$263,803	$271,849
Labor		$73,700	$85,635	$123,768	$160,170	$223,197	$232,096	$251,630	$259,304	$267,213	$275,363
Packaging		$0	$30,783	$50,047	$77,360	$106,293	$135,875	$141,094	$145,398	$149,832	$154,402
Marketing		$10,000	$2,772	$11,274	$20,293	$31,307	$39,977	$48,632	$50,115	$51,644	$53,219
Utilities		$8,500	$10,500	$14,000	$15,000	$16,000	$16,488	$16,991	$17,509	$18,043	$18,593
Professional fees		$6,000	$3,500	$4,061	$4,624	$5,189	$5,347	$5,510	$5,678	$5,851	$6,030
Supplies		$1,890	$3,280	$4,970	$6,560	$7,950	$8,192	$8,442	$8,700	$8,965	$9,239
Gasoline, fuel, oil		$750	$1,500	$1,750	$2,000	$2,250	$2,319	$2,389	$2,462	$2,537	$2,615
Insurance		$9,000	$9,275	$12,000	$12,366	$12,743	$13,132	$13,532	$13,945	$14,370	$14,809
Interest		$0	$0	$0	$0	$0	$0	$0	$0	$0	$0
Taxes		$9,735	$10,528	$12,696	$15,053	$17,542	$19,914	$22,005	$22,676	$23,368	$24,080
Rent/leases		$0	$0	$0	$0	$0	$0	$0	$0	$0	$0
Repairs and maintenance		$11,437	$11,886	$12,416	$13,019	$13,833	$14,260	$14,705	$15,153	$15,615	$16,092

	Year 0	Year 1	Year 2	Year 3	Year 4	Year 5	Year 6	Year 7	Year 8	Year 9	Year 10
Depreciation		$80,154	$152,595	$140,542	$136,490	$145,259	$146,175	$141,144	$113,521	$86,660	$84,919
Miscellaneous		$4,000	$5,000	$7,000	$8,000	$9,000	$9,275	$9,557	$9,849	$10,149	$10,459
Total expenses		$256,655	$412,761	$526,697	$652,540	$824,493	$884,115	$924,050	$920,305	$918,051	$941,667
Taxable income		($256,655)	($375,539)	($232,743)	($77,759)	$43,604	$195,648	$417,291	$461,947	$506,359	$526,188
Loss carry forward		($256,655)	($632,193)	($864,936)	($942,695)	($899,091)	($703,443)	($286,152)			
Income tax @ 40%									($237,235)	($202,544)	($210,475)
Net income		($256,655)	($375,539)	($232,743)	($77,759)	$43,604	$195,648	$417,291	$224,712	$303,816	$315,713
Capital purchases	($690,042)	($453,650)	($44,874)	($53,056)	($60,276)	($81,387)	($42,700)	($44,481)	($45,345)	($47,236)	($48,153)
Depreciation		$80,154	$152,595	$140,542	$136,490	$145,259	$146,175	$141,144	$113,521	$86,660	$84,919
Cash flow	($690,042)	($630,150)	($267,818)	($145,257)	($1,545)	$107,476	$299,123	$513,954	$292,889	$343,240	$352,479

Financial Plan

The following table summarizes the amount of money needed each year to establish the proposed small, premium winery. The money will be used to construct the winery and tasting room, purchase the necessary winemaking equipment, and cover the annual operating expenses. A more detailed look at the disposition of funds is provided in the financial section of the study.

Year	*Amount of money needed*
Year 0	$690,042
Year 1	$630,150
Year 2	$267,818
Year 3	$154,257
Year 4	$1,545
Total over 4 years	**$1,743,812**

The financial section begins by projecting annual revenues, capital asset purchases, operating expenses, and cash flow projections for the small premium winery. A detailed description of the capital asset requirements and operating expenses are then provided.

Wineries are capital-intensive, and the cash flow analysis showed that the winery does not attain a positive cash flow until year 5; thus, an investor could not expect to withdraw any funds prior to the fifth year of operation.

Vineyard Establishment Summary Charts

Table 7 V. vinifera Grape Establishment and Development Costs per Acre, Finger Lakes Region, NY, 2004

Operation	Labor Used	Labor Hours	Equipment Hours	Labor Cost	Equipment Cost	Materials Cost	Total Cost
Site preparation (rounded up or down to the nearest dollar):							
Drainage*	Custom	n/a	n/a	n/a	n/a	$67.00	$1,430
Lime (2 tons/acre)	Custom	n/a	n/a	n/a	n/a	$24.00	$67
Herbicide application	Custom	n/a	n/a	n/a	$9.00	n/a	$33
Stone removal and land maintenance	Unskilled	1	0.8	$10.00	$5.49	$1.50	$15
Soil sampling	Skilled	0.2	n/a	$3.12	n/a	$48.80	$5
Fall fertilization	Skilled	0.6	0.5	$9.36	$3.77	n/a	$62
Plowing	Custom	n/a	n/a	n/a	$15.90	n/a	$16
Disking (×2)	Custom	n/a	n/a	n/a	$22.20	n/a	$22
Total	n/a	1.8	1.3	$22.48	$56.36	$141.30	**$1,650**
First year:							
Floating	Skilled	0.25	0.2	$3.90	$1.27	n/a	$5
Laser planting	Custom	n/a	n/a	$358.23	$358.23	$2,823.33	$3,540
Fertilization (hand application)	Skilled	0.6	0.5	$9.36	$3.43	$15.66	$28
Hilling up	Skilled	1.5	1.2	$23.40	$9.40	n/a	$33
Chemical weed control—trellis+Solubor	Skilled	2.5	2	$39.00	$13.39	$42.40	$95

Operation	Labor Used	Labor Hours	Equipment Hours	Labor Cost	Equipment Cost	Materials Cost	Total Cost
Trellis construction**	Skilled	41	8	$639.60	$61.07	$2,244.00	$2,945
Cultivation	Skilled	0.6	0.5	$9.36	$3.92	n/a	$13
Spray 1	Skilled	0.4	0.3	$6.24	$3.12	$8.46	$18
Spray 2	Skilled	0.4	0.3	$6.24	$3.12	$8.46	$18
Spray 3	Skilled	0.4	0.3	$6.24	$3.12	$8.46	$18
Mowing (×2)	Skilled	1.3	1	$20.28	$8.01	n/a	$28
Total	n/a	50.75	14.3	$1,121.85	$468.07	$5,150.79	$6,741
Total for first year and site prep							$8,391
Second year:							
Pruning and brush removal	Skilled	6	n/a	$93.60	n/a	n/a	$94
Tying and renewal	Unskilled	4	n/a	$40.00	n/a	$3.20	$43
Vine replacement	Skilled	2	2	$31.20	$14.67	$56.47	$102
Spring fertilization	Skilled	0.6	0.5	$9.36	$3.77	$7.48	$21
Chemical weed control—trellis	Skilled	2.6	2	$40.56	$13.39	$44.40	$98
Suckering	Unskilled	5	n/a	$50.00	n/a	n/a	$50
Cluster removal	Unskilled	5	n/a	$50.00	n/a	n/a	$50
Take away	Skilled	3	2.5	$46.80	$19.58	n/a	$66
Hand hoe	Unskilled	8	n/a	$80.00	n/a	n/a	$80
Chemical weed control—row middle	Skilled	0.6	0.5	$9.36	$3.35	$9.60	$22
Hilling up	Skilled	1.7	1.5	$26.52	$11.75	n/a	$38
Spray 1	Skilled	0.4	0.3	$6.24	$3.12	$8.46	$18
Spray 2	Skilled	0.4	0.3	$6.24	$3.12	$8.46	$18

continues

continued

Operation	Labor Used	Labor Hours	Equipment Hours	Labor Cost	Equipment Cost	Materials Cost	Total Cost
Spray 3	Skilled	0.6	0.5	$9.36	$5.20	$8.46	$23
Spray 4	Skilled	0.6	0.5	$9.36	$5.20	$8.46	$23
Mowing (×2)	Skilled	1.3	1	$20.28	$8.01	n/a	$28
Rogueing	Unskilled	1	n/a	$10.00	n/a	n/a	$10
Total	n/a	42.8	11.6	$538.88	$91.15	$154.99	$785
Third year:							
Pruning and brush pulling	Custom	Piece rate***	n/a	$193.60	n/a	n/a	$194
Tying and renewal	Unskilled	10	n/a	$100.00	n/a	$3.20	$103
Vine replacement	Skilled	2	2	$31.20	$14.67	$56.47	$102
Spring fertilization	Skilled	0.6	0.5	$9.36	$3.77	$14.95	$28
Chemical weed control—trellis	Skilled	2.6	2	$40.56	$13.39	$34.10	$88
Suckering	Unskilled	7	n/a	$70.00	n/a	n/a	$70
Cluster removal	Unskilled	8	n/a	$80.00	n/a	n/a	$80
Take away	Skilled	3	2.5	$46.80	$19.58	n/a	$66
Hand hoe	Unskilled	8	n/a	$80.00	n/a	n/a	$80
Spot herbicide treatment	Skilled	0.4	0.3	$6.24	$2.01	$6.00	$14
Chemical weed control—row middle	Skilled	0.6	0.5	$9.36	$3.35	$9.60	$22
Spray 1	Skilled	0.6	0.5	$9.36	$5.20	$12.82	$27
Spray 2	Skilled	0.6	0.5	$9.36	$5.20	$12.82	$27

Labor Operation	Labor Used	Equipment Hours	Labor Hours	Equipment Cost	Materials Cost	Cost	Total Cost
Spray 3	Skilled	0.6	0.5	$9.36	$5.20	$12.82	$27
Spray 4	Skilled	0.6	0.5	$9.36	$5.20	$12.82	$27
Spray 5	Skilled	0.6	0.5	$9.36	$5.20	$28.46	$43
Spray 6	Skilled	0.6	0.5	$9.36	$5.20	$28.46	$43
Spray 7	Skilled	0.6	0.5	$9.36	$5.20	$24.74	$39
Spray 8	Skilled	0.6	0.5	$9.36	$5.20	$29.70	$44
Spray 9	Skilled	0.6	0.5	$9.36	$5.20	$12.26	$27
Spray 10	Skilled	0.6	0.5	$9.36	$5.20	$12.26	$27
Spray 11	Skilled	0.6	0.5	$9.36	$5.20	$46.04	$61
Spray 12	Skilled	0.6	0.5	$9.36	$5.20	$43.06	$58
Mowing (×2)	Skilled	1.3	1	$20.28	$8.01	n/a	$28
Brush chopping (×1)	Skilled	1.2	1	$18.72	$8.01	n/a	$27
Hilling up	Skilled	1.7	1.5	$26.52	$11.75	n/a	$38
Rogueing	Unskilled	1	n/a	$10.00	n/a	n/a	$10
Petiole sampling	Skilled	0.1	n/a	$1.56	n/a	$2.30	$4
Total	n/a	54.7	17.3	$856.52	$146.93	$402.89	$1,406

* See Table 5 for details.

** See Table 6 for details.

*** Note: If one decides not to use piece rate labor the estimated pruning time is 18 hours per acre, and with skilled labor the cost is $280.80. Thus total labor requirements using regular hired labor would be 74.1 hours per acre.

Drainage Construction Costs

Table 5 contains an estimate of drainage construction costs. These costs are transferred to the site preparation section of the establishment and development costs. These costs will vary greatly from site to site depending on the soil conditions and vineyard manager preferences. This study assumed that tile drainage was placed in the middle of every third row, or 27 feet apart.

Table 5   Tile Drainage Costs per acre for *V. vinifera* Grapes, Finger Lakes Region, NY, 2004

Item	Quantity	Price	Total Cost per Acre
Main line: 6-inch pipe	99 feet	$0.69 foot	$68
Laterals: 4-inch pipe	1,613 feet	$0.25 foot	$403
Installation	1,712 feet	$0.52 foot	$890
Total drainage construction per acre			$1,362

Trellis Construction Costs

The total cost for trellis materials is estimated at $2,244 per acre. The costs are included in the first year of establishment and development. Labor and machinery costs for trellis establishment are also included.

The trellis was designed for Vertically Shoot Positioned (VSP) vines. It was made of two pairs of moveable catch wires and two fixed wires for vine support (a total of six wires). Wooden line posts were used for every third vine, and two catch wire clips were used on each post to hold the catch wires in place. Wooden anchor posts were used to support each end post. Rows were 440 feet long, with 11 rows to an acre and 73 vines per row.

Establishment and Development Costs

The costs for labor machinery and materials for site preparation and years 1 through 3 constitute the establishment and development (E&D) costs. First-year costs—including site preparation, trellis construction, and planting—are substantial, amounting to $8,391 per acre. A planting density of 807 vines (6'×9') (vine by row) was assumed. The largest cost in the first year is the expenditure of $2,823 for vines. In year 2, costs are a relatively modest $785 per acre with lower spray costs and less labor required than for mature vines. In the third year, a full spray program is required, and hand harvesting is also necessary to protect the young vines. Total costs for the third year are $1,406 per acre.

Table 8: Summary of Establishment and Development Costs by Year for *V. vinifera* Grapes, Finger Lakes Region, NY 2004

Item	Year 1	Year 2	Year 3
Revenue:			
Yield per acre (tons)	0	0	1
Market price (average of 4 varietals)	n/a	n/a	$1,358
Total revenue	$0	$0	$1,358
Costs:			
Site preparation	$1,650	$0	$0
Annual variable costs			
Preharvest	$6,741	$785	$1,406
Harvest (hand) + hauling	n/a	n/a	$200
Total variable costs and site preparation	$8,391	$785	$1,606
Annual fixed costs:			
Machines and equipment amortization	$358	$358	$358
Buildings amortization	$69	$69	$69
Property taxes	$61	$61	$61
Land opportunity cost	$100	$100	$100
Office supplies, phone, etc.	$50	$50	$50
Insurance	$38	$38	$38
Management	$213	$213	$213
Total fixed costs	$889	$889	$889
Interest on cumulative costs	$371	$453	$571
Total costs	$9,651	$2,127	$3,066

continues

continued

Item	Year 1	Year 2	Year 3
Net returns	($9,651)	($2,127)	($1,708)
Total cumulative costs	$9,651	$11,778	$13,486
Amortization of vineyard			$933
Cash costs of vineyard establishment (3 years)			$10,582

Tax and Trade Bureau Geographic Brand Name Regulations

The federal Tax and Trade Bureau (TTB) is touchy about the use of names on labels. Before you develop brand names for your wines, be sure to look into TTB Chapter 4 of the regulations covering brand name use (www.ttb.gov/wine/chapter4.pdf). The following is a sample direct from the regulations.

Geographic Brand Names

Definitions:

geographic brand name   A brand name with viticultural significance.

viticultural significance   A brand name has viticultural significance if the brand name includes the name of:

 ◆ A U.S. state or foreign equivalent

 ◆ A U.S. county or foreign equivalent

 ◆ An approved American or foreign viticultural area

 ◆ A geographic area that:

    ◆ Actually exists *and*

    ◆ Is described in at least two reference materials as a grape-growing area

"new" geographic brand name   A geographic brand name used on an application for certificate of label approval (COLA) submitted on or after July 7, 1986.

"grandfathered" geographic brand name   A geographic brand name used on a certificate of label approval (COLA) issued prior to July 7, 1986.

Requirement for Use of a "New" Geographic Brand Name

A "new" geographic brand name may be used *provided* the wine meets the appellation of origin requirements for the geographic area named in the brand name.

The "Appellation Requirements" table identifies the appellation requirements for a geographic brand name that includes a state, a county, a viticultural area, etc.

Appellation Requirements

If the Brand Name Includes the Name of …	The Wine …
A U.S. state	1) Must be derived from not less than 75 percent of grapes, citrus, or other fruit or other agricultural commodity grown in the named state *and*
	2) Must be fully finished (except for cellar treatment and blending, which does not result in an alteration of class and type) in the named state or an adjacent state *and*
	3) Must conform to the laws and regulations of the named state
The foreign equivalent of a U.S. state	1) Must be derived from not less than 75 percent of grapes, citrus, or other fruit or other agricultural commodity grown in the named foreign equivalent of a state *and*
	2) Must conform to the laws and regulations of the country in which the wine was produced
A U.S. county	1) Must be derived from not less than 75 percent of grapes, citrus, or other fruit or other agricultural commodity grown in the named county *and*
	2) Must be fully finished (except for cellar treatment and blending, which does not result in an alteration of class and type) in the state in which the named county is located *and*
	3) Must conform to the laws and regulations of the state in which the named county is located

continues

continued

If the Brand Name Includes the Name of ...	The Wine ...
The foreign equivalent of a U.S. county	1) Must be derived from not less than 75 percent of grapes, citrus, or other fruit or other agricultural commodity grown in the named foreign equivalent of a county *and*
	2) Must conform to the laws and regulations of the country in which the wine was produced
An approved American viticultural area	1) Must be derived from not less than 85 percent of grapes grown in the named viticultural area *and*
	2) Must be fully finished (except for cellar treatment and blending, which does not result in an alteration of class and type) in the state in which the named viticultural area is located *and*
	3) Must conform to the laws and regulations of the state in which the named viticultural area is located
An approved foreign viticultural area	1) Must be derived from not less than 85 percent of grapes grown in the named viticultural area *and*
	2) Must conform to the laws and regulations of the country in which the wine was produced
A geographic area that:	*Cannot* be labeled with such a brand name.
	a) Actually exists and
	b) Is described in at least two (2) reference materials as a grape-growing area

The EXAMPLES chart provides example geographic brand names with explanations of the acceptability/unacceptability of each.

Examples

Brand Name and Class and Type Designation	Brand Name Acceptable If	Brand Name Unacceptable Because
Washington Cellars, Apple Wine	1) Not less than 75 percent of the volume of the wine is derived from apples grown in Washington State *and* 2) The wine was fully finished (except for cellar treatment and blending, which does not result in an alteration of class and type) in Washington State *and* 3) The wine conforms to the laws and regulations of Washington State	
Quebec Grande, Sparkling Wine	1) Not less than 75 percent of the volume of the wine is derived from grapes grown in Quebec *and* 2) The wine conforms to the laws and regulations of Canada	
Sonoma Coast Royale, Table Wine	1) Not less than 85 percent of the volume of the wine is derived from grapes grown in the Sonoma Coast viticultural area *and* 2) The wine was fully finished (except for cellar treatment and blending, which does not result in an alteration of class and type) in California *and* 3) The wine conforms to the laws and regulations of California	

Examples

Brand Name and Class and Type Designation	Brand Name Acceptable If	Brand Name Unacceptable Because
Muchacha de Rioja, Red Wine	1) Not less than 85 percent of the volume of the wine is derived from grapes grown in the Rioja viticultural area *and* 2) The wine conforms to the laws and regulations of Spain	
Virgin River Valley Serenade, White Wine		"Virgin River Valley" is the name of a geographic area that: a) Actually exists and b) Is described in at least two (2) reference materials as a grape-growing area *But* "Virgin River Valley" is not an appellation of origin, i.e., it is not a state, county, or approved viticultural area *and* Therefore, the wine cannot meet the appellation of origin requirements for the geographic area named in the brand name

Requirement for Use of a "Grandfathered" Geographic Brand Name

A "grandfathered" geographic brand name may be used *provided:*

◆ The wine meets the appellation of origin requirements for the geographic area named in the brand name.

Note: See the "Appellation Requirements" table earlier *except for* a brand name that includes the name of a geographic area that (a) actually exists and (b) is described in at least two (2) reference materials as a grape-growing area. (See the following "Appellations for 'Grandfathered' Geographic Brand Names" table.)

Or

◆ The wine is *labeled with* an appellation of origin, in direct conjunction with the class and type designation, as outlined in the following "Appellations for 'Grandfathered' Geographic Brand Names" table.

Or

◆ The wine is labeled with a statement that is sufficient to dispel the impression that the geographic area suggested by the brand name is indicative of the origin of the wine.

The "Appellations for 'Grandfathered' Geographic Brand Names" table identifies the specific type of appellation of origin required for a "grandfathered" geographic brand name based on the type of appellation of origin included in the brand name.

Appellations for "Grandfathered" Geographic Brand Names

If the Brand Name Includes the Name of ...	The Wine Must Be Labeled with an Appellation of Origin of ...
A U.S. state or a foreign equivalent of a U.S. state	1) A U.S. state or foreign equivalent of a U.S. state *or* 2) A U.S. county or foreign equivalent of a U.S. county *or* 3) An approved American or foreign viticultural area
A U.S. county or a foreign equivalent of a U.S. county	1) A U.S. county or foreign equivalent of a U.S. county *or* 2) An approved American or foreign viticultural area

continues

continued

If the Brand Name Includes the Name of ...	The Wine Must Be Labeled with an Appellation of Origin of ...
An approved American or foreign viticultural area	1) A U.S. county or foreign equivalent of a U.S. county *or* 2) An approved American or foreign viticultural area
A geographic area that: a) Actually exists and b) Is described in at least two (2) reference materials as a grape-growing area	1) A U.S. county or foreign equivalent of a U.S. county *or* 2) An approved American or foreign viticultural area

Tax and Trade Bureau Report of Wine Premises Operations

During the course of your winery operation, the TTB keeps tabs on all wine movements both for excise tax purposes and for label regulations that apply to blending and volume of grape varieties. The following form is the one you use to report all wine activity in your winery (www.ttb.gov/epayment/wine_operations_report_guide.pdf).

OMB No. 1513-0053 (8/31/2005)

DEPARTMENT OF THE TREASURY
ALCOHOL AND TOBACCO TAX AND TRADE BUREAU (TTB)
REPORT OF WINE PREMISES OPERATIONS

PERIOD	OPERATED BY (Name, Address and Telephone)
MONTH _____ YEAR _____ (If applicable)	
REGISTRY NUMBER	

INSTRUCTIONS

1. The reporting period for this form shall be monthly, except that proprietors who qualify under the exception stated in 27 CFR 24.300 (g)(2) may file this form on a calendar year basis unless required to file monthly by the Alcohol and Tobacco Tax and Trade Bureau (TTB). A proprietor who files monthly reports but does not expect any reportable operations in a subsequent month or months may indicate in Part X that no monthly reports will be filed until a reportable operation occurs. (§24.300 (g)(1))

2. Prepare this form in duplicate and file it by the fifteenth day after the end of the report period *(month or year)*. Keep the copy on your bonded wine premises for inspection by TTB officers. Send the original to TTB at this address:

   Director, National Revenue Center
   Alcohol and Tobacco Tax and Trade Bureau
   550 Main St, Ste 8002
   Cincinnati, OH 45202-5215

3. Explain any unusual operations in Part X.

4. The quantities "on hand end" will ordinarily be "book inventory" figures, that is the quantity required to balance each summary. Use the "on hand end" from your report for the previous period as the "on hand beginning" of the current report. On reports for any period when you take a physical inventory, report the difference as losses for bulk wine and shortages for bottled wine, or as gains, as the case may be.

5. If the quantity of wine previously reported on TTB F 5120.17 is affected by adjustments made on a tax return, TTB F 5000.24, adjust the current TTB F 5120.17 in Section A *(and Section B, if bottled wine is involved)*. Explain the entries in Part X.

PART I - SUMMARY OF WINES IN BOND (GALLONS)

ITEM	NOT OVER 14 PERCENT (a)	OVER 14 TO 21 PERCENT (Inclusive) (b)	OVER 21 TO 24 PERCENT (Inclusive) (c)	ARTIFICIALLY CARBONATED WINE (d)	SPARKLING WINE (e)	HARD CIDER (f)
SECTION A - BULK WINES						
1. ON HAND BEGINNING OF PERIOD						
2. PRODUCED BY FERMENTATION[1]					BF	
					BP	
3. PRODUCED BY SWEETENING						
4. PRODUCED BY ADDITION OF WINE SPIRITS						
5. PRODUCED BY BLENDING						
6. PRODUCED BY AMELIORATION						
7. RECEIVED IN BOND						
8. BOTTLED WINE DUMPED TO BULK						
9. INVENTORY GAINS						
10.						
11.						
12. TOTAL						
13. BOTTLED[2]					BF	
					BP	
14. REMOVED TAXPAID						
15. TRANSFERS IN BOND						
16. REMOVED FOR DISTILLING MATERIAL						
17. REMOVED TO VINEGAR PLANT						
18. USED FOR SWEETENING						
19. USED FOR ADDITION OF WINE SPIRITS						
20. USED FOR BLENDING[4]						
21. USED FOR AMELIORATION						
22. USED FOR EFFERVESCENT WINE						
23. USED FOR TESTING						
24.						
25.						
26.						
27.						
28.						
29. LOSSES (OTHER THAN INVENTORY)						
30. INVENTORY LOSSES						
31. ON HAND END OF PERIOD						
32. TOTAL						
SECTION B - BOTTLED WINES						
1. ON HAND BEGINNING OF PERIOD						
2. BOTTLED[2]					BF	
					BP	
3. RECEIVED IN BOND						
4. TAXPAID WINE RETURNED TO BOND						
5.						
6.						
7. TOTAL						
8. REMOVED TAXPAID						
9. TRANSFERRED IN BOND						
10. DUMPED TO BULK						
11. USED FOR TASTING						
12. REMOVED FOR EXPORT						
13. REMOVED FOR FAMILY USE						
14. USED FOR TESTING						
15.						
16.						
17.						
18. BREAKAGE						
19. INVENTORY SHORTAGE[3]						
20. ON HAND END OF PERIOD						
21. TOTAL						

TTB F 5120.17 (5/2005)

[1] Enter in col. (e) on line marked "BF" the quantity of sparkling wine produced by fermentation in bottles, and on line mark "BP" the quantity of sparkling wine produced by bulk process.

[2] Section A line 13 and Section B line 2 should show the same quantities. Enter in col. (e) on line marked "BF" the quantity of finished bottle fermented sparkling wine bottled, and on line marked "BP" the quantity of finished bulk process wine bottled.

[3] Fully explain in either Part X, or on a separate signed statement submitted with this report. Failure to satisfactorily explain shortages of bottled wine may result in the assessment of taxes applicable to those shortages.

[4] Only report blending if wines of different tax classes are blended together.

PART II - (RESERVED)

PART III - SUMMARY OF DISTILLED SPIRITS (Proof Gallons)

ITEM	WINE SPIRITS					DISTILLATES CONTAINING ALDEHYDES[v]		SPIRITS FOR USE IN NON BEVERAGE WINES
	FOR ADDITION TO WINE[v]				FOR PREPARATION OF DOSAGES OR ESSENCES (e)	(f)	(g)	(h)
	GRAPE (a)	(b)	(c)	(d)				
1. ON HAND BEGINNING OF PERIOD								
2. RECEIVED								
3. INVENTORY GAIN								
4. TOTAL								
5. USED								
6. TRANS. TO COL. (e)								
7.								
8. LOSSES								
9. ON HAND END OF PERIOD								
10. TOTAL								

PART IV - SUMMARY OF MATERIALS RECEIVED AND USED

ITEM	GRAPE MATERIAL				KINDS OF MATERIALS OTHER THAN GRAPE[v] (Pounds or Gallons)			SUGAR	
	GRAPES		JUICE (Gallons) (c)	CONCENTRATE (Gallons) (d)	(e)	(f)	(g)	DRY (Pounds) (h)	LIQUID (Gallons) (i)
	UNCRUSHED (Pounds) (a)	FIELD CRUSHED (Gallons) (b)							
1. ON HAND BEGINNING OF PERIOD									
2. RECEIVED									
3. JUICE OR CONCENTRATE PRODUCED									
4. TOTAL									
5. USED IN WINE PRODUCTION									
6. USED IN JUICE OR CONCENTRATE PRODUCTION									
7. USED IN ALLIED PRODUCTS									
8. REMOVED									
9. ON HAND END OF PERIOD									
10. TOTAL									

PART V - (RESERVED)

PART VI - SUMMARY OF DISTILLING MATERIAL AND VINEGAR STOCK (Gallons)[v]

ITEM	DISTILLING MATERIAL[v]		VINEGAR STOCK	
	(a)	(b)	(c)	(d)
1. ON HAND BEGINNING OF PERIOD (Storage Tanks)				
2. PRODUCED				
3. RECEIVED FROM OTHER BONDED WINE PREMISES				
4.				
5. TOTAL				
6. REMOVED TO DISTILLED SPIRITS PLANTS				
7. REMOVED TO OTHER BONDED WINE PREMISES				
8. REMOVED TO VINEGAR PLANTS				
9.				
10. ON HAND END OF PERIOD (Storage Tanks)				
11. TOTAL				

PART VII - IN FERMENTERS END OF PERIOD (Gallons)[v]

TOTAL	(a)	(b)	(c)	(d)	(e)	TOTAL
1. IN FERMENTERS (ESTIMATED QUANTITY OF LIQUID)						

PART VIII - SUMMARY OF NONBEVERAGE WINES (Gallons)

ITEM	NOT OVER 14 PERCENT ALCOHOL (a)	OVER 14 TO 21 PERCENT ALCOHOL (Inclusive) (b)	TOTAL (c)
1. PRODUCED			
2. WITHDRAWN			

PART IX - SPECIAL NATURAL WINES AND 27 CFR 24.218 WINES (Gallons)

ITEMS	VERMOUTH (a)	OTHER SPECIAL NATURAL WINES				TOTAL (cols. a, b, c, d and e) (f)	27 CFR 24.218 WINES (g)
		NOT OVER 14 PERCENT ALCOHOL (b)	OVER 14 TO 21 PERCENT ALCOHOL (c)	ARTIFICIALLY CARBONATED (d)	SPARKLING (e)		
1. PRODUCED							
2. TAXABLE REMOVALS							
3. ON HAND END OF PERIOD							

PART X - REMARKS

Under penalties of perjury I declare that I have examined this report, including the documents submitted in support thereof, and to the best of my knowledge and belief, it is true, correct, and complete.

PROPRIETOR	BY (Signature and Title)	DATE

[v] State kind - apple, blackberry, etc.
[v] Distilling material includes lees, filter wash and other residues used for production of wine spirits. See 27 CFR 24.306.

PAPERWORK REDUCTION ACT NOTICE

TTB F 5120.17 (5/2005)

Resources

This appendix includes a list of United States and Canadian province alcohol control offices plus a partial list of wine distributors, custom crush facilities, federal government liaison offices, and online wine industry software. Each list is critical for getting started with the alcohol permit application and your overall business plan.

Alcohol Control Boards

Every state, the District of Columbia, Puerto Rico, and every Canadian province has an alcohol control board office that issues permits to produce alcohol and regulations under which your business must operate. After you decide where you will live and start your winery, you'll need to contact both federal and local alcohol control offices for permit applications.

In the United States, you can start the federal process online at www.ttb. gov/forms/5000.shtml, or you may want to hire a government liaison to help you through the process. For a local permit, you begin the process by contacting the alcohol control board in the state or province you've selected for your business.

Alabama (Control State)

**Alabama Alcoholic Beverage
Control Board**
2715 Gunter Park Drive West
Montgomery, AL 36109
334-271-3840
www.abc.alabama.gov/index.aspx

Alaska

Alaska Revenue Department
Alcoholic Beverage Control Board
5848 E. Tudor Road
Anchorage, AK 99507
907-269-0350
www.revenue.state.ak.us

Arizona

**Arizona Department of Liquor
Licenses and Control**
800 W. Washington, 5th Floor
Phoenix, AZ 85007
602-542-5141
Or:
400 W. Congress, #150
Tucson, AZ 85701
520-628-6595
www.azliquor.gov

Arkansas

Alcohol Beverage Control
1515 W. Seventh Street, Room 503
Little Rock, AR 72201
501-682-1105
www.state.ar.us/dfa/abc_administration/
abcadm_index.html

California

**California Department of Alcoholic
Beverage Control**
3927 Lennane Drive, Suite 100
Sacramento, CA 95834
916-419-2500
www.abc.ca.gov/

California Board of Equalization
450 N. Street
Sacramento, CA 94279-0073
916-445-6464
www.boe.ca.gov

Canada

**Liquor Control and Licensing
Branch (LCLB)**
Ministry of Public Safety and Solicitor
General
PO Box 9282, Stn Prov Govt
Victoria, BC
V8W 9J7
250-356-9596
www.pssg.gov.bc.ca/lclb

**Canadian Association of Liquor
Jurisdiction**
382 Elm Road
Toronto, ON M5M 3V8
416-780-1851
www.calj.org

Colorado

**Colorado Department of Revenue
Liquor Enforcement Division**
1881 Pierce #108A
Lakewood, CO 80214-1495

Mail:
1375 Sherman Street
Denver, CO 80261
303-205-2300
www.revenue.state.co.us

Connecticut

Connecticut Department of Consumer Protection
Liquor Division
State Office Building
165 Capitol Avenue
Hartford, CT 06106
860-713-6200
www.ct.gov/dcp

Delaware

Alcoholic Beverage Control Commission
Carvel State Office Building, 3rd Floor
820 N. French Street
Wilmington, DE 19801
302-577-5210
www.licensesandpermits.com/
us_abcd2.htm

District of Columbia

Alcoholic Beverage Regulation Administration
941 North Capitol Street, NE, Suite 7200
Washington, DC 20002
202-442-4423
www.abra.dc.gov

Florida

Florida Department of Professional Business Regulations
Division of Alcoholic Beverages
1940 N. Monroe
Tallahassee, FL 32399-0783
850-488-3227
www.myflorida.com/dbpr

Georgia

Georgia Department of Revenue
Alcohol and Tobacco Tax Division
1800 Century Center Boulevard, N.E.
Room 4235
Atlanta, Georgia 30345-3205
404-417-4900
www.dor.ga.gov

Hawaii

Honolulu:
Liquor Commission City and County of Honolulu
Pacific Park Plaza
711 Kapiolani Boulevard, Suite 600
Honolulu, HI 96813
808-523-4458
www.co.honolulu.hi.us/liq

Department of Liquor Control
County of Hawaii
101 Aupuni Street, Suite 230
Hilo, HI 96766
East HI: 808-961-8218
West HI: 808-327-3549
co.hawaii.hi.us/directory/
dir_liquor.htm

Kauai:
Department of Liquor Control
County of Kauai
Lihue Civic Center
Mo'ikeha Building
4444 Rice Street, Suite 120
Kauai, HI 96766
808-241-6580
www.kauai.gov/Government/
Departments/LiquorControl/
tabid/128/Default.aspx

Maui:
Department of Liquor Control
County of Maui
2145 Kaohu Street, Room 107
Wailuku, HI 96793
808-243-7753
www.co.maui.hi.us/departments/
Liquor

Idaho (Control State)

Idaho State Liquor Dispensary
1349 E. Beechcraft Court
Boise, ID 83716
Mailing address:
PO Box 179001
Boise, ID 83717-9001
208-947-9400
www.liquor.idaho.gov

Illinois

**Illinois Liquor Control
Commission**
100 West Randolph Street,
Suite #5-300
Chicago, IL 60601
312-814-2206

Or:
101 West Jefferson, Suite 3-525
Springfield, IL 62702
217-782-2136
www.state.il.us/LCC

Indiana

Alcohol and Tobacco Commission
Indiana Government Center South
302 W. Washington Street, Room
E-114
Indianapolis, IN 46204
317-232-2430
www.in.gov/atc

Iowa (Control State)

Iowa Alcoholic Beverages Division
1918 S.E. Hulsizer Avenue
Ankeny, IA 50021
515-281-7400
www.iowaabd.com

Kansas

**Kansas Department of Revenue
Alcohol Beverage Control**
915 SW Harrison Street, Room 214
Topeka, KS 66625-3512
785-296-7015
www.ksrevenue.org/abc.htm

Kentucky

**Kentucky Alcoholic Beverage
Control Department**
1003 Twilight Trail, Suite A-2
Frankfort, KY 40601
502-564-4850
www.abc.ky.gov

Louisiana

Louisiana Department of Revenue
Alcohol and Tobacco Control Office
8549 United Plaza Boulevard,
Suite 220
Baton Rouge, LA 70809
225-925-4041
www.rev.state.la.us

Maine (Control State)

Main Department of Public Safety
Licensing
164 State House Station
Augusta, ME 04333-0164
207-624-7220
www.state.me.us/dps

Maryland

Alcohol and Tobacco Tax Bureau
Louis L. Goldstein Treasury Building
PO Box 2999
Annapolis, MD 21404-0466
410-260-7314
www.compnet.comp.state.md.us/
MATT_Regulatory_Division/
Alcohol_and_Tobacco_Tax

Montgomery County Department of Liquor Control
(Control State—Montgomery County only)
16650 Crabs Branch Way
Rockville, MD 20855
240-777-1900
www.montgomerycountymd.gov/dlc

Worcester County Liquor Control Board
5363 Snow Hill Road
Snow Hill, MD 21863
410-632-1250
www.msa.md.gov/msa/mdmanual/
36loc/wo/html/woe.html

Massachusetts

Alcoholic Beverages Control Commission
239 Causeway Street, Floor 1
Boston, MA 02114-2130
617-727-3040
www.mass.gov/abcc

Michigan (Control State)

Michigan Liquor Control Commission
7150 Harris Drive
PO Box 30005
Lansing, MI 48909-7505
517-322-1345
www.michigan.gov/dleg/0,1607,7-
154-10570---,00.html

Minnesota

Liquor Control Division
Alcohol and Gambling and
Enforcement Division
444 Cedar Street, Suite 133
St. Paul, MN 55101-5133
651-296-6979

Mississippi (Control State)

Alcoholic Beverage Control Office
PO Box 540
Madison, MS 39110-0540
601-856-1301
www.dps.state.mn.us/alcgamb/
alcgamb.html

Missouri

Division of Alcohol and Tobacco Control
PO Box 837
Jefferson City, MO 65102
573-751-2333
www.atc.dps.mo.gov

Montana (Control State)

Montana Liquor License Bureau
125 N. Roberts
Helena, MT 59620
406-444-0700 or 406-444-6900
mt.gov/revenue/forbusinesses/
alcohol.asp

Nebraska

Nebraska Liquor Control Commission
301 Centennial Mall South
PO Box 95046
Lincoln, NE 68509-5046
402-471-2571
www.lcc.ne.gov

Nevada

Nevada Department of Taxation
Carson City:
1550 E. College Parkway, Suite 115
Carson City, NV 89706
775-687-4892
www.tax.state.nv.us

Reno:
4600 Kietzke Lane
Building O, Room 263
Reno, NV 89502
775-688-1295
www.tax.state.nv.us

Elko:
850 Elm Street #2
PO Box 1750
Elko, NV 89803
775-738-8461
www.tax.state.nv.us

Las Vegas:
Grant Sawyer Office Building
555 E. Washington Avenue,
Suite 1300
Las Vegas, NV 89101
702-486-2300
www.tax.state.nv.us

New Hampshire (Control State)

New Hampshire State Liquor Commission
Robert J. Hart Building
Storrs Street
PO Box 503
Concord, NH 03302-0503
603-271-3134
www.nh.gov/liquor

New Jersey

New Jersey Department of Law and Public Safety
Division of Alcoholic Beverage Control
140 East Front Street
PO Box 087
Trenton, NJ 08625-0087
609-984-2830
www.state.nj.us/lps/abc/index.html

New Mexico

New Mexico Regulation and Licensing Department
Alcohol and Gaming Division
725 St. Michael's Drive
PO Box 25101
Santa Fe, NM 87504-5101
505-827-7066
www.ukcites.gov.uk/license/
GN15%20Timber%20Guidance_
P1.doc

New Mexico Department of Public Safety
Special Investigations Division
6301 Indian School NE, Suite 310
Albuquerque, NM 87110
505-841-8053
www.ukcites.gov.uk/license/
GN15%20Timber%20Guidance_
P1.doc

New York

New York State Liquor Authority
Division of Alcoholic Beverage Control
Zone 1:
State Liquor Authority
317 Lenox Avenue, 4th Floor
New York, NY 10027
212-961-8385
www.abc.state.ny.us

Zone 2:
State Liquor Authority
80 S. Swan Street, Suite 900
Albany, NY 12210-8002
518-474-3114
www.abc.state.ny.us

Syracuse District:
State Liquor Authority
333 E. Washington Street, Room 205
Syracuse, NY 13202
315-428-4198
www.abc.state.ny.us

Zone 3:
State Liquor Authority
535 Washington Street, Suite 303
Buffalo, NY 14203
716-847-3035
www.abc.state.ny.us

North Carolina (Control State)

North Carolina Alcoholic Beverage Control Commission
3322 Garner Road
Raleigh, NC 27610-5632
919-779-0700
www.ncabc.com

North and South Dakota

North Dakota Office of the State Tax Commissioner
Alcohol Tax Section
600 East Boulevard Avenue
Bismarck, ND 58505-0599
701-328-2702
www.nd.gov/tax

Ohio (Control State)

Ohio Department of Commerce
Division of Liquor Control
6606 Tussing Road
Reynoldsburg, OH 43068-9005
614-644-2411
www.com.ohio.gov

Oklahoma

Alcoholic Beverage Law Enforcement Commission (ABLE)
4545 N. Lincoln Boulevard, Suite #270
Oklahoma City, OK 73105
405-521-3484
www.ok.gov/able

Oregon (Control State)

Oregon Liquor Control Commission
9079 S. E. McLoughlin Boulevard
Milwaukie, OR 97222
503-872-5000
Licensing: 503-872-5124
www.oregon.gov/OLCC/index.shtml

Pennsylvania (Control State)

Pennsylvania Liquor Control Board
Commonwealth of Pennsylvania
Northwest Office Building
Harrisburg, PA 17124-0001
Licensing: 717-783-9454
www.lcb.state.pa.us

Puerto Rico

Luis Perez-Rivera, Director
Negociado de Bebidas
PO Box S-9024140
San Juan, PR 00904
www.hacienda.gobierno.pr/
search/search.asp?zoom_per_
page=20&zoom_query=bebidas

Rhode Island

Division of Commercial Licensing and Regulation
Liquor Enforcement and Compliance
233 Richmond Street, Suite 230
Providence, RI 02903
401-222-2416
www.dbr.state.ri.us/divisions/
commlicensing/realestate.php

South Carolina

South Carolina Department of Revenue and Taxation
Alcohol Beverage Licensing Section
301 Gervais Street
PO Box 125
Columbia, SC 29214-0137
803-898-5864
www.charlestoncounty.org/
index2.asp?p=/rulesof.htm

South Dakota

See also: North and South Dakota

South Dakota Department of Revenue
Division of Special Taxes and Licensing
700 Governor's Drive
Pierre, SD 57501-2276
605-773-3311

Tennessee

Tennessee Alcoholic Beverage Commission
226 Capitol Boulevard Building, Room 600
Nashville, TN 37219-0755
615-741-1602
www.tennessee.gov/abc

Texas

Texas Alcoholic Beverage Commission
5806 Mesa Drive
PO Box 13127
Capitol Station
Austin, TX 78711-3127
512-206-3333
www.tabc.state.tx.us

Utah (Control State)

Utah Department of Alcoholic Beverage Control
1625 South 900 West
Salt Lake City, UT 84130
801-977-6800
www.alcbev.state.ut.us

Vermont (Control State)

Vermont Department of Liquor Control
Green Mountain Drive, Drawer 20
Montpelier, VT 05620-4501
802-828-2345
www.state.vt.us/dlc

Virginia (Control State)

Virginia Department of Alcoholic Beverage Control
PO Box 27491
Richmond, VA 23261
804-213-4413
www.abc.virginia.gov

Washington (Control State)

Washington State Liquor Control Board
3000 Pacific Avenue
PO Box 3098
Olympia, WA 98504-3098
360-664-1600
www.liq.wa.gov

West Virginia (Control State)

West Virginia Alcohol Beverage Control Commission
Enforcement and Licensing Division
322 70th Street S.E.
Charleston, WV 25304-2900
304-558-2481 or 1-800-642-8208
www.wvabca.com

Wisconsin

Wisconsin Alcohol and Tobacco Enforcement
Department of Revenue
2135 Rimrock Road
Madison, WI 53713
608-266-2776
www.dor.state.wi.us/pubs/pb302.pdf

Wyoming (Control State)

Wyoming Liquor Commission
1520 East 5th Street
Cheyenne, WY 82002
307-777-7231
www.revenue.state.wy.us

Wine Industry Directory/Buyer's Guide

The best overall directory for services to the wine industry is the one put out by *Wines and Vines Magazine*. In it, you'll find equipment manufacturers and dealers, vineyard nurseries, designers, professional consultants, and all manner of suppliers, plus a complete list of wine distributors.

Wines and Vines
1800 Lincoln Avenue
San Rafael, CA 94901
866-453-9701
www.winesandvines.com

Wine Distributors by State (Partial List)

Far fewer alcohol distributors operate today as, say, 30 years ago. But still, the choices number in the hundreds. This partial list is a means to get you started in your search for a distributor that may be right for your size wine company.

Alabama

M and J Personal Selections/ M and J Wines
26355 Fell Road
Elberta, AL 36530
251-987-5660
www.mjwines.com

Alaska

Specialty Imports
4119 Ingra Street
Anchorage, AK 99503
907-563-9100
www.specialtyimports.com

Arizona

Fine Wine Selection Co.
23620 N. 20th Drive, Suite 20
Phoenix, AZ 85085
623-581-1101
www.finewineselection.com

Arkansas

Barrett Hamilton
3801 W. 65th Street
Little Rock, AR 72209
501-955-2808

California

Chambers and Chambers Wine Merchants
14011 Ventura Boulevard, #210 E
Sherman Oaks, CA 91423
818-995-6961
www.chamberswines.com

Colorado

Organic Vintners
1628 Walnut Street
Boulder, CO 80302
303-245-8773
www.organicvintners.com

Connecticut

Eder Brothers, Inc.
11 Eder Road
West Waven, CT 06516
203-934-8381

Delaware

Delaware Importers, LLC
PO Box 271
New Castle, DE 19720
302-656-4488

Florida

Altamira Wine Distributors
2511 N.W. 16th Lane, Bay 2
Pompano Beach, FL 33064

Southern Wine and Spirits
PO Box 60489
Jacksonville, FL 32254
904-783-1320
www.southernwine.com

Georgia

Grape Expectations
3427 Oakcliff Road, Suite 106
Atlanta, GA 30340
770-455-9573
www.grapeexpectationsgeorgia.com

Hawaii

Fine Wine Imports
500 Ala Kawa Street, Suite 214
Honolulu, HI 96817
808-841-7302

Idaho

J W Thornton Wine Imports
PO Box 2289
Ketchum, ID 83340
208-725-3876
jtwineimports@velocitus.net

Illinois

Winevine/I and B Imports
1734 N. Sedgwick Street
Chicago, IL 60614
312-355-9463
lindam@iandbimports.com

Indiana

Graybull Organic Wines, Inc.
7365 Lakeside Drive
Indianapolis, IN 46278
317-797-2186
graybullwines@comcast.net

Iowa

Vine Adventures, Inc.
1438 Tulip Tree Lane
West Des Moines, IA 50266
515-222-0866
redwine2@msn.com

Kansas

Handcrafted Wines of Kansas, Inc.
PO Box 11461
Shawnee Mission, KS 66211
913-327-1977
www.handcraftedwines.net

Kentucky

Bryant Distributing Co.—Louisville
PO Box 14191
Louisville, KY 40214
502-366-4574
www.bryantdistributing.com

Louisiana

International Wine and Spirits, Inc.
4927 Bloomfield Street
Jefferson, LA 70121
504-736-9577
intwine@bellsouth.net

Maine

Chartrand Imports
PO Box 1319
Rockland, ME 04841
207-594-7300
www.chartrandimports.com

Maryland

The Charmer Sunbelt Group
525 Progress Drive, Suite K
Linthicum, MD 21090
410-401-9300
www.charmer-sunbelt.com

Massachusetts

Classic Wine Imports
975 University Avenue
Norwood, MA 02062
781-352-1100
www.classicwineimports.com

Michigan

Decanter Imports
54790 Grand River
New Hudson, MI 48165
jdunn@decanterimports.com

Minnesota

V I P Wine and Spirits, Ltd.
763 Kasota SE Avenue
Minneapolis, MN 55414
612-701-5902
www.batrounmountains.com

Mississippi

Silver Leaf Wines and Spirits, Inc.
6954 Old Canton Road, Suite C
Ridgeland, MS 39157
601-206-4638
www.silverleafms.com

Missouri

J K Wines
8500 River Park Drive, Suite 237B
Parkville, MO 64152
816-382-3900
www.jkwines.com

Montana

Cardinal Distributing
1750 Evergreen Drive
Boseman, MT 59715
406-586-0241
kkulbeck@cardinaldistributing.com

Nebraska

Nebraska Wine and Spirits
4444 S. 94th Street
Omaha, NE 68127
402-399-9444

Nevada

Nevada Wine Agents
6231 McLeod Drive, Suite K
Las Vegas, NV 89120
702-895-7592
info@nevadawineagents.com

New Hampshire

Vinilandia New Hampshire Wine Distributors
35 Station Drive
Dover, NH 03820
603-674-7763
www.vinilandiausa.com

New Jersey

Winebow, Inc.
75 Chestnut Ridge Road
Montvale, NJ 07645
201-930-2323
www.winebow.com

New Mexico

Boutique Wines of New Mexico
2538 Camino Entrada, Suite 301
Santa Fe, NM 87507
505-471-1757
boutiquewines@quest.com

New York

Metropolis Wine Merchants
527 W. 45th Street
New York, NY 10036
212-581-2052
www.metropoliswine.com

North Carolina

Dionysus Wine Distributors, LLC
3216 Wellington Court, Suite D
Raleigh, NC 27615
919-790-8205
dionysusdist1@bellsouth.net

North Dakota

Republic National Distributing Co.
1402 N. 30th Street
Fargo, ND 58102
701-282-0985
www.rndc-usa.com

Ohio

Tramonte and Sons, LLC
4457 Bethany Road, Building G
Mason, OH 45040
513-770-5501
www.whimports.net/Distributors.aspx

Oklahoma

Select Wines and Spirits, LLC
6833 E. Reading Place
Tulsa, OK 74115
918-835-2511
larryw@selectwinesandspirits.com

Oregon

Bacchus Fine Wines
8800 Enchanted Way SE
Turner, OR 97392
503-362-4338
www.bacchusdistributing.com

Pennsylvania

Specialty Wines and Liquors, Inc.
631 Skippack Pike, Suite 7
Blue Bell, PA 19422
215-646-1812
www.specialtywines.com

Rhode Island

Blue Water Wine
114 Minnesota Avenue
Warwick, RI 02888
401-739-7744
www.bluewaterwine.com

South Carolina

Capital Wine and Beverage
3150 Charleston Highway
West Columbia, SC 29172
803-739-0188

Tennessee

B and T Distributing Co.
6520 Baum Drive
Knoxville, TN 37919
865-602-2233
dhenry@bandtdist.com

Texas

Prestige Wine Cellars
10430 Shady Trail, Suite 108
Dallas, TX 75220
214-823-9272
chad@prestigewinecellar.com

Utah

Vine Lore, Inc.
258 E. 100 S
Salt Lake City, UT 84111
801-359-0244
vinelore@aol.com

Vermont

Dewitt Beverage
PO Box 596
Brattleboro, VT 05301
802-254-6063

Virginia

Hand Picked Selections, Inc.
226 E. Lee Street
Warrenton, VA 20186
540-347-9400
www.handpickedselections.com

Washington

Cascade Trade
2414 S.W. Andover Street, #F102
Seattle, WA 98106
206-223-0410
www.cascadetrade.com

Washington, D.C.

House of Wines, Inc
6500 Chillum Place NW
Washington DC, 20012
202-882-3333

West Virginia

Beverage Distributors
PO Box 866
Clarksburg, WV 26301
304-624-9720
jiaquinta@beveragewv.com

Wisconsin

Neuburg Wine Co.
6836 N. Yates Road
Fox Point, WI 53217
414-352-9409
www.neuburgwinecompany.com

Wyoming

Wyoming Liquor Division
1520 E. 5th Street
Cheyenne, WY 82002
307-777-6457
www.revenue.state.wy.us

Custom Crush Services by State (Partial List)

If you choose the custom crush route for your business, you can start with this partial list of companies for each state or province. Interview one and then find another or two more if possible, to compare with the first one you interview.

Alabama

Perdido Vineyards
22100 County Road 47
Perdido, AL 36562
251-937-9463
www.perdidovineyards.com

Arizona

Page Springs Cellars, Inc.
1500 N. Page Springs Road
Cornville, AZ 86325
928-639-3004
www.pagespringscellars.com

Arkansas

Post Familie Vineyards and Winery
1700 St. Mary's Mountain Road
Altus, AR 72821
479-468-2741
www.postfamilie.com

California

Crushpad
2573 3rd Street
San Francisco, CA 94107
415-864-4232
www.crushpadwine.com

Colorado

Vintages Handcrafted Wine
120 W. Olive Street
Fort Collins, CO 80524
1-800-748-2226
www.vintageswine.com

Florida

Chatauqua Vineyards and Winery, Inc.
364 Hugh Adams Road
Defuniak Springs, FL 32433
850-892-5887
www.chautauquawinery.com

Georgia

BlackStock Vineyards and Winery
5200 Town Creek Road
Dahlonega, GA 30533
706-219-2789
www.bsvw.com

Idaho

Thousand Spring Winery
18854 Highway 30
Hagerman, ID 83332
208-837-4001
www.thousandspringswinery.com

Illinois

Cellars De Santim, Inc.
69 Roosevelt Road
Carbondale, IL 62901
618-534-6282
www.santomwine.com

Iowa

Grape Escape Vineyard and Winery
1185 40th Place
Pleasantville, IA 50225
515-848-3094
www.grapeescapeiowa.com

Kentucky

Felice Vineyards
829 E. Market Street
Louisville, KY 40206
502-819-5898
www.felicevineyards.com

Maine

Sweetgrass Farm Winery and Distillery
347 Carroll Road
Union, ME 04862
207-785-3024
www.sweetgrasswinery.com

Michigan

Peninsula Cellars
2464 Kroupa Road
Traverse City, MI 49686
231-223-4050
www.peninsulacellars.com

Minnesota

Northern Vineyards
223 N. Main Street
Stillwater, MN 55082
651-430-1032
www.northernvineyards.com

Missouri

Native Stone Vineyards
4317 Native Stone Road
Jefferson City, MO 65109
573-584-8600
carastauffer@aol.com

Nebraska

The Last Chance Winery
PO Box 308
Craswford, NE 69339
308-665-2712
www.thelastchancewinery.com

Nevada

Churchill Vineyards
1045 Dodge Lane
Fallon, NV 89406
775-423-4000
cpfrey@phonewave.net

New Jersey

Cava Winery and Vineyard
4 Havenhill Road
Hamburg, NJ 07419
973-920-2083
ariccio@accessqhs.com

New Mexico

La Vina Winery
4201 S. Highway 28
La Union, NM 88021
505-882-7632
www.lavinawinery.com

New York

Fox Run Vineyards
670 State Route 14
Penn Yan, NY 14527
1-800-636-9786
www.foxrunvineyards.com

North Carolina

Silver Coast Winery
6680 Barbeque Road
Ocean Isle Beach, NC 28469
910-287-2800
www.silvercoastwinery.com

Oregon

Coelho Winery, Inc.
PO Box 618
Amity, OR 97101
503-835-9305
www.coelhowinery.com

Pennsylvania

Naylor Wine Cellars, Inc.
4069 Vineyard Road
Stewartstown, PA 17363
717-993-2431
www.naylorwine.com

Tennessee

**Savannah Oaks Winery and Gift
Shop**
1817 Delano Road
Delano, TN 37325
423-263-1513
www.savannah-oaks-winery.com

Texas

Water 2 Wine, Inc.
2211 N.W. Military Highway, Suite
128
Castle Hills, TX 78213
210-344-9463
www.water2wine.us

Vermont

Shelburne Vineyards, LLC
70 Pierson Drive
Shelburne, VT 04582
802-734-1386
www.shelburnevineyard.com

Virginia

**Prince Michel Vineyard and
Winery**
154 Winery Lane
Leon, VA 22725
510-547-3707
www.princemichel.com

Washington

Frye Winery
15011 S. Meridian, Suite B
Puyallup, WA 98373
253-845-1177
fryewinery@aol.com

Wisconsin

Lil' Ole Winemaker Shoppe
10101 Market Street, Suite C20
Rothschild, WI 54474
715-355-9700
www.lilolewinemaker.com

Wyoming

Irvin Cellar
101 Webbwood Road
Riverton, WY 82501
307-856-2173
rivirvincellar@msn.com

Custom Crush Canada

Adora Estate Winery
6807 Highway 97
Summerland, BC VOH 1Z9
250-404-4201
info@adorawines.com

Stoney Ridge Estate Winery
3201 King Street, Box 566
Vineland, ON L0R 2C0
905-562-1324
store@stoneyridge.com

Vignoble Bourg Royal
1910 Rue du Vignoble
Charlesbourg, QC G2L 1R8
418-681-9119

Government Liaison

This government liaison service can help you with labels and trademarking:

Government Liaison Services
200 N. Glebe Road, Suite 321
Arlington, VA 22203
1-800-642-6564

Software Providers

These software providers can help you merge your business accounting, government reporting, and online wine sales systems:

Inertia Beverage
www.inertiabev.com

Winery Solutions
www.ewinerysolutions.com

D

Common Winery Conversions

Dealing with weights and measures is a big part of operating a vineyard and winery. The standard weights and measures used in the United States often differ from those used throughout most of the globe. Therefore, you often find yourself having to convert liters into gallons or grams into ounces, and so on.

This appendix gives you a few basic conversions that generally apply to the wine industry. (The conversion numbers are rounded when necessary.) You can find just about any conversion chart online at www.onlineconversion.com.

Weight

Grapes are weighed by the ton or kilogram, and winery chemistry is normally weighed by the ounce or gram.

> 1 ounce = 28.350 grams
>
> 1 pound = 2.205 kilograms
>
> 1 ton = 2,000 pounds
>
> 1 ton = 907.185 kilograms
>
> 1 ton grapes = approximately 150 gallons wine

Temperature

Of course, outside temperature has an effect on grape-growing, but fermentation temperature and the temperature of resulting wine must be carefully watched and controlled.

Starting at 32°, every 1° Fahrenheit (plus or minus) equals .56° Centigrade (plus or minus).

0°F = –17.92°C

32°F = 0°C (freezing point)

50 to 60°F = 10 to 16°C (optimum wine storage temperature range)

50 to 68°F = 10 to 20°C (general range for fermenting white wine)

68°F = 20.16°C (common temperature for testing wine in the lab)

77 to 90°F = 25 to 32°C (general range for fermenting red wine)

Gallons, Liters, and Other Liquid Measures

When you report your wine production figures to the federal government, you do so in gallons, but some states may have you report in liters. Also, wine storage and packaging may be expressed in gallons or in liters and milliliters.

1 gallon = 3.785 liters

150 gallons = 567.810 liters

1 liter = .265 gallon

1 (750-milliliter) bottle = 25,361 ounces

12 bottles = 1 case wine

1 case wine = 2.382 gallons

Acres and Hectares

In some cases, you may find land values expressed in hectares rather than in acres.

1 acre = .404 hectares

1 hectare = 2.471 acres

Sugar and Alcohol

Every degree of Brix (sugar in grape juice) fermented by yeast produces approximately .55 percent alcohol by volume. For example, 23 Brix fermented all the way should equal 12.65 percent alcohol. But sugar doesn't completely ferment out; there's always a trace of it, even in the driest wine. That 23 Brix fermented would produce somewhere between 12 percent and 12.65 percent alcohol by volume. Some winemakers claim that with new yeast strains, the conversion rate has jumped from .55 to .60 plus. Most yeast manufacturers dispute the claim.

You may find alcohol expressed as "proof," i.e., 40 proof or 80 proof. Proof is twice the alcohol percentage volume. A wine at 12 percent by volume is 24 proof.

Index

CHECK OUT THESE BEST-SELLERS

More than 450 titles available at booksellers and online retailers everywhere!

978-1-59257-115-4

978-1-59257-900-6

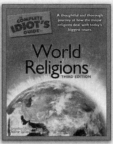

978-1-59257-855-9

978-1-59257-222-9

978-1-59257-957-0

978-1-59257-785-9

978-1-59257-471-1

978-1-59257-483-4

978-1-59257-883-2

978-1-59257-966-2

978-1-59257-908-2

978-1-59257-786-6

978-1-59257-954-9

978-1-59257-437-7

978-1-59257-888-7

ALPHA   idiotsguides.com